The Shepherd's Assistants

A Handbook For Church Elders or Deacons

Arthur J. Clement

Scripture is taken from the HOLY BIBLE, NEW INTERNATIONAL VERSION®. NIV®. Copyright © 1973, 1978, 1984 by International Bible Society. Used by permission of Zondervan Publishing House. All rights reserved.

The "NIV" and "New International Version" trademarks are registered in the United States Patent and Trademark Office by International Bible Society. Use of either trademark requires the permission of International Bible Society.

All rights reserved. No part of this publication may be reproduced, stored in a retrieval system, or transmitted in any form or by any means—electronic, mechanical, photocopying, recording, or otherwise—except for brief quotations in reviews without prior permission from the publisher.

Sixth printing, 2012
Fifth printing, 2010
Fourth printing, 2009
Third printing, 2008
Second printing, 2008

Library of Congress Control Number: 2007920152
Northwestern Publishing House
1250 N. 113th St., Milwaukee, WI 53226-3284
© 2007 by Northwestern Publishing House
Published 2007
Printed in the United States of America
ISBN 978-0-8100-2047-4

INTRODUCTION

Often the men elected to the office of church elder or deacon have feelings of apprehension and inadequacy about serving their church in this capacity. And this is understandable. While they are to be closely associated with the pastor, the spiritual shepherd of the people, and assist him with spiritual affairs, they do not benefit as he does from formal training in the ministry of the Word.

At times the lack of training actually hinders the elder in carrying out his duties with efficiency and effectiveness. It is sad but true that many a situation has been lost in dealing with church members under discipline simply for the reason that the right words were not spoken at the right moment. This occured because the elder had little knowledge of how to meet and talk with the people he was asked to counsel.

The need is surely there for thoroughly trained church elders. I have written this book in an attempt to help fill this need. My suggestion is that this volume be used not only as a reference work and handbook by the individual elder or deacon, but that it also be used by the pastor in board meetings as a training manual for the men who are to assist him in the spiritual care of the flock.

It is with a humble heart that I offer this volume for use in the church. By no means an expert in this field, I regard my work as a small contribution toward the training of the shepherd's assistants. I pray that the church will benefit by it.

                                              Arthur J. Clement

                                              Summer, 1989
                                              Sun Prairie, WI

Inquires regarding this book may be made to:

    Pastor Art Clement
    302 Nellie Ct
    Clinton MI 49236-9748
    PH# 517-456-4893

TABLE OF CONTENTS

CHAPTER ONE
(Pages 1-9)

THE ELDERS AS MINISTERS OF CHRIST AND ASSISTANTS TO THE SHEPHERD (THE PASTOR)

1) Office of deacon: forerunner of office of elder (Acts 6:1-6) .... pp. 1f.
2) The laity: Carrying on a spiritual ministry in the congregation. .... pp. 2-9
   a. Apprehensions concerning lay involvement in spiritual tasks .... p. 2f.
   b. All believers are ministers of Christ; clergy are to train them .... pp. 3-5
   c. Lay involvement in the early church .... pp. 5f.
   d. The laity are to be given opportunity to carry on a spiritual ministry .... pp. 6f.
3) The pastoral office: A special ministry within the priesthood of believers. .... pp. 7-9
   a. The pastoral office is carried on for the spiritual welfare of the laity. .... pp. 7f.
   b. The office of elder: A valuable tool of the pastoral office in public ministry. .... pp. 8f.

CHAPTER TWO
(Pages 10-28)

THE ELDERS' QUALIFICATIONS, CHARACTERISTICS, DUTIES, DO'S AND DON'TS

1) Office of elder involves spiritual duties which give assistance to the pastor. Spiritual qualifications are required. .... pp. 10f.
2) The qualifications of an elder .... pp. 12-14
3) Scriptural characteristics that ought to be found in every elder. .... pp. 14-16
4) Duties of elders .... pp. 16-24
   a. The worship service .... pp. 16-18
   b. Care of the pastor .... pp. 18f.
   c. The congregation's spiritual life and Christian service .... pp. 20f.
   d. Visits. .... pp. 21-23
   e. Stewardship. .... p. 23

v

	f. Membership	pp. 23f.
	g. Records	p. 24
	h. Prayer	p. 24
5)	Do's and Don'ts for elders	pp. 24-27
	a. Do	pp. 24-26
	b. Don't	pp. 26f.
6)	What enables the elder to carry on his work	pp. 27f.

CHAPTER THREE
(Pages 29-44)

THE ELDERS AT WORK: WINNING PEOPLE'S CONFIDENCE

1)	The elder must not only know God's Word but be able to communicate it	pp. 29f.
2)	St. Paul's philosophy of dealing with people, as an example	pp. 31-35
3)	The elder's approach to people to win their confidence	pp. 35-44
	a. The elder should be accomodating, adaptable	pp. 35f.
	b. The elder should be a friend	p. 36
	c. The elder should be loving	pp. 36f.
	d. The elder should be caring	pp. 37f.
	e. The elder should have a sympathetic heart	p. 38
	f. The elder should meet people on their own turf	pp. 38-40
	g. The elder should have respect for others and have empathy	pp. 40f.
	h. The elder should demonstrate loving concern for the burdened	pp. 41f.
	i. The elder should be knowledgeable and have sense of humor	p. 43
	j. It is, finally, the Word of God that changes hearts	p. 44

CHAPTER FOUR
(Pages 45-69)

THE ELDERS AT WORK: SCRIPTURAL DISCIPLINE AND THE ELDERS' INVOLVEMENT

1)	Christian discipline (generally) and church discipline	p. 45
2)	What the Scripture says concerning discipline	p. 45-69
	a. Scripture #1: Galations 6:1-2 — Restoring the sinner	pp. 45-48
	b. Scripture #2: Matthew 18:15-18 — The four steps	pp. 48-58
	c. Scripture #3: 1 Corinthians 5:1-5 — Failure to act	pp. 58-62
	d. Scripture #4: 1 Corinthians 5:11 — Isolation	pp. 62f.
	e. Scripture #5: 1 Timothy 1:19b-20 — Apostasy	pp. 64f.
	f. Scripture #6: Titus 3:10-11 — Divisiveness	pp. 65-69

CHAPTER FIVE
(Pages 70-87)
THE ELDERS AT WORK: ADMONISHING THE OFFENDER
1) Discipline is to carried out in the proper spirit. . . . .   pp. 70f.
2) What admonishing the offender requires of the elder-counselor . . . .   pp. 71-75
3) Admonishing the offender requires communication skills. . . . .   pp. 75-78
4) Confronting the offender with his sins . . . .   pp. 78-80
5) Admonishing the offender involves reproof, warning, encouragement . . . .   pp. 80f.
6) The Scripture is the Spirit's instrument to work change . . .   pp. 81f.
7) The elder needs to be proficient in the Scripture . . . . . .   pp. 82f.
8) The offender needs to accept scriptural admonition . . .   pp. 83f.
9) Announcing forgiveness to the repentant offender . . . . .   pp. 84-86
10) The restored offender is to live a restored life. . . . .   pp. 86f.

CHAPTER SIX
(Pages 88-116)
THE ELDERS AT WORK: MINISTERING TO DELINQUENTS
1) Delinquency a vexing problem, often not given proper attention . . . .   pp. 88-90
2) Scripture's witness against inactive church membership . . . .   pp. 90-93
3) Why church members become delinquent . . . .   pp. 93-99
4) Preventing delinquency . . . .   pp. 99f.
5) Signs of impending delinquency . . . .   pp. 100f.
6) How soon should initial contact be made? . . . .   pp. 101-103
7) How to admonish delinquents. . . . .   pp. 103-112
   a. Treat delinquency as sin. . . . .   pp. 103f.
   b. Questions that may be asked . . . .   pp. 104-106
   c. Pitfalls to avoid in ministering to delinquents . . . . .   pp. 106-111
   d. The significance of excuses or objections . . . .   pp. 111f.
8) Bringing things to a head . . . .   pp. 113-116
   a. How many times should visits be made? . . . .   pp. 113f.
   b. Final action . . . .   pp. 114f.
   c. Members who have moved away . . . .   p. 115
   d. Helping the former delinquent with his problem . . . .   pp. 115f.

CHAPTER SEVEN
(Pages 116-121)
THE ELDERS AT WORK: WRITING LETTERS
1) Caution must be exercised with letters . . . .   pp. 117-119
   a. Rarely can letters take the place of personal contact. . . . .   pp. 117f.

	b. Temptation to use letters to save time	p. 118
	c. Temptation to use letters to update membership list..	p. 118
	d. Letters can't properly deal with unbelief.........	p. 118
	e. Letters may be threatening when shouldn't be ...	pp. 118f.
	f. Care taken with letters emphasizing communion attendance	p. 119
2)	Letters to those who have moved from visiting area ...	pp. 120-122
	a. When does contact by letter become necessary? ...	p. 120
	b. Letters of transfer	p. 121
3)	Individual letters are called for.....................	p. 122

ADDENDUM ONE
(Pages 123-127)

A PRESENTATION OF GOD'S PLAN FOR OUR SALVATION

ADDENDUM TWO
(Pages 128-133)

THE LAW AND THE GOSPEL

ADDENDUM THREE
(Pages 134-155)

RESPONDING TO EXCUSES OR OBJECTIONS

1)	"I don't get anything out of the sermon/church"	p. 135
2)	"I was sick and nobody visited me".................	p. 136
3)	"A friend of mine ... couldn't have the wedding music she wanted"..	pp. 136f.
4)	"The pastor refused to conduct the funeral for ..."...	pp. 137f.
5)	"I don't like the minister"..........................	pp. 138f.
6)	"Members of my family don't attend, etc."............	p. 139
7)	"I feel bitter about a bad experience with someone..."...	pp. 139f.
8)	"I have no money to give the church"................	p. 140
9)	"All the church wants is my money/ ... keeps asking for money"	p. 141
10)	"I can't tolerate being in a crowd"..................	pp. 141f.
11)	"I never feel good in the morning"..................	p. 142
12)	"I work so hard during the week ... too tired, etc."...	pp. 142f.
13)	"I really want to come ... just can't get started, etc."	p. 143
14)	"I can worship God at home ... don't need church"...	pp. 143f.
15)	"I just don't see good of going every Sunday ... bores me"	pp. 144f.
16)	"I guess you're right — I should go to church, etc."...	p. 145
17)	"The church demands too much of me ... too strict, etc."	pp. 145f.

18)	"I don't think it is a sin not to go to church"	p. 146f.
19)	"Too many hypocrites . . . turns me off"	p. 147
20)	"Church doesn't seem that important. I'll come when I want"	p. 148f.
21)	"I don't want to be told I have to go to church"	p. 149
22)	"I don't have to go to church to be a good Christian"	pp. 149f.
23)	"It's none of your business whether or not I come"	pp. 150f.
24)	"Why don't you pick on someone else, etc.?"	p. 151
25)	"I'll take my chances"	pp. 151f.
26)	"My money is all mine, and no one can tell me . . ."	pp. 152f.
27)	"I haven't the time to come to church, etc."	p. 153
28)	"Right now my life is all messed up, etc."	pp. 153f.
29)	"I have to work on Sundays"	pp. 154f.

ADDENDUM FOUR
(Pages 156-196)

SCRIPTURE TOPICS INDEX

ADDENDUM FIVE
(Pages 197-218)

SAMPLE LETTERS

1)	Letter #1: To member who hasn't attended for past month	p. 197
2)	Letter #2: To communicant who hasn't communed	p. 198
3)	Letter #3: To delinquent, about forth-coming visit	p. 199
4)	Letter #4: To communicants who have moved away (#1)	pp. 200f.
5)	Letter #5: To communicants who have moved away (#2)	pp. 201f.
6)	Letter #6: To communicants who have moved away (#3)	pp. 202f.
7)	Letter #7: To communicants who have moved away (#4)	pp. 203f.
8)	Letter #8: To communicants who have moved away (#5)	pp. 204ff.
9)	Letter #9: A commendatory letter of transfer (#1)	pp. 206f.
10)	Letter #10: A letter of transfer relax member (#2)	pp. 208f.
11)	Letter #11: To member who has evaded discipline by disassociating himself (notification of congr. action)	pp. 209ff.
12)	Letter #12: To member who has dissociated himself for no apparent reason (notification of congr. action)	pp. 211ff.
13)	Letter #13: To member who has been released to join a church of another fellowship (notification of congr. action)	pp. 213f.

14) Letter #14: To member under discipline (3rd step), urging him to attend a congregational meeting to hear testimony .... pp. 215f.
15) Letter #15: To member who has been excommunicated (notification of congr. action) .... pp. 217f.

ADDENDUM SIX
(Pages 219-225)

THE ELDERS ORGANIZE
1) Geographical divisions (area, district, elder assistants) ... pp. 219-221
2) The board as administered by congregation's constitution...................................... pp. 221-225

ADDENDUM SEVEN
(Pages 226-233)

NOTES AND BIBLIOGRAPHIES

CHAPTER ONE

THE ELDERS AS MINISTERS OF CHRIST AND ASSISTANTS TO THE SHEPHERD (THE PASTOR)

INTRODUCTION

Christians are to care for the physical and spiritual welfare of other Christians. Jesus said so (Matthew 25:34-36; 18:15-17). The trouble is, the job that belongs to everyone so often becomes the job that no one does, or that isn't done efficiently by the few who attempt it.[1] Often lacking is proper organization. Duties need to be defined and people have to be called, appointed or elected to carry them out. Even the mother church in Jerusalem ran into problems for lack of organization and efficiency. It was soon discovered that the apostles couldn't possibly carry on the work of the church alone. The complaint was heard from the Grecian Jews that their widows were being over-looked in the daily distribution of food. Clearly it was time to introduce an auxiliary office in the church. Acting upon the command of the apostles, the congregation appointed seven Spirit-filled men (deacons) to take over the care of the needy (Acts 6:1-6). The first attempt at organization afforded much-needed assistance to the apostles, who served as the pastors of the congregation. As the result, the widows were all fed and the pastors were released from time-consuming mundane labors so they could give their attention to ministering in spiritual matters.

The seven men who were chosen to minister the congregation's welfare fund are not referred to directly in the Acts account as deacons (literally, "helpers"). However, it is safe to assume that they held the office of deacon or elder in its primitive form, which was to "wait on tables" in the daily distribution of food, in order to free the apostles for "the ministry of the Word of God" (Acts 6:2). Two of the deacons, Stephen and Philip, also preached.

Eventually the office of deacon became established in congregations other than the mother church in Jerusalem. This office is referred to in the introduction of St. Paul's Letter to the Philippians, where he wrote: "To all the saints in Christ Jesus at Philippi, together with the overseers (i.e. the pastors) and deacons" (Philippians 1:1). Paul also mentioned the office of deacon in his first Epistle to Timothy, and drew up a list of qualifications for those holding the office (1 Timothy 3:8-10, 12).

The appointment of seven men in the Jerusalem congregation to the position of almoners does not constitute God's command to his church to have elders or other officers. Nowhere in the New Testament are we commanded to have a particular kind of church organization. On the other hand, the office of deacon in the early church, established by apostolic command under divine guidance, certainly serves as an antecedent of our present day church boards and establishes a precedent for them.

And so, taking its cue from the apostles and the early church, the church of today has made provision for the office of elder or deacon to assist the shepherd(s), the pastor(s), in caring for the spiritual needs of the flock. The elders receive the call to their spiritual work as the pastor(s) does – from the congregation. But the pastor(s) has a greater responsibility as shepherd of the flock. The elders are therefore subject to the pastor's guidance. Elders or deacons are not assistant pastors but are assistants to the pastor(s), carrying on the public office of the Word in the congregation. They are spiritual men called by their fellow Christians to help in specific areas of ministry as defined by their congregation.

The church has created other offices as well to handle both spiritual and practical matters of government. History has proven the wisdom of efficiency through proper organization. Offices, boards, committees, and organizations may be added or deleted as this best serves the gospel and the Christian love and care that flow from it.

THE LAITY:

CARRYING ON A SPIRITUAL MINISTRY IN THE CONGREGATION

Apprehensions Concerning Lay Involvement in Spiritual Tasks

Some apprehensive souls may question the right of the laity to carry on a spiritual ministry in the congregation. "Pay and pray" are all too often the only tasks — besides mowing the church lawn, cleaning God's house, ushering, and organizing the church potlucks — that the laity are challenged or even permitted to do.

However, elders elected to the board should have no problem with, or apprehension about, assuming labors in the congregation that are of a deeply spiritual nature. Nor should those who elect them. Without question, the laity are spiritually empowered with spiritual duties in the church. Without question, the spiritual care of Christians is not solely in the hands of the pastor. This is not to say that the laity throughout church history have always exercised their God-given right to carry on spiritual duties. Frequently the work of the ministry has suffered simply for the reason that either the pastor tried to do all the work himself and cut the laity out, or the laity expected him to do the work alone. The laity either didn't acknowledge, or refused to accept, their God-given prerogative to minister in spiritual matters.

All Believers Are Ministers of Christ and Should Be Trained by the Clergy for Spiritual Tasks

Among those Scripture references that entrust the ministry of the Word to every believer, are those that speak of the use of the Keys as the possession of every believer. Our risen Savior bestowed the use of the Keys to the believers on Easter Sunday evening as they were gathered behind locked doors in the upper room. The evangelist Luke reports that not only were the apostles present at this meeting, the two disciples from Emmaus and others were present as well (Luke 24:22). To this gathering of apostles and disciples, Jesus gave the use of the Keys: "Receive the Holy Spirit. If you forgive anyone his sins, they are forgiven; if you do not forgive them, they are not forgiven" (John 20:22-23).

That the authority to use the Keys, that is, to forgive and retain sins, has been given to the whole church — to all Christians — was taught, moreover, by our Lord when he charged the local congregation, and not just the clergy, with excommunicating the impenitent sinner from the congregation (Matthew 18:17-18).

Then there are those passages of the Scripture that teach what is commonly referred to as the priesthood of believers. The apostle Peter assured the Christians: "You are a chosen people, a **royal priesthood**, a holy nation, a people belonging to God, that you may declare the praises of him who called you out of darkness into his wonderful light" (1 Peter 2:9). The apostle John referred to the Christians as a "kingdom and **priests** to serve his (Christ's) God and Father . . ." (Revelation 1:6). And so, as priests of God, the believers in Jesus Christ not only have direct access to God through Christ and his sacrifice, they are also given the wonderful privilege and duty to teach the gospel of Christ to others (1 Peter 2:9).

On the subject of the ministry as it pertains to all believers as priests of God, Luther wrote: "As priests we are worthy to appear before God to pray for others and to teach one another divine things . . . Thus Christ has made it possible for us, provided we believe in him, to be not only his brethren, co-heirs, and fellow kings, but also his fellow priests."[2] Luther emphasized the truth that the New Testament church is a priesthood of all believers, not a special hierarchy of clerics.[3] Commenting on the titles bestowed on the believers in 1 Peter 2:9 ("royal priesthood, holy nation, people belonging to God"), Oscar J. Feucht, in *Everyone a Minister*, observes: "These titles raise all believers to the status of 'ministers.' They put all Christians in the role once performed by the Old Testament priests. The coming of Christ brought to the church a whole new dispensation, a new order — an order of the laos (i.e. the people) including every Christian, both man and woman."[4]

When are believers consecrated to the office of priest? St. Paul reminded the Ephesians that in Christ the believers are sealed with the promised Holy Spirit (1:3). This occurs in baptism, the washing of regeneration (Acts 2:38; Titus 3:5). And so, when the believers are baptized and given the gift of the Holy Spirit, who imparts faith to their hearts and takes up residence in them, they are thereby consecrated to the priesthood. There is no order of priests in the New Testament except the order that includes all who believe in Jesus Christ, who have thus received the Holy Spirit.

Among the Scripture passages that entrust the ministry of the Word to all believers are the following promises of Jesus made to believers generally: "I tell you the truth, anyone who has faith in me will do what I have been doing. He will do even greater things than these, because I am going to the Father" (John 14:12); and "'Whoever believes in me, as the Scripture has said, streams of living water will flow from within him.' By this he meant the Spirit" (John 7:38-39). Jesus promised the believers that they would do greater miracles than the physical ones he did during his ministry here. These "greater miracles" are nothing less than the conversions performed by the Holy Spirit through their testimony of the Savior. The Holy Spirit acts like streams of living waters flowing from the Christians out to others. He is active in the testimony of each and every Christian — clergy and laity — to work the miracle of saving faith in others, thus quenching their thirst for salvation.

The laity are indeed empowered by God to exercise spiritual duties toward their fellow Christians. But not only toward their brothers and sisters in the faith. They are empowered to exercise spiritual duties toward all human creatures as well. Saving souls out in the world through preaching the gospel depends on the efforts of God's believers generally. Saving souls and keeping saved souls saved is not holy ground upon which the pastor alone may venture. Laymen have a spiritual duty to laymen, a duty for which they are to be trained by the clergy. Instead of doing the work of the ministry alone, the pastor has the privilege and duty to train the laity for their God-given role of ministers of Christ. This is soundly scriptural. St. Paul wrote in Ephesians: "It was he who gave some to be apostles, some to be prophets, some to be evangelists, and some to be pastors and teachers, **to prepare God's people for works of service**, so that the body of Christ may be built up until we all reach unity of faith and in the knowledge of the Son of God and become mature . . ." (Ephesians 4:11-13).

Laymen in the Early Church Preached the Word

That the early Christians interpreted Christ's command to preach the gospel as binding on all believers is attested to by St. Luke in Acts. He reports that the murder of Stephen, a deacon of the Jerusalem church, set off a general persecution of the Christians in that city. As a result they were scattered throughout Judea and Samaria. And they took their faith with them, serving as Christ's public witnesses. St. Luke informs us that "those who had been scattered preached the Word wherever they went" (Acts 8:4). Later on this apostle reports that while some of the scattered Christians told the message only to the Jews (traveling as far as Phoenicia, Cypress, and Antioch) some when in Antioch "began to speak to Greeks also, telling them the good news about the Lord Jesus." The result was that "the Lord's hand was with them, and a great number of people believed and turned to the Lord" (Acts 11:19-20). The laity went to the world, preaching and witnessing and confessing, just as the Savior commanded his church to do. As the result of this activity by the laity, many congregations were founded.

Laymen in the Early Church Were Called into the Public Service of the Word, Some of Whom Eventually Became Pastors

Laboring as leaders and as pastors and missionaries, the apostles did not do what they did alone. They had much help from the laity, and recognized and commended the laity for it. There were Acquila and his wife Priscilla, who were co-workers with St. Paul, not only in tent-making, but in the work of evangelism as well. Paul called them "my fellow workers in Christ Jesus" (Romans 16:3). This husband-wife team taught the Word of God to Apollos, an Alexandrian Jew who became a believer in Christ. Apollos himself was an eloquent speaker who used his gifts for the Lord. During Paul's absence from Ephesus, Apollos preached in the synagogue there. Later, after becoming more proficient in parts of Christian doctrine where he had been lacking, Apollos was encouraged by the believers to go to Achaia. "On arriving, he was a great help to those who by grace had believed. For he vigorously refuted the Jews in public debate, proving from the Scripture that Jesus was the Christ" (Acts 18:27b, 28). Corinth was a city in Achaia, and Apollos served the Christian church there.

Silas is another example. At first he was a member of the Jerusalem church. Later he became a companion and co-worker of St. Paul, accompanying this apostle on his second missionary journey. He preached in Berea and carried Peter's letter from Rome to the churches of Asia Minor (Acts 15-18).

Stephanas was one of the first believers in Corinth and rose to the position of leader in the congregation. Paul urged the Corinthian believers to be obedient to Stephanas (1 Corinthians 1:16; 16:1-5, 17). Philip was one of the first deacons of the church. He took to evangelistic preaching and was one of the first to go out beyond Jerusalem and even outside the Jewish nation with Christ's message (Acts 6:5; 8:5-40; 21:8). Epaphroditus, from the Philippian congregation, was referred to by Paul as "my brother, my fellow worker and fellow soldier" who "almost died for the work of Christ" (Philippians 2:25, 30). Tychicus was a Gentile convert from Ephesus whom Paul labled "a dear brother, a faithful minister (deacon) and fellow servant in the Lord" (Colossians 4:7).[5]

Were laity called or appointed to the gospel work that began at Jerusalem and then spread to other cities and even to other countries as well? Did the apostles recognize laity as ministers of Christ with them in the public service of the Word? No other conclusion is warranted. What is true of the laity today concerning the ministry of the Word? It is this, that the ministry of the Word has been made the responsibility of every believer in Jesus Christ. There is also urgent need for congregations to call from the laity those who will function faithfully with the gifts God has given them in specific areas of the ministry of the Word (Romans 12:4-8; 1 Corinthians 12:4-11).

The Laity Are to Be Given Opportunity to Carry on the Spiritual Ministry God Has Given Them

The claim is rightly made that Luther restored the people to their proper place by saying to them the Word of God: "Thou art a priest." "He laid God's hands upon the heads of the laity and ordained and consecrated them to the priesthood."[6] However, has the church since the time of the Reformation practiced the doctrine of the priesthood of believers as it should?

> If the church at any time lacks enough workers, it is because she has forgotten the practice of the priesthood of all believers. She may still hold to the doctrine in her verbalizations, but has she failed to really practice this doctrine? . . . God wants his people to be led by competent shepherds. But nowhere does God give "clergy" exclusive rights. Rather, God has vested all authority in the whole Christian assembly. A

church that is wholly operated by professionals is not a healthy church. There is truth to the couplet:

> Ill fares the church to hastening ills a prey
> Where a few are paid to work and others give the pay.[7]

The doctrine of the priesthood of all believers must be faithfully taught in churches to every generation. Yet our churches must not only *teach* the doctrine that every Christian is a priest, but actually *practice* it, affording the laity ample opportunities to function in their role of priests.

> What spiritual opportunities do the lay members of our congregations have, to train and develop them for larger responsibilities? Why is it that in many congregations the lay members are engaged for the most part, if not exclusively, in organizational and administrative functions, which deal primarily with the external needs of the parish, when the priestly functions God has assigned to them are largely spiritual in nature? If our congregations are to be what God has called them to be — launching pads for Christ's mission to the world — then the Christians in our congregations must be trained and given opportunity to translate their commitment to Jesus Christ into action. E. Stanley Jones has well said: "A religion that does not start with the individual does not start; and a religion that stops with the individual stops."[8]

The board of elders furnishes an excellent example of Christians being allowed — and even appointed — to express themselves as priests in a most significant manner. Election to the post of elder is the congregation's mandate to the Christian to use his office of priest to assist the pastor in his care of the flock. Each and every elder should be thankful for the privilege of serving as a priest of God or minister of Christ in this special way!

THE PASTORAL OFFICE: A SPECIAL MINISTRY
WITHIN THE PRIESTHOOD OF BELIEVERS

The Pastoral Office is Carried on for the Spiritual Welfare of the Laity

The Old Testament church had its prophets and priests to teach and preach the Word. The New Testament witnessed Jesus' calling of the twelve apostles, whose office, then, was the forerunner of a number of the aspects of the pastoral office today. While many of the first congregations were founded by the laity who, at the time, were on the move due to the scattering effect of persecutions, nevertheless the care of these churches was not left to the laity. After congregations were established, the office of preaching was also established so that the believers could have continued indoctrination and edification carried out according to the manner ordained by God (Acts 14:23; 20:28).[9]

Joined together in a Christian congregation, the New Testament Christians (as priests of God) have the authority to call men into various forms of *public* ministry, including the pastoral office (Romans 10:14-15; Titus 1:5, 7). However, this form of public ministry certainly is given only to qualifying individual's (1 Timothy 3:1-11; Titus 1:6-9). The pastoral ministry is a special office within the priesthood of believers and is an extension of the ministry that belongs to all believers. The pastor is charged not only with administering the Word to humanity in general — a charge that all believers have — but of administering the means of grace to the congregation. The pastor labors to save the souls committed to his care. In the process he feeds them, trains them, disciplines them, encourages them, inspires them and comforts them. He also aids them in recognizing and using their Spirit-given gifts. He is the trainer, motivator and activator of God's priests for their work of the ministry (Ephesians 4:11-12), and is their overseer (Acts 20:28).

The Scripture uses a variety of terms to describe the pastor in his office of ministering God's Word to the congregation under his care. He is called a **shepherd**. This term that gives us our English word "pastor," reminds us of the pastoral scene of the shepherd tending and feeding his flock (1 Peter 5:2; Ephesians 4:11; John 21:15-17). He is designated as an **overseer** or **superintendent**, a term that is translated in some Bibles as "bishop" (1 Timothy 3:1, 5; Acts 20:28). The term **elder** was originally applied to the pastor to designate him according to his dignity (Acts 14:23; 1 Timothy 5:17). Though still used in some churches today to designate the pastor, in Lutheran circles it is applied to a man who serves on the auxiliary board charged with assisting the pastor. The Scripture also calls the pastor **teacher** (1 Corinthians 12:27-28; Ephesians 4:11), **ambassador** or **representative** (2 Corinthians 5:20), **steward** or **manager** (1 Corinthians 4:1), and **leader** (Hebrews 13:17).

The Office of Elder: A Valuable Tool of the Pastoral Office in Public Ministry

Not only do the believers, banded together in congregations, have the right to call men into the pastoral office of public ministry, they also have the right to establish other offices of public ministry which they deem expedient.

The office of elder is one of these. Furthermore, the office of elder is very much needed. It has long been the experience of the church that the pastor must be supplied with the necessary help in caring for the spiritual needs of the congregation. The time and energy of even the most efficient and dedicated pastor are governed by limits. He is, after all, only human. The pastor who tries to do everything himself is hurting the work and he is hurting himself. He isn't making his family happy either. Sooner or later he will suffer physically and mentally from trying to do too much. It's called "burnout."

Pastors really can't do all the work themselves. The pile-up of names on the discipline list, the carry-over of congregational problems from year to year, the oft-heard complaint that the pastor doesn't call on his members (especially the elderly) as frequently as they would like — these are just a few of the indicators that no pastor can, and none should, work all alone.

The laity are there to help, and even as pastors have to be trained for their office, the laity have to be trained for their work as ministers of Christ. Even more important and necessary is the thorough, ungoing training of the church elders. The pastor should conduct his office under the premise that a necessary part of his work is that of recruiting and training others to do the work of public ministry *with* him, equipping God's priests for God's work within and without the community of saints.

The precedent of supplying the pastor with helpers is well established in the Scripture (Exodus 18:13-26; Acts 6:1-4; Romans 16; Acts 15-18; Philippians 2). Moreover, God outfits individuals with the very gifts needed in the office of elder, even as other gifts are given to individuals to qualify them for various duties in the church (Romans 12).

While serving in public ministry of the Word together with the pastor, the elders are under his supervision. He is the leader, the shepherd, the overseer. Full responsibility rests, finally, with him. However, it is the congregation that prescribes the elders' duties and responsibilities, having established their office. The pastor as the "elder" who labors in the Word and doctrine (1 Timothy 5:17), and as the overseer of the congregation (Acts 20:28), is always a member of the board of elders — as he is a member, by virtue of his office, of every other board and committee.

† † † † † †

CHAPTER TWO

THE ELDERS' QUALIFICATIONS, CHARACTERISTICS, DUTIES, DO'S AND DON'TS

INTRODUCTION

The duties of the pastoral office in the congregation are *spiritual* duties, succinctly described by the apostles as "prayer and the ministry of the word" (Acts 6:4). Work of a mundane nature is not the work of the pastoral office. This is a task for the laity (Acts 6:3-4). However, as was shown in the previous chapter, this does not mean that the laity cannot be assigned spiritual tasks in the congregation. God has already assigned spiritual tasks to them by giving them the use of the Keys and by making them an order of priests.

Since the pastoral office needs assistance, members of the laity can be elected by the congregation to an auxiliary office to serve under the pastor, who has overall responsibility.[1] This office is commonly referred to in our circles as the office of elder (less frequently, office of deacon). Briefly, the elders are charged with assisting the pastor(s) in the spiritual care of God's people in the local congregation.

The material or external affairs of the congregation are best placed into the hands of a separate and distinct board, the board of trustees. The congregation is both a spiritual fellowship centering in the Word of God, and a chartered corporation involved with physical properties and assets.

The antecedent of our present-day board of elders was the board of deacons established in the mother church in Jerusalem. Deacons were appointed also in other congregations, and St. Paul laid down the qualifications for deacons in his first letter to Timothy (3:8-12). According to Lutheran scholar Theodore Graebner, the references by the church fathers to the office of deacon describe the deacons as generally having the function of keeping order in the church, especially in the worship service. They also lit the candles, read lessons from the Scriptures and announced prayers and hymns. Especially did they care for the poor, the widows and orphans. There was no fixed rule circumscribing their duties. Nor was there a special calling or appointment to some definite function. The Christian congregation simply instructed the lay elders or deacons to perform such duties as circumstances and special occasions required, to help the pastors in their work.[2]

In the matter of establishing the office of elder or deacon, the congregations were, and are, free to act according to the needs of the time, and have received no direct divine command. Thus the duties of the office of elder are not prescribed in Scripture and, therefore, remain a matter of Christian freedom. The list of duties contained in this chapter is compiled from various sources, including church constitutions. To a great extent the duties simply reflect the use of sanctified judgment aimed at filling an important need in the church.

The qualifications of elders are spelled out in the qualifications laid down for the deacons in the primitive church (1 Timothy 3:8-12). Moreover, we can associate other Scripture references with the elders to emphasize certain spiritual characteristics that they should possess. These passages call on Christians in general to cultivate faith and godliness. How they apply in producing a list of characteristics that church elders should manifest ought to be obvious: what is expected of *all* Christians by way of faith and conduct must be expected also of the elders, only to a *marked degree*. Simply stated: what the church needs is deeply spiritual people to do spiritual work. And so, men are chosen to serve as elders who are valued highly for their spiritual qualities, qualities that distinguish God's regenerate from the world's unregenerate. And for their skills, spiritual gifts, wisdom, experience, and traits of character and personality necessary in those who assist the pastor in his spiritual calling.

Any man elected to the board of elders ought always be aware of the trust placed in him by the congregation, and for this reason, too, he should strive for constant personal spiritual development. And he should strive for the development and use of all those traits, abilities and gifts that he owns, that are so necessary to the proper conduct of his office.

THE QUALIFICATIONS OF AN ELDER

† † † *Brothers, choose seven men from among you who are known to be full of the Spirit and wisdom. (Acts 6:3)* † † †

In this passage are listed two outstanding qualifications for deacons in the early church which can and should be applied to the present-day board of elders, whose work is mainly of a spiritual nature:

"Full of the Spirit" One who is full of the Spirit is one whose spiritual life and knowledge are not lacking. He is one whose manner of living and speech everywhere show the influence of the Holy Spirit. Being full of the Spirit, he lives a useful, productive life for the Lord. The more he is filled with the Spirit, the more he puts his sinful flesh out of commission. Thus, to be full of the Spirit is to be filled with the Holy Spirit's presence and power. The filling of the Holy Spirit must be sought where it is to be found: in God's Word. One who is full of the Spirit is filled with the knowledge of God's Word, which he humbly and fully accepts by faith.

"Full of Wisdom" This qualification goes along with being full of the Spirit. Wisdom involves the knowledge of God's Word, which knowledge comes from the Holy Spirit; and it involves "the ability and readiness to apply Christian knowledge to the practical affairs of life,"[3] which ability also comes from the Holy Spirit at work in the individual believer.

† † † *Deacons, likewise, are to be men worthy of respect, sincere, not indulging in much wine, and not pursuing dishonest gain. They must keep hold of the deep truths (mysteries) of the faith with a clear conscience. They must first be tested; and then if there is nothing against them, let them serve as deacons ... A deacon must be the husband of but one wife and must manage his children and his household well. (1 Timothy 3:8-12)* † † †

"Worthy of Respect" The elders are not to be frivolous, shallow, but have a dignified, serious bearing which commands respect. Their very demeanor influences people positively toward them, causing people to speak highly of them and to put stock in what they say. Their demeanor, by inviting respect, also invites imitation.

"Sincere" To be sincere means, literally (according to the original language), "not to be double-tongued." If an elder says one thing to one person and another thing to another, he is speaking with a double-tongue, thus not sincerely. His words are only words: words spoken more for convenience or ulterior motive than for the sake of truth and edification. What advice an elder gives in one situation should be the same advice he gives in another, similar situation. He must give the same answer to the same question, no matter who asks it. He must not say something and then later deny that he said it. Members of a congregation will be quick to discover discrepancies in what the elder has to say. The confidence of the people in the elder is shattered when they discover that he is double-tongued, that is, not sincere. An elder in the church should be among the first to always speak the truth, and to speak with consistency that bears out the facts. Also, elders should always say what they mean, and mean what they say.

"Not Indulging in Much Wine" Church elders have the freedom to use wine, but being an intoxicant, wine must be used in moderation. One must not become addicted to wine or any other intoxicant so as to have an inordinate thirst for it. Today we could add a warning against addiction to drugs as well. The elder's personal reputation, as well as his work in the congregation, demands that he be a model of sobriety: clear-headed and plainly in control of his own desires.

"Not Pursuing Dishonest Gain" This can be a warning to the elders not to pilfer funds (alms) entrusted to them (as Judas Ischariot did). Also a warning not to accept bribes, and not to take unfair advantage of people in business dealings. If they do these things they are, of course, sinning, and at the same time they earn the reputation for themselves of being mercenary and greedy, of being evildoers. Pursuit of dishonest gain is indicative of hearts that love money, hearts full of discontentment, hearts erring from the faith. It betrays hearts that are not filled with love for God and the joy of serving him and the church. Pursuing dishonest gain is sin that needs to be repented of, and cannot be accepted in the lives of the elders.

"Keep Hold of the Truths (Mysteries) of the Faith With a Clear (clean) Conscience" The profound truths of God that are accepted by the elders' faith must reside in a clean conscience. The elders must be men of heart-felt spiritual conviction, who sincerely believe the divine mysteries revealed in God's Word and do not hold secret reservations concerning them. Moreover, the elders' faith and manner of living must agree. If they live in sin while professing faith, they do not have a clear (clean) conscience. The old axiom: "Do what I say, not what I do," has no place in the eldership. The elders must be men who constantly and consistently practice their faith: who live what they believe — yes, are compelled to do so.

"They must first be tested; and then if there is nothing against them, let them serve as deacons." What is involved here is not a period of probation after their appointment as elders. Rather, men found to be blameless when their doctrine and lives are scrutinized, are the ones who are chosen for the office of elder. They are chosen because they are men whose speech and lives do not invite accusation of teaching false doctrines, schism, or of living in sin. They are chosen because they have been observed to display the knowledge and wisdom, characteristics and skills that are needed for such a high office in the church. This office is worthy of the best the congregation can offer. It is worthy of men who are tried and true. They are not placed into office to make them more devout, but are chosen for their evident devotion to God, his Word, the welfare of the congregation and the welfare of the pastor. They live careful, not careless Christian lives. They have not been causes of problems in the congregation, but rather have shown steady heads and willing, capable hands in solving problems.

"Husband of but one Wife and Must Manage His Children and His Household Well." A basic test of a man's piety is the way he treats his wife and children. The man who qualifies for the office of deacon (or the present-day office of elder) is faithful and kind to his wife, of which he has only one, and good to his children. He lovingly and efficiently cares for his family in accordance with sound Christian principles. He gives his household a good example of faith and godliness to follow, and expects and receives obedience from his children and godly submission from his wife (whose respect he cherishes and is careful to earn). The Word of God reigns supreme in his household: he is the teacher of Scripture to his wife and his children.

SCRIPTURAL CHARACTERISTICS THAT OUGHT TO BE FOUND IN EVERY ELDER

The godly characteristics that ought to be found in every Christian as a member of the universal priesthood of God ought to be found in every elder — even more so! All Christians, for example, are commanded in the Scripture:

Be on your guard; stand firm in the faith; be men of courage; be strong. Do everything in love. (1 Corinthians 16:13)

Whatever happens, conduct yourselves in a manner worthy of the gospel of Christ . . . contending as one man for the faith of the gospel without being frightened in any way by those who oppose you. (Philippians 1:27-28)

Grow in the grace and knowledge of our Lord and Savior Jesus Christ. (2 Peter 3:18)

Let the Word of Christ dwell in you richly as you teach and admonish one another with all wisdom. (Colossians 3:13)

(Speak) as one speaking the very words of God. (1 Peter 4:11)

Respect those (the pastors) who work hard among you, who are over you in the Lord and who admonish you. Hold them in the highest regard in love because of their work. (1 Thess. 5:12, 13)

Devote yourselves to prayer, being watchful and thankful. (Colossians 4:2)

Be imitators of God, therefore, as dearly loved children and live a life of love just as Christ loved us and gave himself up for us. (Ephesians 5:1-2)

Each one should use whatever gift he has received to serve others, faithfully administering God's grace in its various forms. (1 Peter 4:10)

Clothe yourselves with compassion, kindness, humility, gentleness and patience. Bear with each other and forgive whatever grievances you may have against one another. (Colossians 3:12-13)

Love your wives and do not be harsh with them. (Colossians 3:19)

Live by the Spirit, and you will not gratify the desires of the sinful nature. (Galatians 5:16)

Put to death, therefore, whatever belongs to your earthly nature: sexual immorality, impurity, lust, evil desires and greed. (Colossians 3:5)

Rid yourselves of... anger, rage, malice, slander, and filthy language from your lips. Do not lie to each other. (Colossians 3:8-9)

Live in order to please God (that)... your daily life may win the respect of outsiders. (1 Thessalonians 4:1, 14)

Summary

Elders are counselors in the congregation. Their work includes setting the proper example for others, motivating others, solving problems, restoring peace, helping others to greater faith and diligence and, in general, promoting faith, righteousness and harmony in the Christian community.

Therefore, the men selected as elders must be recognized for their faith — tried and true Christian men. Men who live exemplary Christian lives, irreproachable within and without the congregation. Honest men, full of integrity, who keep their word. They must be men who are regular in church and communion attendance, who participate faithfully in Bible class and also study their Bibles in private. Elders must be willing to confess their faith and show their loyalty to God's Word by taking a firm stand against false doctrine and sin, at the same time promoting the Word of truth in the congregation. The heart of their office is the gospel. They must be men who are mature in their faith and attitudes; men who display wisdom and sound judgment. They must be sober and temperate in all things; their lives characterized by chastity and their speech by decency. Elders must love people and be capable of expressing themselves as they give heart-to-heart Christian counsel — always displaying patience, kindness and brotherly concern. They must be men who are kind to their wives and good to their children: men whose households reflect training in the Scripture. They must be men who are full of the Holy Spirit, by whom the power of Christ's love is unleashed in them. They must be willing to be trained and have the ability to use their training in practical situations. Elders must be willing to spend themselves and be spent for Christ in the congregation.

DUTIES OF ELDERS

Since giving assistance to the pastor in carrying out the duties of his office is incumbent upon the board of elders by congregational decree, the following duties therefore suggest themselves: (Note: See Addendum Six.)

DUTIES: The Worship Service

The Elders Should:

1. Oversee the church services: the church lighted, heated (or ventilated) and open for services; the services held regularly and on time and conducted with decency and order. Help the ushers maintain decorum before, during and following the services, which are to be conducted in such a manner as to make the hour or so spent in church a time of spiritual enrichment for all.[4]

2. In an emergency read the sermon and, if necessary, conduct the entire service when no pastoral replacement is available. In all cases the service must go on.

3. Help the pastor find pulpit replacements and guest organists.

4. Assist at Holy Communion in every way assigned by the congregation: e.g. under the supervision of the pastor see to the placing of the communion ware and the supply of elements before the service, and the care of the communion ware and leftover elements following the service.[5] Supervise the altar guild's work if these matters are charged to the ladies. See that a good supply of wine and bread waffers is kept on hand and properly stored for good keeping. Assist the pastor to maintain "close" communion.[6] Commune the pastor in the event the congregation appoints an elder(s) to this.[7] See that accurate communion attendance records are kept. Discuss at board meetings possible reasons for members not communing, and solutions to the problem. Oversee the ushering of people for communion, giving assistance to the infirm.

5. Assist at baptisms. Serve as official witnesses, especially at private baptisms, and be responsible for filling the baptismal bowl and for ushering the baptismal party. Oversee the altar guild's work of cleaning the baptismal bowl and its storage. See to the supply of baptismal napkins or towels and certificates. Make certain the baptism is entered in the record.

6. Assist at weddings. Light the candles or have church ushers or acolytes light them. Also snuff them after the service (elders have the final responsibility). See that proper decorum is maintained before, during and after the ceremony (no pictures taken during the service except those cleared by the pastor). Public weddings are worship services and should be conducted from beginning to end as such. Welcome the strangers who are in church and offer assistance. Supervise the ushering. Make certain the wedding is entered in the record.

7. Keep accurate attendance records for all worship services and discuss at board meetings possible reasons for low attendance — if this is the case — and solutions to the problem.

8. Take charge of welcoming visitors and have them sign the guest book (address and phone number). Appoint and train official greeters.

9. Promote Christian fellowship after the church service.

10. Watch for persons in the church service who appear to have special needs, and give them aid.

11. Watch for people following the church service who are looking for attention: for people to notice them and talk with them. These are people of need. Speak with them and introduce them to others. When necessary, arrange a personal conference for them with the pastor. Their personal need cannot be neglected or ignored.

12. Discuss the services at board meetings. What can be done to improve the singing? Are the sermons getting through? What can be done to improve the general tone of the service? Discuss any problems that have arisen. Discuss with the pastor ways to make the church services more worshipful and meaningful, and help inaugerate the improvements agreed upon.

13. Help the pastor and voters plan and schedule special services.

14. Approve and disapprove new forms of worship, liturgies and hymns for use in the public worship.[8]

15. Maintain a supply of worship-related items: hymnals, communion wine and bread waffers, communion cards, baptismal napkins or towels, certificates, candles, Bibles, pencils, subscriptions to devotional booklets, tracts, etc.).

16. Together with the trustees, watch over the condition of the hymnals and see that they are rebound or replaced as conditions warrant it.

17. See that the PA system is in good repair and operational for each service.

18. Recruit, train and supervise the ushering staff and conduct refresher courses as necessary. Be ready to discuss problems with them.

19. Supervise the Altar Guild.

20. Supervise the nursery staff.

DUTIES: Care of the Pastor
(Note: the care of the teachers is placed under the board of education.)

The Elders Should:

1. Watch over the pastor and his needs, seeing to it that his wages keep up with his and his family's needs. Of all church boards, it is from the elders

especially that the pastor should receive care, lest he become the forgotten one.[9]

2. Do everything possible to help the new pastor "settle in" and feel welcome.

3. Do what is possible to shelter the pastor and his family from unnecessary aggravation. Be the protectors of the pastor and his family.

4. Aid the pastor in supervising doctrine and practice in the church and school.

5. Watch over the doctrine and life of the pastor without being watchdogs poised to pounce on him, and without feeling or showing distrust in the pastor's character and abilities. Help him in a spirit of brotherly love and harmony to feed and care for his flock with the pure Word, to maintain the practices of the church, and to set a proper example for the sheep and the lambs. Where pastoral abuses are evident, deal with them sensibly, employing words of admonition spoken in private and breathing patience, kindness, love and understanding. The intent cannot be to destroy the pastor but to treat him with utmost respect, gentleness and love — both as a pastor and Christian brother. The intent must be to assist the pastor to see his mistakes, to confess his sins and make amends, thus to win him from his error and restore him as a good, faithful and honorable shepherd of the flock. Only if such assistance and admonition is fruitless should the matter be taken to the Circuit Pastor.[10]

6. Help the pastor, however possible, in his office but not take charge of him or of the spiritual duties of his office, nor ever interfer with his official duties.

7. Give assistance to the pastor and his family in time of illness or calamity.

8. Honor the pastor and teach the members of the congregation to honor him, thus helping to honor and maintain the pastoral office in the congregation. The elders should be the first to step in and silence those who attempt to slander the pastor.

DUTIES: The Congregation's Spiritual Life and Christian Service

The Elders Should:

1. Care for their own spiritual life first of all (and that of their families), being fully devoted to the means of grace. Be regular in church and communion attendance and faithful in Bible class attendance. Practice faithfully the various aspects of stewardship: willing to use time, talents and treasure in God's service.

2. Emphasize every-member participation in the work of the church. People have to be challenged, taught and led by being confronted with opportunities to get involved.

3. Inform the pastor of spiritual problems in the congregation (which he might be unaware of), and also of cases of sickness and hardship.

4. Be peacemakers and peacekeepers in the congregation. Help to restore harmony. Work to cultivate brotherly love and patience among the members.

5. Work for strict adherence to sound doctrine and practice throughout the congregation.

6. Encourage the newcomers to enroll in Bible class, adult doctrine class, evangelism class, etc. Encourage Bible reading and study by all.

7. Encourage the newcomers who are men to apply for membership in the voters' assembly; those who are women, to apply for membership in the women's auxiliary.

8. Encourage personal witnessing for Christ.

9. Encourage the children to attend Sunday school and catechism class and youth group.

10. Be concerned about people and their spiritual (but also their physical) welfare. Have a heart for people and their problems and bear with their weaknesses (Romans 15:1).

11. Be ready at all times to give appropriate counsel from God's Word.

12. Integrate the new members into the spiritual life and fellowship of the church, as well as into the various opportunities for Christian service.

Don't be satisfied if they come to church.[11] Perhaps appoint a "fellowship" friend to assist the new member over the first year.[12] The new member needs carefully planned and executed integration into the congregation.

13. Develop a deeper spiritual life in all the members through regularly scheduled home visits (at least once or twice a year).

14. Encourage programs of fellowship.

15. Keep a finger on the spiritual pulse of the congregation, and study and discuss at board meetings ways to improve the congregation's spiritual condition.

16. Care for the children of the congregation, even the "wee" ones.

17. Know the individuals in the congregation appointed to the elder's watch care.

18. Be devoted to prayer, to study of the Scripture, to crucifying the sinful flesh, to godly meditation, to setting always a good example for others.

19. Encourage spiritual programs in the societies of the congregation generally.

DUTIES: Visits

The Elders Should:

1. Make visits to the sick. It is, of course, the pastor's duty to make sick calls regularly. However, the elders should fill in for the pastor or supplement his visits whenever asked to do so, thereby demonstrating his loving concern for the members' physical, as well as spiritual welfare.

2. Make visits to those who have suffered tragedy or trauma, in order to comfort and encourage them, and thus help to carry each other's burdens (Galations 6:2). Pray *for* them and, as the occasion requires it, pray *with* them.

3. Make visits to those who have enjoyed good fortune. Rejoice with them. Congratulate them and pray God's continued blessings upon them. In all cases remind them that good fortune comes from God, who is

gracious. (James 1:17; Romans 8:32; Psalms 23, 46, 103, 106:1, 107, 121; 1 Samuel 12:24; Genesis 32:10, and many more.)

4. Make visits to the needy. The elders should be made aware of the plight of members, and should be instrumental in alleviating their suffering by administering the charity fund, supervising collections of food and/or money. In seeking contributions to the charity fund the congregation may be reminded of Jesus' words, Matthew 25:35, 40; and of God's promise given through Isaiah (58:10). (Also: Luke 6:38; Proverbs 22:9; 1 John 3:17; 2 Corinthians 9:7; 2 Corinthians 8:3-5). Upon consultation with the pastor, some cases may best be referred to appropriate social service agencies in the community, while the congregation gives what aid it can. Confidentiality, except for unique cases, should be extended to the recipients.

5. Make visits to the delinquents and others requiring Christian admonishment. Keep a calling file in which is recorded pertinent information regarding the visits that are made. Every member of the congregation should be listed in this file, and only the pastor and the elders have access to it.[13] However, it should not be thought that discipline is left only in the elders' hands, they alone assisting the pastor in counseling the erring. As wisdom dictates, the elders should take other members along on visits to those who require Christian admonishment. And when there are calls to make, they should be made and not put off. The salvation of blood-bought souls is involved. Nor should bad weather interfer.

6. Make visits to newcomers. Every new member should be assigned immediately to the watch care of an elder. Very soon the elder should take a copy of the constitution, the congregation budget and a box of offering envelopes to new members (except when these tasks are assigned to other officers or boards).

7. Make visits in the company of the pastor at his request.

8. Make visits which the pastor asks the elders to make in his behalf.

9. Make visits on a regular basis (once or twice a year) to all the members in his assigned area or on his assigned list. Official visits are not made for idle chitchat and never for gossip. The purpose of these visits can be set up by the board at the monthly meetings with the pastor. Strategy

should be carefully mapped out, and printed materials (for handouts) should be prepared or purchased.

10. Make visits to individual families or persons as these are deemed necessary. The spiritual course of the conversations will be determined by the reasons for the visits. The pastor stands ready to counsel the elders regarding such visits. Report back to the pastor whenever this reporting is called for.

DUTIES: Stewardship

The Elders Should:

1. Refer the new members to the stewardship committee for further information on the church's finances and to receive encouragement to begin immediately a program of regular, proportionate giving.

2. Take under discussion at board meetings the congregation's response to the Bible's injunctions concerning Christian giving, and, where there is a stewardship committee or board, make recommendations.

3. Work to cultivate an awareness of all aspects of Christian stewardship and actively encourage the membership of the congregation to develop and use their God-given abilities for the Lord.

DUTIES: Membership

The Elders Should:

1. See to the prompt receipt of transfers for newcomers.

2. See to the prompt transfer or release of members leaving the congregation.

3. Evaluate all transfers and releases that have been sent to the congregation, and make appropriate recommendations to the council and/or voters' assembly.

4. On the basis of the work that has been done by the board, make reports and appropriate recommendations to the council and/or voters' assembly regarding cases of discipline and delinquency.

5. See to the publishing and distribution once a year of an up-to-date

membership list containing addresses and phone numbers together with the names of all communicants and soul members.

DUTIES: Records

The Elders Should:

1. Make certain that the official records of the congregation are kept up-to-date and safely stored.
2. See that a separate family record, listing all pertinent information of the baptized, communing and voting members is kept. This record can be sent along with the transfer of a removing member or family.
3. Maintain a personal record of each family committed to the elders care along with pertinent information.

DUTIES: Prayer

The Elders Should:

1. Pray for the Lord's guidance and help in doing the work of an elder.
2. Pray for spiritual strength and wisdom and understanding of the Scripture.
3. Pray for everyone under the elder's care; when propitious, pray with them.
4. Pray for hardship cases, for the sick and for others who have need.
5. Pray for the pastor and for the teachers.
6. Pray for the welfare of the congregation and school.

DO'S AND DON'TS FOR ELDERS

DO ...

1. Have a love for souls.
2. Be devoted to your Lord, your church, your pastor.
3. Be an exemplary Christian.

4. Be patient; cultivate an even temperment.

5. Cultivate good, pleasing personal habits; be neat and clean in appearance.

6. Know your Bible; be well-grounded in Christian doctrine and practice.

7. Be humble and repentant.

8. Communicate on the people's level, and relate to their problems and needs.

9. Have a high degree of respect for the pastoral office and help uphold it.

10. Work closely and capably with the pastor and teachers.

11. Be responsible, faithful, dependable and trustworthy — and so win the people's confidence.

12. Be thoroughly trained for the office of elder.

13. Be willing to take on even "small" tasks and do them well.

14. Keep alert to special needs while in people's homes.

15. Listen to what people have to say.

16. Leave the home you are visiting while they still want you to stay.

17. Report back concerning any visit you make where it is necessary to do so.

18. Be friendly — a smile wins; be courteous — no one likes a boor.

19. Let God's Word have its say.

20. Be faithful to your Master, your church, your pastor, your calling. Keep the promises you made when you assumed your office.

21. Be thoughtful. You are thoughtful when you think highly of others and are not insensitive to their feelings and needs.

22. Be diligent. If you have some elder work to do, do it. Immortal souls are at stake. "Always give yourselves fully to the work of the Lord, because you know that your labor in the Lord is not in vain" (1 Corinthians 15:58).

23. Be patient. God is. Patience prevents hasty action, or "shooting from the hip" with words ill chosen, unwisely spoken.

24. Put up with discouragement and disappointment. Success doesn't always come with the first try . . . or the second . . . or . . .

25. Be courageous. People will not always be eager to hear you out, or even to welcome you. God is always with you. The treatment you receive is really rendered to Christ. You are merely his representative. But he has sent you, so go fearlessly in his name.

26. Be straight-forward. It saves time. It shows sincerity. You also avoid giving people the impression that you are patronizing them.

27. Be imaginative, innovative, ingenious, inventive.

28. Above all, be God's man, always.

DON'T . . .

1. Don't do all the talking. At times you should listen more than you speak.

2. Don't jump to conclusions, but carefully weigh and sort out the facts.

3. Don't be untrained for your office.

4. Don't take a seat in people's homes where you must constantly turn your head to talk with them, and don't compete with the TV set, letting it destroy your call.

5. Don't forget to be appreciative of the welcome you receive from people.

6. Don't forget to pray: before, during and after your visit.

7. Don't gossip.

8. Don't allow anyone to undermine the office of the pastoral ministry or the man who holds it. Don't accept an accusation against the pastor. The fault finder must talk to his pastor himself about any differences that exist between them.

9. Don't argue. You never win by winning an argument. Present God's Word clearly and expect and allow it to work.

10. Don't make it a rigid rule to call ahead on the phone for an appointment with members. Sometimes it is wiser not to call ahead.

11. Don't be apologetic concerning your work. You have nothing to apologize for in carrying out your office and duties assigned to you. You are doing the Lord's work and you are doing it because you love people's souls. You are doing the people in the congregation a great service. If you apologize you invite a curt reception and you becloud the spiritual issues involved in your visit and your right to address them.

12. Don't make your visits too long. As someone has observed: this is a nervous age. Leave while they still want you to stay.

13. Don't determine to see your visit through if there is strong indication that it just isn't the proper time. Use your sanctified common sense. Be flexible.

14. Don't forget that you, too, are a sinner, saved by the grace of God.

15. Don't neglect to weep with those who weep, and rejoice with those who rejoice.

16. Don't speak when you should listen. Don't listen when you should speak.

17. Don't forget to report back on any call where this is required.

18. Don't discuss elder affairs with your wife. As soon as you've told someone (though she won't tell another soul) the matter is no longer confidential.

WHAT ENABLES YOU TO CARRY ON YOUR OFFICE OF ELDER?

You are an elder, but first of all, you are a believer. You are not your own, and the work you do is not your own. You are Christ's and the work you do is his. Christ gives you spiritual gifts through the Holy Spirit to enable you to carry out your appointed duties. In the words of St. Paul: "And God is able to make all grace abound to you, so that in all things at all times, having all that you need, you will abound in every good work" (2 Corinthians 9:8). And in the words of St. Peter: "Each one should use whatever gift he has received to serve others, faithfully administering God's grace in its various forms. If anyone speaks, he should do it as one speaking the very words of God. If anyone serves, he should do it with the strength God provides, so that in all things God may be praised through Jesus Christ. To him be the glory and the power for ever and ever. Amen" (1 Peter 4:10-11).

Your attitude as an elder ought always be one of dependence upon God for his grace to help you do your duties. The Holy Spirit, given you as a believer, is, then, your source of strength, competence and zeal. Since you carry on your office only by the grace of God operating in you, cultivate this grace through regular, intense Bible study and meditation upon God's truths. Request this grace through diligent prayer. And so, with God's grace working in you, faithfully discharge your duties as elders, doing all things to God's glory and for the welfare of his church.

† † † † † †

CHAPTER THREE

THE ELDERS AT WORK: WINNING PEOPLE'S CONFIDENCE

INTRODUCTION

As an elder you have the duty to aid the pastor in caring for the spiritual needs of the congregation. On occasion it is necessary for you to visit individuals for the purpose of speaking God's Word to them. This includes — as circumstances warrant it — conducting brief devotions with the sick, the injured and the dying in order to comfort and encourage them. It also includes giving out words of admonition to those who are remiss in their duties of membership, that is, the delinquents and those who have otherwise sinned and given offense. Most would agree that visits made for the purpose of disciplining church members are by their very nature difficult — often for the reason that the elder is unsure of both the situation and himself, and he suspects that the visit will be anything but pleasant.

You are, of course, aware of the grave importance of your visit. A soul purchased with the blood of Jesus Christ is at stake. If he is delinquent in his duties of membership or has fallen into other grievous sin, his hold on eternal life has been jeopardized — hence the reason for your visit. You go to him that his problem might be brought out in the open and placed under the light of God's Word for close scrutiny and solving. Together with the pastor and other members of the board, you work to bring the fitting Word of God to people in spiritual need. You are an instrument of God, with the Holy Spirit working on hearts through the testimony you give from God's Word.

If anything will be accomplished by your visit to a member of the congregation, God's Word — accurately quoted and correctly applied — will accomplish it. In your work as an elder there can be no substitute for a thorough knowledge and understanding of God's Word. St. Paul's charge to Timothy is certainly in keeping with the duties of the elder also: "Do your best to present yourself to God as one approved, a workman who does not need to be ashamed and who correctly handles the Word of truth" (2 Timothy 2:15).

But knowing the Word of God is one thing, while being able to communicate effectively with people you are assigned to visit is another. The power is in the Word of God. Let there be no question about this. Still, you can't communicate God's Word to people if you don't gain their confidence or if you have lost it. You can turn people off to your message through an approach that is careless, thoughtless, abrasive, impatient, loveless, tactless, pompous — or that lacks what we could simply call "plain old common sense." You are God's representative, the church's elected official and the pastor's trusted helper. But whatever God, the church and the pastor hope to accomplish through your work can be jeopardized if you approach people in such a way that you do not relate to them or their problem, if you show no feeling for them, if your speech and mannerisms unduly antagonize them and build up a wall between them and you. Your work is jeopardized by your failing to establish rapport. You must be able to communicate with people in such a way that you, the *human* instrument, do not get in the way of God's Word, the *divine* instrument.

To be an effective and efficient human agent or elder, you need ability from the Holy Spirit to approach an individual with deep love in your heart for him, using great care and perception, tact and understanding. Then you will have his confidence, friendship and trust — as well as his ear. If you are unable to communicate with the individual who has a spiritual problem — if he does not have confidence in you, resulting in his refusal to listen to what you have to tell him — God's Word cannot testify to him. Tact will open the door to you. Lack of tact will close it, even slam it in your face. People expect to be treated with courtesy and respect. It has been said that courtesy evokes courtesy, that courtesy is the most essential element of tact.[1] The point has also been made that people are social beings, that we were made that way by God. Thus counseling needs to take into account the strong influence of interpersonal dynamics.[2]

In your approach to people in which you work to gain their confidence, you must be caring. If you genuinely care for people, you will use every God-pleasing means at your disposal to reach the particular individual who has been entrusted to your watch care. First and foremost, you must be a caring person, vitally involved to the depth of your being with the welfare of others. Learn from one who cared. Let the apostle Paul show you out of his own abundant personal ministry the approach he used in bringing people under the influence of God's Word. Make his Spirit-induced philosophy for communicating with others your own. Writing in 1 Corinthians, Paul revealed his personal philosophy for approaching people:

> *Though I am free and belong to no man, I make myself a slave to everyone, to win as many as possible. To the Jews I became a Jew, to win the Jews. To those under the law I became like one under the law. To those not having the law I became like one not having the law*

(though I am not free from God's law but am under Christ's law), so as to win those not having the law. To the weak I became weak, to win the weak. **I have become all things to all men so that by all possible means I might save some.** *(9:19-22)*

Paul took care in communicating God's Word to people so that he might save whatever souls he could. That's your purpose in communicating with people too: to save whatever souls you can.

ST. PAUL'S WILLINGNESS AND ABILITY TO ACCOMODATE HIMSELF TO PEOPLE

Take special note of Paul's words in the above quotation that so succinctly describe his philosophy for approaching people to communicate God's Word to them: "I have become all things to all men." A simple explanation of these words of Paul is that he adapted or accomodated himself to everyone in their situation. Paul had empathy. He knew people. He understood the other person's religious feelings and beliefs. He knew what direction they were coming from, and dealt with them accordingly. Paul was well-educated and ingenious, possessing the ability to relate to others. He put out conscious effort to gain people's confidence by his actions and words, and to avoid antagonizing people, if at all possible. In accomodating himself to others, in adapting himself to the local situation, he took into consideration the people's nationality, language, customs, and religious backgrounds and beliefs — also the measure of their spiritual development. Paul aimed at establishing rapport: a *harmonious* rather than an *acrimonious* relationship with people. He gained their friendship, respect and confidence that would ultimately enable him to testify the truth of God to them. Paul was well aware of the fact that if the people rejected him as a person, they would certainly also reject his testimony to them about their sins and their Savior. Paul took great care to avert this possibility.

Paul's Adaptability to the Jews

The apostle illustrated his philosophy of adapting or accomodating himself to people — his being "all things to all men" — by summarizing his manner of dealing with the Jews. He became "like a Jew" to the Jews to win the Jews. Paul didn't say that he *became* a Jew, that he reverted back to the Jewish religion when he was among Jews. Only that he became "like" a Jew. He became "like one under the law," to those under the law. Thus when the apostle Paul was laboring among Jews who were not converted to Christ and who still felt bound to the old laws, he was careful to conduct himself in such ways as to be accepted — if not always for his message, at least for his person — by the Jews. Paul adapted his own life-style to the life-style of those who were living under the old Mosaic laws and national customs. As an example: Paul was a tentmaker by trade and employed his skills to earn his living while working as a missionary. When he plied his trade among Jews who still observed the Sabbath, Paul also rested from work on that day. Furthermore, he was careful about his eating habits while laboring among those who were still bound in their consciences to the old prohibitions, lest he cause offense. If Paul would not have conducted himself "as under the law" while among those under the law, he most certainly would have caused deep offense and aroused antagonism — not just against himself but, more importantly, against the gospel he preached, and even against the Savior he represented.

Though Paul was careful not to offend the Jews by flagrant, unJewish conduct while in their midst, he did not, on the other hand, teach others to abide by the Jewish customs and Mosaic laws. He was acting with gentlemanly grace and dignity as Christ's ambassador, blending his actions with the actions of the Jews among whom he preached — people who were scrupulous about legal prescriptions.[3]

But Paul had to consider his role of becoming all things to all men — his being like a Jew among Jews — not only when working among non-Christian Jews, but even while working among Christian Jews, especially in Jerusalem. The Christian Jews in that city, exposed daily to the old emphasis on the Mosaic law (Moses was still read and revered) still clung to some of the Jewish regulations. It was a matter of custom with them: they remained, for a time, with the old, retaining a Jewish flavor in practicing their Christianity. While in their midst, Paul accomodated himself to their life-style to keep from offending them. Indeed, he accomodated himself to the Jews whether Christian or non-Christian. Paul had empathy. Yet he did not surrender to Jewish doctrine and declared that he was not under the (Jewish) law.

Moreover, when Paul preached to the Jews in the synagogue it was with a rabbi's skill. He knew his Bible, having acquired the skills that the Jews required and respected in their teachers. What an example to present day pastors and church elders. Know your Bible!

Paul's preaching was a presentation of God's truth. He was wholly committed to the truth (Acts 27:22-25; Romans 9:1; 2 Corinthians 11:10; 1 Thessalonians 2:13). But in presenting God's truth to the Jews, Paul showed a profound use of human psychology. He was careful to try to win their confidence by presenting his message of truth in such a manner that he not only showed that he knew what he was talking about, but that he was also convinced in his own heart. He could not inspire confidence in others concerning his message if he himself did not portray confidence and conviction.

Paul's Adaptability to the Gentiles

As has already been pointed out, Paul found himself preaching a great deal to the Gentiles, not just to the Jews. He wrote: "To those not having the law I became like one not having the law (though I am not free from God's law, but am under Christ's law), so as to win those not having the law." The Gentiles did not have the Word of God and, therefore, were without the Old Testament legal code by which God regulated his chosen nation Israel until Christ came. Paul accomodated himself to the non-Christian Jews when he was among them by keeping some of their laws and customs outwardly. By the same token, since he also wanted to gain the Gentiles for Christ and not in any way lay the stumbling block of antagonism before them, he also then adapted to their customs when he was among them (except, of course, where these conflicted with God's truth and righteousness). The custom of the Gentiles was not to observe Mosaic laws and Jewish customs, and so, while in their midst, Paul didn't either. Paul was not converting the Gentiles to the Jewish religion but to the Jewish Messiah, whom God had promised through Abraham to all people.

Paul testified: "Though I am not free from God's law, but am under Christ's law . . ." Inspite of Paul's flexibility when dealing with the Gentiles, we dare not infer that he was unprincipled. While Paul didn't observe in their midst the Old Testament ceremonial laws governing such things as days and sacrifices and food and drink, nevertheless, his conduct was godly and moral since it was determined by *Christ's law*. His whole sphere of mission activity was carried out in the tradition of Christ's law of love. Christ loved Paul and gave himself for him. Paul loved Christ, and out of that love served his Savior by preaching his name and salvation and by keeping up a morally decent and upright life. His whole manner of living and working was ruled by love in his heart that was engendered by faith in Christ and the cross. And so, Paul remained an exemplary Christian among Jew and Gentile alike.

Christ's law, the law of Christian love, is the sphere of your activities as an elder too. You must stand at the cross of Christ looking up. You stand cleansed of your sins by Christ's blood. It is with the cross of Christ, and the love it demonstrated, laid upon your personal conscience that you go forward in your work as an elder, bearing God's Word to those who have special need of it. While you can neither be snobbish to the poor and the common, nor intimidated by the rich and prestigious, you can — and you must — love them all in Christ, and love to be of service to them.

Paul's Adaptability to the Weak

There was yet another group of people with whom Paul employed his philosophy of becoming all things to all men. He wrote: "To the weak I became as weak, to win the weak." Paul's business was not only to save the non-Christian but to keep the Christian saved. And that is your special work as an elder too. The weak, especially, need the watch care of the pastor and the elders. The weak stand in constant danger of being led away from Christ because of their lack of understanding and their shallow spiritual depth (Luke 8:12). They waver between truth and error, between faith and doubt.

Paul was willing and able to relate to the weak, to accomodate himself as much as possible to their perilous spiritual condition. He went to them, not to pass judgment on their weak faith, but to be sympathetic, desiring only to coax the weak faith to grow strong. In reading Romans chapter fourteen, we can see how carefully Paul taught Christian love and understanding and patience toward those who were still unsure in their own minds concerning the freedom from the law of Moses that the gospel of Christ gives to Christians. Paul emphasized that no one should put a stumbling block, or occasion to fall, in his brother's way by eating meats which offended the brother's weak conscience, meats which the brother still regarded as ceremonially unclean. The spiritually strong are to take care how they conduct themselves around the spiritually weak (Romans 14:19; 15:1-2). Weak Christians have to be given the chance to grow in their knowledge and faith and appreciation of the gospel. Strong Christians are to help them (1 Thessalonians 5:14). "The thought seems to be that some people need to borrow from another's strength on occasion."[4]

And so, you as an elder must learn to be patient and understanding with the weak, and not be harsh. The bottom line is brotherly love (the law of Christ). The spiritually weak suffer from spiritual malnutrition. They need to be fed God's Word, which can make them grow in their knowledge and faith (1 Peter 2:2; 2 Peter 3:18; John 17:17). Lovingly and patiently, with deep feeling for their spiritual needs, offer the weak the food of God's Word. Coax them to partake. Help them to understand and appreciate God's Truth. Endeavor to interest them in reading their Bibles on their own; endeavor to seat them at the pastor's feet where he, as a shepherd under Christ, can feed them the spiritual food the Holy Spirit provides.

Why Paul Did What He Did, the Way He Did It

The book of Acts gives us some record of Paul's work and the results. So do his epistles. Paul did not win *all* the people to whom he witnessed Christ. He won *some*. And, all things considered, even that was a true miracle — as is always the working of faith in the human heart by the Holy Spirit (John 14:12). But winning at least some is what the Lord had sent the apostle to do, and that is the work Paul was pleased to carry on for the Lord. He confessed: "I have become all things to all men so that by all possible means I might save some."

To win even some, Paul found it necessary to pour his heart and soul into his work. He has to learn to accommodate himself to people, to have empathy or understanding and feeling for them and their situation. And Paul did this exceedingly well.

THE ELDER'S APPROACH TO PEOPLE TO WIN THEIR CONFIDENCE

The aim of Paul's philosophy of being all things to all men was to establish and maintain a cordial and harmonious relationship with those to whom he was sent with the gospel. Paul endeavored to keep the lines of communication open between himself and the people by accommodating or adapting himself as much as possible to them, without compromising the Lord's Word or his position as the Lord's servant. Some applications to your work as an elder have already been made from Paul's philosophy. There are other things that may be said in order to encourage you to expend intense effort and great care in establishing and maintaining rapport with the people you are assigned to serve.

Be Accomodating, Adaptable

You should recognize that as an elder you must adapt yourself as best you can (without compromising the Word of God or your office) to the person, to the time, to the circumstance and to whatever else is involved that makes the counselee and his case unique. In other words, you will seek to avoid a rigidity in your personal behavior and in your methods of ministration that would make it impossible for him to accept you as his counselor and maintain confidence in you. You may find that you will have to discard a certain approach to an individual for the reason that he is unable at the time spiritually, emotionally, or even physically to accept it. In adapting yourself to the individual you will have to learn how to exercise patience: how to make your way slowly and deliberately.

The counselee may or may not respond in the manner you hope for. He may be immediately receptive, or immediately hostile. He may treat you with warmth, or he may treat you with indifference, even coldness. He may act quiet and withdrawn or he may show obstreperous behavior. He may be a person of principle or a person lacking in principle. Whatever the case, you will purposely try every godly recourse to maintain a basis for counseling the person, at the same time avoiding everything that would hinder or destroy a meaningful and fruitful dialog (interaction).

Be a Friend

Strive to establish and maintain an atmosphere of cordiality and friendship with the counselee. Friendship is highly important to gaining his confidence so that he accepts you as his confidant and counselor. If you go to him in a spirit of bitterness, or with a hostile attitude, wearing a chip on your shoulder — yes, if you go to him as his enemy — you will not gain his friendship or his confidence. The point is that circumstances, especially the sin he is involved with, could make it easy enough to go to the counselee in an unfriendly, uncaring, even harsh and belligerent mood. But adapt yourself to his needs. He needs your friendship; he needs a patient, caring, tender and kind attitude on your part — even when you must talk firmly to him about his sin. "There is a friend who sticks closer than a brother" (Proverbs 18:24).

Be Loving

Yes, you should love him even when he is stubborn and disagreeable and unloving toward you: "A friend loves at all times" (Proverbs 17:17).

> It is a mistake to think that all who disagree with us are dishonest at heart and that they will never accept the truth. Let us try to show them all the love and respect we can and thus try to gain their confidence. If these people persist in their stubborness, they will need rebuke; but even words of rebuke should be spoken in the spirit of love and helpfulness. Let us remember we are not better than they, with the exception that the grace of God has renewed us and kept us. Hence, we must deal with obstinate sinners as God has dealt with us. Any assumed superiority on our part will repel, will not attract them.[5]

Everyone can relate to a loving heart. As an elder you simply must have a heart that is filled to the brim with love for the souls under your care. Christ had it and you learn from him: "Christ loved the church and gave himself for it" (Ephesians 5:25). Those words, "He *gave himself* for it," tell us much. In giving himself, Christ — who is the Lord of glory — endured shame, terrible shame. He who made the world later walked on it and was finally crucified on it, that in his wounds we might have redemption, the forgiveness of sins. Learn from the Savior's love to love other souls. Learn to love, even when you do not feel loved. Learn from the Savior's acts of humble service to be a humble servant. If you do, you will not be guilty of patronization. In love and patience Jesus waited for repentance in his own people. He longed for their acceptance of him as Lord and Messiah, but was rejected time and again. Before he threatened Jerusalem's destruction, he first wept over it. His sobs keep us from regarding any of his words of rebuke and warning as bitting and harsh. Learn of Jesus. "There is no substitute for a genuine love of souls. People feel it instinctively whether you like them or not. Jesus wept over souls. Have you ever wept over souls?"[6]

You are not a piece of glass that transmits heat but remains cold yourself. You transmit the Lord's love toward sinners through your own warm, loving heart. Out of a heart that basks in the sunshine of God's love you speak to those under your care about sin, about the Savior from sin, about the Christian life. You are able to communicate Christ to others because you experience Christ yourself.

And don't forget to smile. Let your facial expression radiate love. Warm people with a smile and a friendly face that expresses the love you *feel* for them in your heart. An exchange of smiles, and the warmth behind them, can change the whole tone of a meeting.

Be Caring

The counselee needs a caring heart in you, his counselor and confidant. And he needs to experience it; he needs to see evidence of it in your attitudes, mannerisms and speech. People have a way of sensing whether other people really care or are just acting. Don't be artificial; strive to be genuine. If you genuinely care for people, you will not merely go through the motions but you will show your caring spirit in the way you relate to them.[7]

Your purpose in counseling the individual is to help change his heart and life. You must let him know that you accept him as a person and that you care for him deeply regardless of his problems or his sins. And that it is because you care that you want him to change. He must not be made to feel threatened when he sits down to counsel with you as his confidant. He must know that you love him and are deeply concerned for his welfare and happiness — which depends on his relationship with God — and that you are especially concerned over where he will spend eternity.

Especially when it comes time to warn the person of impending doom for his impenitence, a spirit of love and deep caring must govern your words and attitudes.

> Let us present the message of retribution. One missionary so preaches the doctrine of retribution as to produce this impression on the sinner: If you do not repent and believe, you will be damned; your case is hopeless; and *I don't care if it is*. Another missionary puts it this way: If you do not repent and believe, you will be lost; *but my heart is breaking with sorrow over your dreadful mistake* (emphasis added).[8]

Which of the two in his approach to the impenitent is most like his Savior? It has been said that ministry has many tools and that care is the handle that fits them all.[9]

Have a Sympathetic Heart

In adapting or accomodating yourself to the people you are to counsel, and to their particular situation, also maintain a sympathetic heart. The people you counsel desperately need this in you. These people are in trouble or sin, or are enduring grief. They need help, guidance, admonishment and comfort from you. But you will blunder in your approach and shut yourself off from them if you do not have sympathy in your heart and give evidence of it. Jesus had sympathy and showed it often in his ministry. He wept at Lazarus tomb. He sobbed over doomed Jerusalem. He was deeply touched by the suffering of others, thus fulfilling the prophet Isaiah's words: "Surely he took up our infirmities and carried our sorrows" (Isaiah 53:4). And now in heaven, at the throne of grace, Jesus continues to treat us with sympathy: "For we do not have a high priest who is unable to sympathize with our weaknesses" (Hebrews 4:15). We sympathize with others when we appreciate what they are going through and we deal with them with the tenderness and understanding that such appreciation instinctively calls for. A sympathetic heart can understand people and place you in a position to communicate with wisdom and tact, and to greatly influence the people you are called on to counsel.

Meet People on Their Turf: Talk Their Language

Accomodating or adapting yourself to other people requires you to be ingenious enough to speak to them in language they understand (their language), and to meet them on turf they are familiar with. Thus ask the Holy Spirit to give you the ability to adapt yourself to people's background, culture, experience, education, interests, as well as to their present circumstances and needs; even to individual human temperment. It has been said that sanctified ingenuity is a gift to be prized highly, both for its value and for its rarity. Strive to be ingenius. Ask the Holy Spirit to guide you to methods of approach to people that will open the door and keep it open to your visits: methods of approach that will fit the individual person and the particular situation at hand.

One of the delinquent members of a small town congregation was an auto repairman and owner of his own shop. Frustrated by earlier failures to persuade the man to attend church, the pastor finally hit on an ingenius approach which met the repairman on his own turf and enabled him to deliver God's message. Visiting the man one day in his shop, the pastor found him kneeling on the floor, putting a wheel back on a car that he had repaired. Crouching down beside the repairman, the pastor began the conversation with the question: "Is it necessary that all of these wheel nuts be tight?" "Certainly," came the quick reply, "if even one of these nuts were not tight, the wheel could eventually work loose and come off the car." Each wheel nut is important for each has its job to do. And the only way that it can do its job is to be tightened down securely. If only one does not do its job the performance of the wheel and even the safety of the car itself is jeopardized. Seeing his opening, the pastor proceeded to point out to the repairman that the individual member of a congregation has his part to play and his job to do. When a member does not attend the worship services, he is missed. Things aren't the same. Each and every member is important to God and to the congregation. No one can say that it is not important or necessary for him to take an active part in the congregation. Without being facetious, the pastor asked the mechanic where he fit in. Was he being a responsible Christian and member of the church? Was he doing his job or had he, so to speak, come loose? By his neglect of the worship service was he causing a bad effect on the congregation? His point was well taken. He had spoken to the man in terms he could relate to.

Another pastor used a fireplace to come to terms with a longtime acquaintance who was a lapsed church member. During the course of the evening, the pastor, without saying a word, merely removed one of the smaller logs from the pile of logs that was burning fiercely. As the two campers watched in silence, the blaze of the solitary log gradually died out. The unchurched acquaintance got the message: to withdraw from God's people is to invite spiritual death.[10]

Christ, too, was ingenious, as well as practical. Recall the time he asked for a drink of water in order that he might invite a sinner to partake of the living (spiritual) water he has to offer. In the process he slaked his own physical thirst.

Have Respect for Others. And Have Empathy: Put Yourself in the Place of Others, Treating Them as You Would Want to be Treated

When you treat others the way you yourself would like to be treated, you find that people are not turned off or intimidated by your presence. They experience rapport with you. When approaching people to counsel them, try to wear like an old pair of shoes or fit like an old pair of gloves. Simply stated: be comfortable to have around.

For example: respect the other person's time as you want your own time respected. Respect his feelings as you want your own feelings respected. Respect his right to entertain company without interference from "outsiders," even as you would like the same privilege for yourself. Respect his working and sleeping habits as you like others to respect yours. Respect his right to well-earned (and perhaps much needed) leisure time, and the freedom of choice as to how he will use it — even as you want your leisure time respected.

And so, don't go ahead with your visit when you learn that your counselee is entertaining guests (presuming that you did not call ahead for an appointment). If a number of cars are parked out front, you have good reason to believe that he has company. Go on by. Try again another time. What you have to say to him is a private matter anyway. Keep yourself informed of your counselee's working and sleeping hours. Neither get the person out of bed to counsel him, nor keep him from his regular routine. Don't keep him and his family up. Don't stay late. Don't belabor the matter at hand. If you can't tend to all your business within a reasonable length of time in one call, make an appointment to return another time. And when you say good-by or good night, leave. Don't dwaddle. Don't carry on your conversation outside the door.

Don't stay long when you see that the family is in commotion. You won't accomplish much if the person is preoccupied with some crisis that has just surfaced. What you have to say to the person requires *his* undivided attention, and *yours*.

Do be a gentleman and a gentle man at all times. If the person is a talker and is used to having people give him their attention, don't lose his confidence by doing too much of the talking (especially at first) and don't interrupt him. On the other hand, when you have the floor, in a gentlemanly way impress him with the fact that you expect the same courtesy. Don't allow yourself to be interrupted or sidetracked from your line of conversation. On the other hand, avoid wordiness. Don't preach.

Don't neglect the children in the household. Greet them when you enter the house, if they are present. Talk with them. Show interest in them. This holds true also of the person's spouse. Be friendly and outgoing. Also be understanding of the spouse's position in the matter at hand.

Don't use steamroller tactics, which no one likes. Don't use intimidation. You are not there in his home to pressure him but rather to counsel him with the Word of God employed with wisdom and tact. You may, indeed, win your argument; you may carry the discussion, and yet lose the case. You can't browbeat a delinquent or a sinner into submission. The Word of God must carry the hour. Quite often you will find that it is necessary to sow the seed of the Word and then let it have a chance to take root and grow. In future visits you can water and nurture the tender faith that springs up. Give the Holy Spirit a chance to work on the counselee's heart. Don't think that you must, or that you will, see the fruitage of your labors immediately.

Demonstrate Loving Concern for the Burdened

The point is well made that bringing the solace of the church to the sick and the aged is a special kind of visiting and is the finest way of making the member realize that the church cares about him.[11] It has also been observed that at times the prayer of a layman said at a bedside has a much more telling impact than the prayer of a clergyman. That while people expect the minister to pray, the act of prayer by a fellow church member seems to plumb depths unreachable by the man of the cloth.[12]

Perhaps a person who is under discipline — someone you have been counseling — has been seriously injured, stricken with illness, even hospitalized. It would be a wonderful demonstration of loving concern to go to his bedside (if it is a woman, how practicle and wise it would be to take your wife along). By being there to share his burden in even a small way you show your love and the congregation's concern. The very fact that you show this loving care for him in his time of suffering will do much to soften his attitude toward the work that you as an elder are called on to do. In receiving a visit from you when he is ill, or otherwise down and out, the member under discipline is given an excellent example of the wonderful benefits of Christian fellowship and love that accrue to the members of the congregation. Not only will your prayers offered in his behalf reach the ears of God in heaven, your sympathy and loving concern — and that of the congregation — will be cherished by the person for years to come.

There is the case of a man, well-known in the community where he lived, who had been without a church and a pastor for over sixty years. He became seriously ill and had to receive surgery. His condition for a time was grave. A local pastor with an intense love for human souls had been visiting this man on and off in his home, but with little success. When the pastor heard of the man's hospital confinement, he made it a point to be often at his bedside where he offered up fervent prayer in the man's behalf. By God's grace the patient recovered. Later he and his wife received formal instructions from the pastor and became faithful members of the church. Several times this elderly convert related the love he had for the man of God who so faithfully saw him while he was in the hospital and prayed for his recovery. He saw his recovery as nothing short of an act of God. He needed no more convincing as to what yet needed to be done in his life. But please note: the pastor who wanted so much to save the man's soul, also had deep feelings for the man's physical hurt. And these tender feelings finally drew hearts together, making it possible for the pastor to speak to him and his wife the words of Christ that are spirit and life.

There is also the account of a man who was won *back* to the Lord and the church by the care a pastor gave to his hospitalized wife. The husband had been confirmed as a youth in the Lutheran Church, and had eventually strayed, remaining away from the church for many years. His wife did not belong to any church and had never been baptized. One day, near death, she was rushed to the hospital. A pastor visited her after her condition stabilized. She was very weak and semi-comatose. Hoping that she could hear him and understand what he was saying, the pastor spoke to her briefly about her merciful Lord who forgives sins and helps people in their troubles. Then, speaking close to her ear, he prayed a brief but fervent prayer in her behalf, little knowing what effect if any his words had on her injured brain. By God's grace she recovered. Led further by his grace she requested Christian instructions and joined the church. Her husband reaffirmed his faith before the entire congregation. The woman then proceeded to turn two other families to Christ. She once told her pastor: "I heard every word you said to me at the hospital. You will never know how much it meant to me that you came and prayed for me."

Here, then, is a challenge for you in your work as an elder. Make it a point to show your sincere, loving concern. With the help of the pastor, and perhaps also the office secretary, keep track of the seriously ill and injured. Your pastor will be glad to counsel you regarding any visits that you wish to make to the sick and injured. At times he will even request that you make certain visits as part of your work.

Be Knowledgeable

You will find it an asset to your work as an elder to possess the ability to speak intelligently on a wide range of topics, and to show interest in those things that are of interest and importance to the person you are attempting to reach. A man may be ridiculed for his ignorance, but who is shamed for his knowledge? When you speak to others as a bearer of God's truth, take care not to lose the person's confidence by showing ignorance either of the Bible or of things that are of general interest and concern. And if you can speak with him intelligently on matters of specific concern, or at least show genuine interest in them, so much the better. Be a well-read person. Strive for a well-rounded personality. Continually work at becoming better educated. Possess the knowledge that will enable you to deal with all kinds of people as their equal. Above all, keep growing in your knowledge of the Bible and in your ability to apply the fitting word as the occasions arise.

Don't Forget Humor

In *A Bit of Honey*, W.E. Thorn makes this observation:

> When God reached down and took a little earth and formed man, he crowned him with intelligence. He gave him the ability to reason and to make decisions. Within this complicated creature known as man, God deposited a little bit of honey known as a sense of humor. Man is not complete without it. A man without a sense of humor is like a car without a bumper. Sir Herbert Tree said: "A sense of humor is a test of sanity." A man without a sense of humor will not go far without running into difficulty. A man without a sense of humor is a real cripple. A noted psychiatrist said recently, "Woe unto the man who loses his sense of humor, for laughter is the finest antidote for the acidity that eats ulcers in the stomach."[13]

To be a successful elder and counselor you need to know human nature and how to adjust to human nature's variety of needs. One of human nature's needs is humor. Having a sense of humor includes the ability to laugh at yourself, and that is important in your communicating with people. We are to take ourselves seriously, but not too seriously, for then we become pompous. Tasteful humor can be an appropriate tension-buster. Long faces do nothing for the kingdom of God. A smile and a little bit of honey in the form of good humor costs us nothing and is so much appreciated by the other person. As the saying goes, "A smile is easily caught." Good humor, a warm smile and even some laughter — all have their place in the kingdom work.

IN CONCLUSION

While it is important to be tactful, sympathetic and understanding; while it is important to accomodate yourself as much as possible to the person you counsel; while it is necessary to meet him on his own turf and communicate with him in terms he can understand, and in a manner that will build rapport, always bear in mind that the Word of God is, finally, what changes hearts and souls for Christ. And this Word is charged with power from on high through the Holy Spirit. It is the Word that must do it, and you as an elder are obligated to speak the Word of God truthfully, with confidence and without apology, as one who believes it yourself, whose eternal destiny depends on it, whose own life is daily guided and guarded by it. Know the Word. Use the Word. Depend on the Word. Pray for the success of the Word. Teach the Word to others.

† † † † † †

CHAPTER FOUR

THE ELDERS AT WORK: SCRIPTURAL DISCIPLINE AND THE ELDERS' INVOLVEMENT

INTRODUCTION

Scriptural discipline of church members falls into two categories:

1. **Christian discipline carried on generally.** This is the everyday variety of Christian discipline, the interaction of Christians as they call upon each other to be strong in the faith, to serve God and remove sin[1] (Romans 15:14; Matthew 18:15ff.; 2 Timothy 3:16).

2. **Church discipline.** This is admonishment on an official level, and includes also the steps that may proceed beyond it, which the church, the congregation, administers to erring or offending members: excommunication or exclusion, and the action of isolation. Though the process of admonishing or disciplining the offending party may have been started by an individual member, finally, due to the turn of events, it moves also to the care of those who are specifically charged with carrying out admonishment in the name of the church: the pastor and the board of elders. And it may move to that group charged with taking *final* action in the case: the voters' assembly, which acts in the name of the entire congregation.

The few Scripture references that have been selected should give a fairly good idea of how individual Christians as well as the church (congregation) should proceed in the matter of discipline, the pitfalls to avoid and the blessings that may result.

WHAT THE SCRIPTURE HAS TO SAY CONCERNING DISCIPLINE

Scripture #1: Restoring the One Who Sinned

Brothers, if someone is caught (overtaken) in a sin, you who are spiritual should restore him gently. But watch yourself, or you may be tempted. Carry each other's burdens, and in this way you will fulfill the law of Christ. (Galations 6:1-2)

The meaning of Paul's words is not that we have overtaken or surprised our brother while he is in the act of committing some transgression, but that he was overtaken or caught by a temptation and didn't save himself by fleeing from it as the Scripture exhorts Christians to do (1 Timothy 6:11; 2 Timothy 2:22; 1 Corinthians 6:18). He let down his guard for the moment and, as a result, temptation moved in and had him before he realized what was happening. King David, who committed adultery and, later, murder; and the apostle Peter, who denied three times that he knew Jesus, are examples of this. Paul's words do not describe cases of deliberate or wilful sin, but of falling prey, suddenly, to the deceptive power of sin.

God wants the Christian who has fallen prey to sin rescued. And there are those who "are spiritual," to come to the rescue — Christians who walk in the Spirit, who are not themselves involved in the same or similar sins and are recognized for their exemplary lives. They have an important job to do. They are to help him mend his sinful way so that he comes back to his former condition of not committing sins such as the one that has overtaken him. He must be restored as a righteous servant of Christ.

But it is not enough to get the person overtaken by sin to stop his sin. He must be helped to see what a terrible wrong he has done and to hate his sin, to confess his sin, to ask forgiveness for his sin and to quit his sin. The brother stepped away from God when he was overtaken in sin; the brother steps back to God and is restored when he confesses his sin (turning from it) and accepts the forgiveness offered in the gospel. Restored in heart, he will also live a restored life.

Consider the episode of King David's sins. He committed adultery with his neighbor's wife and then murdered his neighbor to hide the sin. After months of public scandal, Nathan went to David and confronted him with his sin, admonishing him. David then made this confession: "I have sinned against the Lord." Nathan announced God's forgiveness: "The Lord has also put away your sin. You will not die." When David regarded his sins with fear and deep sorrow, and then accepted the Lord's forgiveness, he was restored (cf. 2 Samuel 12:1-23). In Psalm 32 David confessed to God: "I acknowledge my sin to you . . . I said, 'I will confess my transgressions to the Lord' — and you forgave the guilt of my sin" (v. 5). While taking comfort in God's forgiveness, David also prayed for rescue from the power of sin: "Create in me a pure heart, O God, and renew a steadfast spirit within me" (Psalm 51:10). David had been restored.

Paul wrote that the one overtaken or caught in a sin should be restored gently —literally, in a spirit of humility or meekness, which then breeds gentleness and courtesy. The Christian counselor's sanctity is not under discussion. He isn't to compare himself with the offending brother in order to remind him: "You have committed a sin I have not committed. How could you do it?" Such a better-than-thou attitude is, needless to say, disgusting and self-defeating. Rather, the restoring brother goes to the offending brother in a posture of humility, readily confessing his own sinfulness. All Christians have the old sinful flesh, and, therefore, have the capability for sin which that flesh produces (Matthew 15:19; Galatians 5:19). The restoring brother looks back with shame upon the times he himself fell into sin's clutches. He goes humbly, thus gently, to his erring brother as a fellow sinner who loves him and wants to save him.

The story is told about a minister who went to a prison to visit a condemned man. He stood outside the bars of the man's cell and officiously reproached him for his crime, warning him to repent or suffer the eternal consequences. He got nowhere with the condemned man. But another minister tried a different tack. He went right into the man's cell, sat down beside him on the prison cot, and putting his arm around the man's shoulders, spoke to him in a spirit of humility and gentleness. "Isn't it wonderful that we have a Savior who died for sinners like you and me?" he asked the condemned man. Christ won that sinner's heart and restored him. It is well said that the devil is thwarted by humility.

> Deal gently with the erring; Oh, do not thou forget,
> However darkly stained by sin, He is thy brother yet.
> Heir of the selfsame heritage, Child of the selfsame God,
> He has but stumbled in the path, Thou hast in weakness trod.

And note the added warning: But watch yourself, or you also may be tempted." If the restoring Christian is arrogant and self-righteous, or if he is concerned only with the fallen brother's trespasses, recklessly forgetting his own evil flesh and thinking that it can't happen to him, he, too, may be tempted. And so, the restoring brother must first be concerned about his own spiritual condition.

Paul further urged: "Carry each other's burdens, and in this way you will fulfill the law of Christ." Sin in the brother becomes a burden to his fellow Christians as well, who will do what they can, with God's help, to relieve him of it. First, by helping him to see and acknowledge his sin, and second, by leading him to the cross and the blood of the Lamb that was shed there for him. What greater devotion of love can a Christian show than to restore a brother who has been overtaken or caught in a sin (John 13:34; Romans 12:10)?

THE BOARD OF ELDERS' INVOLVEMENT

The Lord should always be able to count on the elders of the church as being among "those who are spiritual:" men who are filled with the Holy Spirit and thus live victorious Christian lives. The Lord, working through his church to carry on discipline, should always be able to count on the elders to help lead the way in restoring members who have fallen prey to sin. With God's help the elders ought to steadfastly endeavor never to disqualify themselves by being personally overtaken in sin. Furthermore, the elders will follow the standards for dealing with the erring as outlined in this Scripture which we have just discussed. (Consider also the message in Luke 15:3-10.)

Scripture #2:   The Brother Who Sins — The Four Steps of Discipline

If your brother sins against you, go and show him his fault, just between the two of you. If he listens to you, you have won your brother over. But if he will not listen, take one or two others along, so that "every matter may be established by the testimony of two or three witnesses." If he refuses to listen even to the church, treat him as you would a pagan or a tax collector. I tell you the truth, whatever you bind on earth will be bound in heaven, and whatever you loose on earth will be loosed in heaven. (Matthew 18:15-18; see a similar account in Luke 17:3)

Here is the central passage of the Scripture — our Savior's own words — mandating discipline of a Christian brother who has fallen into sin. As Jesus shows here, the erring or offending brother must be given opportunity to repent and receive forgiveness, and if he does not repent, the church must have the opportunity to speak in the matter (i.e. to exclude the person).

The hoped for outcome of church discipline is clearly stated in Jesus' words: "If he listens to you, you have won your brother over." True admonishment (discipline) is always to be entered upon in a spirit of love. The object is not to punish the guilty but in love to win him over so that he repents and his sins can be forgiven.

What sins are included in Jesus' exhortation: "If your brother sins against you, go and show him his fault"? Each and every sin is to be repented of, not only the so-called "mortal sins" (1 Corinthians 6:9-10; Galations 5:19-21). There are no inconsequential sins. Therefore, there are no sins that per se require no admonishment, no discipline of the offender. This is not to say that a Christian will pounce on every sin his brother commits and does not repent of. Christians would grow weary of each other if a case were made on the basis of each and every sin that may have been committed in a moment of weakness, and if a greater degree of admonishment were given than is actually called for by the occasion. The Christian would do well to make his admonition timely and meaningful, and suited to the individual as well as to the sin. Sometimes stunned silence, or a look registering shock and disapproval, and a shaking of the head, suffice to admonish the offender concerning his sin. But when verbal confrontation is called for, where anything less would weaken the admonition, then the restoring brother ought to proceed to speak up about the sin and the offending brother's need to repent of it. But he will admonish his brother in a gentle fashion (Galations 6:1f.) for his purpose is not to condemn him, but to help him make his confession.

STEP ONE: *If your brother sins against you, go and show him his fault (literally: 'reprove,' 'rebuke' him), just between the two of you. If he listens to you, you have won your brother over (v. 15).*

The sin the brother commits may or may not directly involve his fellow Christian who takes it upon himself to admonish him for it. No matter. In any case he has committed sin that is apparent to others, and every sin is an affront to the bond of Christian faith, of love, of fellowship that exists between brothers in Christ.

Now then, when the sinning brother gives evidence that he does not experience contrition regarding his sin, the one who knows about the sin has the duty to take the initial step in turning the brother to repentance. "Go and show him his fault," Jesus said. Literally, he is to go and seek his brother out in order to rebuke him, which necessitates laying his sin out before him. The counseling brother dare not wait for his offending brother to come to him. Stubborn impenitence, sinful pride, shame, even ignorance of his sin, or lack of awareness of the gravity of the sin, may keep him from seeking out the offended party to make his confession. When several Christians know about a sin, each should, nevertheless, consider it his duty to go to the offender.

"Go and show him his fault, just between the two of you," Jesus commanded. The words of rebuke are meant only for the ears of the offender. He must be rebuked privately, for the whole object is to save him, not to embarrass him before others. The point is, that if he should repent at this first step, no other step is necessary, no other persons need to be brought in and the case is closed — except where the situation calls for stating an apology or otherwise making amends to the person or persons who were wronged.

Note that Jesus used the term "brother:" "If your *brother* sins . . ." And so, a Christian does not go to the sinner as one who is his enemy, with whom he is going to have a fight, but as one who is his brother, whom he will try to restore. Love breeds patience. Humility results in gentleness (Galations 6:1). The counseling brother doesn't go to the offending brother to threaten him with excommunication, which it is pointless even to mention in the first step, but to censure him for his sin in order to coax him to repent, confess and ask forgiveness. It goes without saying that the counseling party ought to pray diligently in behalf of the offending party, as well as for himself, asking for divine grace and blessing.

The proper reaction on the part of the offending party to the admonishment that is offered him is to "listen." This means to hear the counseling brother out and to respond with the requested repentance and confession, genuinely feeling it in his heart. If the offender repents he is to be forgiven (Luke 17:3). In that event the brother has been won over and he should be deeply grateful to his counseling brother for the great debt of love he has paid him: "My brothers, if one of you should wander from the truth and someone should bring him back, remember this: Whoever turns a sinner away from his error will save him from death and cover a multitude of sins" (James 5:19-20; see also Psalm 141:5).

But what if the offender doesn't "listen" to his brother? Should his counselor move immediately on to the next step? "A lot of Christians, and even some preachers, I'm afraid, make the mistake of thinking that Matthew 18 is a handy-dandy three-step program for kicking people out of the church . . . One, two, three, and you're out."[2] The point is that many Christians think the steps listed in Matthew 18 have to follow each other in rapid succession with only one attempt at each step to get the brother to repent, and the congregation then excommunicating him in short order.

But Jesus' words "if he will not listen" do not infer: "if he doesn't hear you the very first time," thus ruling out subsequent visits. Love, wisdom and patience may very well indicate that additional visits be made under the first step ("just between the two of you"). This first step continues until he either "listens" or shows by his words and actions that "he will not listen." Love for the sinner and love for the truth will have to determine how much time and how many visits would be proper. If protracted visits weaken the counseling brother's testimony, or give the offender reason to believe he can stall him out of more intensive action, or if the sin continues on, thus involving the brother deeper and deeper in sin, there is no alternative to offering him the additional testimony of witnesses.

One of the reasons for continuing admonition under the first step is failure of communication, the failure of the counseling brother to present his admonishment clearly and scripturally. Lack of all the facts, lack of rapport between the two parties, feelings of shame and embarrassment on the part of the offender that kept him from opening up may constitute valid reasons for another visit by the counseling brother under the first step of discipline. He simply may have to build confidence and receptiveness.

If the sinner repents, confessing his sin and acknowledging faith in Christ and his blood atonement, the counseling brother has the privilege of extending him God's pardon. Jesus charged the believers: "If your brother sins, rebuke him, and if he repents, forgive him" (Luke 17:3); "If you forgive anyone his sins, they are forgiven" (John 20:23b). The matter, once having been confessed by the offender and forgiven by his counselor, is settled and must not be made an issue again. Having forgiven his sin, the counseling brother will help the repentant sinner lay out a course to follow in making amends in changing his life. He must not only stop the sin, but do those things that will help insure his staying on the right track (e.g. the study of God's Word to feed his faith, prayer for help, a daily program of contrition, etc.). Where he has sinned against someone besides the counseling brother, he must remove the offense with an apology; and where restitution is in order, restitution must be made. And the emphasis here is not the law: "You must!" but the gospel: the love of Jesus for sinners. The brother will be told: "Your love for Jesus, returning his love for you, will compel you to please him with a changed and restored life" (John 14:15; 2 Corinthians 5:14).

If the brother doesn't "listen," if he doesn't repent — even after several attempts have been made to reach him in the first step — the counseling brother doesn't give up but proceeds to the next step, which involves witnesses. Here a word of caution is in order. If the brother admits his guilt but refuses to repent, there is reason to call in witnesses. But if he doesn't admit to having committed the sin, and there is no way to establish that a sin has been committed other than by his admission, there would be no grounds upon which to call in witnesses. Without clearly establishing guilt — and sometimes this can be accomplished only with the cooperation of the offender — there would be no case to bring before witnesses. If the admonishing brother is still convinced in his own mind that sin has been committed which has not been repented of, he will have to continue his private testimony to the offender in the hope that it will eventually bear fruit. To proceed to call in witnesses when guilt has not been clearly established is to invite the charge of slander from the accused. The admonishing brother has no recourse but to keep praying and to act with patience and restraint. Furthermore, secret sins have a way of becoming public knowledge. (Luke 12:2; 1 Corinthians 14:23)[3] Once they have come to light more intensive testimony, involving witnesses, is possible.

A word about cases of public offense. In such cases sin is public due to the fact it was either committed in the presence of the congregation or in the presence of a public group outside the congregation, the result being that the matter is public knowledge. There is talk. It may even be a scandal reported by the public press. In such cases neither private admonition nor admonition offered before witnesses is required (Galations 2:11f.; 1 Timothy 5:20). These are cases with which the pastor and board of elders are to deal. Yet private admonition need not be ruled out. What does love for the brother compell us to do in this case? How can his repentance best be achieved? These are questions the answers to which will help decide the value of private admonition in the case of public offence.

STEP TWO: *But if he will not listen, take one or two others along, so that "every matter may be established by the testimony of two or three witnesses" (v. 16).* (Note: Employing witnesses is based on Deuteronomy 19:15.)

The reason for this procedure is clear. By rejecting *private* admonition offered by the Christian brother, the offender's sin, together with his attitude about it, is on the way to being made public in the congregation. This is a very serious thing, for if he fails to hear the congregation (if indeed the case reaches the congregation) he is no longer a believer and no longer saved. But the congregation cannot act on one man's testimony, which is hearsay. Every matter needs to be established by the testimony of two or three witnesses. Witnesses brought into the case can establish the validity of pursuing it. This is not to say that the counseling brother is not required to be certain of his facts before calling in witnesses. Moreover, the witnesses are in a position to evaluate the testimony of the counseling brother to the offender. Is it the correct one, the clearest and strongest one? The witnesses also offer their own testimony to the offender. Perhaps two or three people rebuking the brother for his sin and impenitence can make him realize the gravity of his offense and his need to repent. However, in case he persists in his impenitence, the witnesses can testify to this when later the case is brought to the congregation.

The additional people brought into the case may be friends of the offender, any member of the congregation or even church officers. If the pastor or elders are asked to be witnesses in the second step, they would have to serve outside their official capacity (which fits into the third step). They would be asked to participate as witnesses only because of their recognized knowledge and expertise, or because of special rapport that they might enjoy with the offender. The pastor and the elders would have to weigh the issues carefully and decide whether or not it would be wise to be involved in the case at this stage.

The small group of two or three may speak to the offender several times, just as the testimony of the lone Christian in step one could have been repeated several times. But the same cautions are to be observed as in step one.

If the offender "listens" to this small group, they are to tell him that he is forgiven and the matter is settled with this step. Again, what was said under step one concerning the making of amends and doing those things that would help insure his spiritual safety in the future, hold true in this step.

STEP THREE: *If he refuses to listen to them, tell it to the church (v. 17).*

Church discipline, per se, begins with the entering of the case into this step. The failure of private admonition and of admonition in the presence of witnesses necessitates this third step. A caution is in order: The church does not proceed with discipline in order to conduct a trial to determine guilt or innocence. The guilt must already be well-established by the witnesses, otherwise the church has no occasion to admonish. Admonishment is itself a judgment that a sin has been committed that has not been repented of, therefore making discipline necessary.

The "church" to which the counseling brother and the witnesses appeal the matter of the offending brother's sin and impenitence, is not the church at large, but the local congregation of which he is a member. And, generally, it is not to the entire congregation that the appeal is made, but rather to the smaller body, the voters' assembly, through which the congregation's official business is conducted. In the matter of carrying out discipline for the entire congregation, the voters' assembly is the church carrying out in love the duty assigned to it by our Lord.

The third step, which involves the offender's congregation through the voters' assembly, is entered with the purpose and prayer that the weight of many voices proclaiming his offense a sin, and admonishing him to repent, will finally bring about his hoped for repentance — that he will finally "listen."

Upon learning of the appeal that has been made to the congregation, the pastor and board of elders — being spiritual counselors in the congregation

— may deem it in the best interest of all parties concerned to speak with the offending brother in yet another effort to lead him to repentance. Their success would, of course, make it unnecessary to bring the appeal of the counseling brother and his witnesses to the floor of the voters' assembly. Though this procedure involving the pastor and elders is not commanded by the Scripture, nevertheless, loving concern for the offending brother and a sincere desire to expedite his spiritual care and restoration may decide in favor of it.

In the event that the appeal reaches the floor of the voters' assembly, the facts as they are known have to be carefully weighed. Upon accepting the request for a hearing, the voters' assembly resolves that a letter be written, requesting — yes, urging — the offender to be present at a designated meeting. This letter is either sent by certified mail or hand delivered. The counseling brother, together with the one or two witnesses, are also asked to be present with their testimony. They will have to state which sin has been committed and testify that the offender has been earnestly warned to repent. They will also have to state that, in spite of these warnings and encouragements, the brother has remained impenitent.

It may happen that all parties involved in the case, including the offending brother, are present at the voters' meeting to which the request is made for the case to be heard. The hearing could, then, be conducted at this meeting. At any rate, the object is to have the offender come before the congregation — in this case, the voters — for the purpose of making a final attempt to bring him to repentance.

If and when the offender appears at a meeting of the voters, the sin in question is stated and he is asked if he acknowledges his guilt and is ready to repent. But he is also invited to tell his side of the story and make his defense, if he feels this is necessary. In the event that the church is successful in calling the offender to repentance so that he confesses his sin and asks forgiveness, this forgiveness is announced by either the president or the pastor and the matter is dropped. It is not to be the subject of gossip among the members or cause for scandal. It goes without saying that the offender's confession must clearly cover the sin in question and be made without reservation, and with no strings attached.

Please note that forgiveness is not contingent on the offender first proving his repentance by dropping the sin in question from his life. It is not contingent on a future life of righteousness that the restored member will live. Forgiveness is granted by a gracious God for Jesus' sake to the sinner who repents and in faith asks for forgiveness. And this forgiveness from God is announced to him immediately.

Still the restored member experiences a restored life, thus giving evidence that genuine spiritual restoration has taken place — that he truly repents and believes. And this is important. God expects the repentant sinner to "produce fruit in keeping with repentance" (Matthew 3:8; see also Ephesians 4:28). Knowing the love and forgiveness of God incites the repentant sinner to quit sin and to walk the right paths through life. "(Christ) died for all, that those who live should no longer live for themselves but for him who died for them and was raised again" (2 Corinthians 5:15; see also Galations 2:20; 1 Corinthians 6:11; Titus 2:14, 3:8).

But what if the offender does not appear at the designated voters' meeting after being urged to do so? In that case the admonishing brother and his witnesses will be asked to bring the assembly up to date on their efforts to restore the offender. The voters will then decide whether to proceed with the excommunication or to give the offender the benefit of the doubt regarding his failure to appear. If action on the case is not tabled till a future meeting, the church (the voters' assembly) moves on to the fourth step: excommunication.

Why is excommunication in order in the case of the member who will not attend the voters' meeting, or even asks that his name be removed from the roll? Excommunication would be the only action consistent with the events that have transpired to this point. After the offender consistently refused to listen to his Christian counselors, the church was told about the matter and tried to counsel with him. His response to the church's attempt was, finally, not to "listen." Whether he comes to the meeting but fails to respond with repentance, or comes to the meeting, only to shut off the discussion by disassociating himself, or simply refuses to even attend the meeting — the result, in the final analysis, is the same. He refuses to "listen" to the church. In one way or another he states his position, which is that he will not confess his sin and ask forgiveness.

STEP FOUR: *If he refuses to listen even to the church, treat him as you would a pagan or a tax collector. I tell you the truth, whatever you bind on earth will be bound in heaven, and whatever you loose on earth will be loosed in heaven (v. 17b-18).*

No one is to be excommunicated until and unless he is provided ample opportunity to listen to the church and repent of his sin. Only when he shows that he will not listen to the church's call to him to repent and live does the church through its voters' assembly excommunicate him. (It is essential to the proper understanding of excommunication to know that no person is excommunicated for sin, but for impenitence and unbelief.)

The word "excommunication" is not a Scripture term, yet it certainly is scriptural. With this term the church describes its action over against the offender who has been duly admonished, but has remained impenitent. The action of the church in this case has been clearly prescribed by our Lord himself in the words: "Treat him as you would a pagan or a tax collector." The church establishes publicly where the impenitent person stands in relation to the church and the Christian faith, so that in the future he can be dealt with on the basis of this relationship. The church will in the future deal with him as a person who is outside the faith. That describes a *pagan*. The church will in the future deal with him as a person who is outside the church. That describes a *tax collector* as he was known by his fellow Jews in Bible times. A tax collector was an apostatized Jew who was then excommunicated by his church.

Excommunication merely ratifies the offending member's own actions and words. By his sin, followed by his refusal to heed Christian admonition calling him to repentance, he thus shows his unbelief, testifying that he is no longer living in a converted state. Indeed, he is now living apart from Christ, manifesting the same spirit as the unconverted pagan and the apostatizing tax collector.

Excommunication is the church's testimony to the unrepentant member that his refusal to repent puts him outside the kingdom of heaven. At the same time he is warned that unless and until he repents, he will remain outside the kingdom. The purpose of excommunication is not to destroy the person, but to destroy his sinful pride that will not let him confess his sin and ask God for mercy. It is a testimony to the truthfulness of the gospel, that whoever believes will be saved. He does not believe and therefore he is not saved. If unrepentant sinners were allowed communion with the church, a testimony would be rendered *against* the gospel, for such action would proclaim that even unbelievers can enter the kingdom of heaven — or, remain in it. Far from robbing the unrepentant offender of his church membership, excommunication is a public testimony to the fact that the offender by remaining unrepentant robs the church of the privilege of absolving his sin in God's name, and of helping him to live a restored, spiritual life.

Excommunication is not, then, "loveless condemnation."[4] Rather, it is one more testimony which love makes to the sinner, informing him that he has lost his claim on eternal life; and with this testimony the church hopes he will be jolted from his course of stubborn impenitence and unbelief. Unless the impenitent sinner faces facts and acknowledges the truth he cannot be saved. Excommunication is to help him to do this. Through excommunication the church does not permit the man who was once a Christian brother, but has now fallen from grace, to destroy himself unwarned.

Excommunication must be by unanimous vote since it is an action based on God's Word. The issues must be stated so clearly that there can be no scriptural dissent to the excommunication. Thus, any who protest the excommunication place themselves under church discipline. The burden of the matter will have to rest on them. Finally, if the protestors cannot show from the Scripture that the excommunication is invalid, or that the case has been improperly handled — and if they give evidence that they are willfully disobeying God's Word — they will themselves be subject to excommunication. Only after the protestors have been properly dealt with, does the congregation return to the original case of church discipline. This caution: If a significant number of voting members will not vote for excommunication, the matter cannot be concluded, at least for the time being. The pastor, with the backing of the board of elders, will have to pursue a patient, prayerful course of indoctrination concerning the Law and the Gospel, and in regard to the disciplining of church members.

Whether the erring member repents and is forgiven, or does not repent and is not forgiven, the ministry or use of the Keys is involved. Jesus empowered the church with the Keys (the authority to forgive and not to forgive sins) when he said: "I tell you the truth, whatever you bind on earth will be bound in heaven, and whatever you loose on earth will be loosed in heaven" (v. 18).

The power to forgive sins belongs to God. The power of believers (the church) to forgive sins is not apart from God's power, but truly an exercise of what is divine right. The church's absolution is God's own absolution. In forgiving (loosing) sins or in not forgiving (binding) sins, the believers merely express the conclusion that God himself in heaven has reached. And so, while the admonished sinner stands either penitent or impenitent before the church, he stands either forgiven or not forgiven before God. And it is the church's duty to tell him so.

The door is left open for the excommunicated member — he becomes a mission prospect. He has lost what he once had: faith and membership in the church. He has reverted to the status of an unchurched, unbelieving sinner who needs to be brought to faith and made a member of the church. What he once had and lost, the church should hope and pray that he regains. And the church should work to that end. But when the members of the church deal with the excommunicated person, they must be careful not to convey the impression that all that has been lost is his church membership, and simply express the hope that he will come back. What he has lost first of all is his faith and, with it, forgiveness of sins and eternal life in heaven. The church must try to impress upon the excommunicated member that this is an intolerable loss.

It has been demonstrated that the board of elders can become involved in step three between the time that the request for a hearing with the voters' assembly has been made and the accepting of such an appeal by the voters. Moreover it has been demonstrated that the board of elders, with the pastor, is to work with cases of public sin (scandal). Also, the excommunicated person, being recognized as a mission prospect, can be approached on occasion by members of the board in attempts to bring him back to the Savior. God works in mysterious ways at times to establish such fruitful contacts.

Scripture #3: A Congregation is at Fault for Not Taking Action

It is actually reported that there is sexual immorality among you, and of a kind that does not occur even among pagans: A man has his father's wife. And you are proud! Shouldn't you rather have been filled with grief and have put out of your fellowship the man who did this? Even though I am not physically present, I am with you in spirit. And I have already passed judgment on the one who did this, just as if I were present. When you are assembled in the name of our Lord Jesus and I am with you in spirit, and the power of our Lord Jesus is present, hand this man over to Satan, so that the sinful nature may be destroyed and his spirit saved on the day of the Lord (1 Corinthians 5:1-5).

A tragic matter occuring in the Corinthian congregation had been reported to St. Paul. A man was committing sexual immorality, the kind which did not occur even among the pagans, who commonly practiced all manner of wickedness. A man had taken to himself his father's wife (his stepmother), a sin expressly prohibited by God's law (Leviticus 18:8; Deuteronomy 22:30). The woman was probably pagan.

Why the members of the congregation closed their eyes to such flagrant sin, such unheard of wickedness, is impossible to figure out. The reaction of the congregation should have been one of deepest sorrow: sorrow that the devil had gained such a foothold in their midst, sorrow over a precious soul that had backslid from God to be held once again in Satan's clutches, sorrow that such shame as this had blemished the reputation of the congregation in the community, sorrow that an action of a member was causing God's name to be blasphemed among the pagans, sorrow over the harm that was being done to the spirit of the congregation. They should have been filled with grief, and this grief should have stirred them to action, causing them to put out of their fellowship "the man who did this."

But instead they were proud; they acted in an arrogant manner, as though there was nothing amiss in the congregation — they could do no wrong! Perhaps some of the more spiritual members went to the man and scolded him for his behavior. But that's all he got. A scolding is all that Eli's sons received from their father for their wickedness, and the events that later followed showed how displeased the Lord was with Eli's non-decisive manner of dealing with them (1 Samuel 2:12-25). No, nothing short of the punishment (2 Corinthians 2:6) of being expelled by the congregation would do in the case of the incestuous man — a step the Corinthians arrogantly saw no need to take.

The man's continued perversity was an open sore that festered in the congregation, poisoning the spirits of all the members and working to make the gospel ineffective among them. If flagrant sin is allowed to continue, what purpose, then, has the gospel? What need is there of forgiveness if people are not commanded to turn from their wickedness, and are not warned that eternal death and damnation is theirs if they don't? (Refer: Job 20:5ff.; Ezekiel 18:23; Isaiah 55:7; Matthew 3:12.)

Lack of church discipline robs the church's message to the non-Christian world of a great deal of its force. Not requiring manifest sinners in the church to repent creates the illusion that repentance is not prerequisite to saving faith. By failing to discipline, the church, in effect, preaches forgiveness without repentance and justification that isn't followed by sanctification. How can the church possibly preach a meaningful forgiveness if it doesn't preach repentance? How can it possibly accept a confession of faith that isn't accompanied by the putting off of sin and the putting on of righteous works? (See: Ephesians 4:22-24; 2 Corinthians 5:17; James 2:18, 26; 1 John 3:3-10.) Indeed, for the church to accept the sinner's confession of faith — and with it, his membership in the church — while allowing him to continue in his sins unchecked, presents a most confusing, even false message of sin and grace to the world.

What example did the incestuous man give? What example did the congregation give to the outside world by failing to reproach him for his sin and to take decisive action? The cause of Christ and the gospel were deeply hurt in Corinth.

Over in Ephesus St. Paul was not about to share in the congregation's dereliction of duty. He wrote: "And I have already passed judgment on the one who did this, just as if I were present" (v. 3b). Whereas the congregation had taken no action, Paul moved into action at once on the basis of the report he received. Paul's absence from Corinth and his inability to meet with the troubled congregation didn't mean that he had no feelings in the case. Indeed, his feelings ran deep. He was so incensed by the man's gross behavior that he already passed judgment on him, as though he were right there in the congregation. His judgment was that the man was a manifest impenitent sinner, and that he should be expelled.

The congregation was to call a meeting, and though Paul couldn't be present in person, he would be present with them in spirit, his mind and heart yearning for them to do the right thing. And when they finally obeyed God's Word to expel the offender, Paul would be concurring with them. Through this letter sent by way of Timothy, Paul would have his say in absentia, thus guiding them to do the right thing. And in absentia he would also cast his vote — indeed, had already done so — for the man's expulsion from the congregation.

On the basis of Paul's negative reaction to their misconduct, they would have to see that the matter was clear-cut and not delay any further in acting.

But could we fault Paul for not counseling the congregation to first carry out a period of intensive admonishment before it took action to exclude the man? "A little yeast works through the whole batch of dough," Paul told them. By allowing the case of incest to remain unresolved in the congregation, all the members were being brought under the evil influence of it, and were sharing the man's guilt. No, the time of patient admonishment was past. Under the circumstances future counseling would have to take place outside the bond of fellowship. The time had come to speak to the man by resolute action. He had to be told that no penitent believer lives as he was living, that he had reverted to being a pagan and that he was lost and damned. His exclusion from the fellowship of the visible or outward church was but a mark of his exclusion from the kingdom of heaven.

On the basis of the facts which he received, which indicated the man's impenitence, Paul concluded that he must be excluded from the congregation. Yet Paul did not exclude him. Rather, he commanded the congregation in assembly to exclude him. The most that Paul could do was to give the members of the congregation spiritual direction in the matter, and when they carried out his direction, to concur in it, being with them "in spirit." They did not even need an apostle present when they took action. In fact, they were rebuked because they had not taken action already.

What was true then, is true now. Pastors don't excommunicate. Congregations do. When the pastor announces the excommunication, he declares what the congregation in assembly resolved to do. The pastor voted with the congregation and did not take unilateral action toward the offending member.

By what power does a congregation exclude a manifest impenitent sinner from the congregation? First, Paul stressed that the congregation would be assembled "in the name of Jesus." They would be coming together on the basis of Jesus' teachings, foremost of which is the gospel, and it would be for the purpose of carrying out his teachings to his glory. Second, Paul stressed that when members of the congregation assembled together to exclude the manifest impenitent sinner they would be doing so "with the power of our Lord Jesus." What this power is we learn from Jesus' own words in Matthew 18:18: "I tell you the truth, whatever you bind on earth will be bound in heaven, and whatever you loose on earth will be loosed in heaven." This power of Jesus is given to his church to use in his behalf.

Paul described exclusion or excommunication as handing the "man over to Satan so that the sinful nature may be destroyed and his spirit saved on the day of the Lord." In effect the excluded member is told: "Satan, not Christ, has you in his power. You no longer stand with Christ and his church but with Satan and his wicked angels. Unless you repent you will find yourself in the ranks of the damned on judgment day, to be sent away — along with the devil and his angels — into the eternal fires of hell." This strong language is in place. Satan has reclaimed the impenitent person's soul, perhaps without a struggle. In handing him over to Satan, the church is giving him one last powerful testimony that may yet snatch him away from Satan, a testimony that may sink in.

"So that the sinful nature may be destroyed and his spirit saved on the day of the Lord" (v. 5). Handing the impenitent man over to Satan is for the destruction of his flesh or sinful nature. In effect the person is told: "You gave yourself to Satan — you belong to him now — let Satan have you. He controls you, and you will walk more and more in his wicked ways 'storing up wrath against yourself for the day of God's wrath, when his righteous judgment will be revealed'" (Romans 2:5). And so, Satan is free to work unchecked in the excluded, impenitent person's life. But the person will find that unbridled wickedness has its own kind of reward — and he may learn to loathe it. The lost son is a case in point for he came to loathe his terrible condition and determined to return to his father to ask his forgiveness (Luke 15:14-20). By excesses the flesh defeats itself. Remembering the church's warning about his being damned along with Satan, and remembering, too, the sweet mercy of which he was once assured in the gospel, the sinner may then come to his senses. If he does, his flesh is destroyed: its wicked control is once again ended. And his spirit — his spiritual life — rekindled, will be saved "on the day of the Lord." His spirit will triumph in salvation when Jesus on the day of judgment renders the verdict of not guilty toward him.

That this purpose was accomplished in the case of the man who committed incest, is borne out by the testimony of Paul's second letter to the Corinthian congregation. Evidently the man repented and Paul then urged the people in the congregation to receive him back, forgiving him. Paul had already in his own heart forgiven him when he received the report of his repentance. Paul counseled them:

> *The punishment inflicted on him by the majority is sufficient for him. Now instead, you ought to forgive and comfort him, so that he will not be overwhelmed by excessive sorrow. I urge you, therefore, to reaffirm your love for him . . . If you forgive anyone, I also forgive him. And what I have forgiven — if there was anything to forgive — I have forgiven in the sight of Christ for your sake, in order that Satan might not outwit us (2 Corinthians 2:6-8, 10-11).*

Once the congregation forgave the man with God's own forgiveness (Matthew 18:18b) and reinstated him in the Christian community, thus pledging their love for him, the case was closed.

The elders, by their continued testimony to the excommunicated person, may very well be involved in restoring him. They may have occasion to testify to the voters' assembly concerning the excommunicated person's words of repentance and request for reinstatement. Also to bring their own recommendations to the voters.

Scripture #4: Isolating the Manifest Sinner

> *But now I am writing you that you must not associate with anyone who calls himself a brother but is sexually immoral or greedy, an idolater or a slanderer, a drunkard or a swindler. With such a man do not even eat (1 Corinthians 5:11).*

This reference, given in the context of calling for the excommunication of the incestuous man, must be interpreted in its full strength. The person who has been a professing Christian and a member of the congregation (calling himself a brother), but has turned his back to Christ and the regenerate life which the restored image of God in the believer produces

(Romans 6:4, 11; Ephesians 4:24), can no longer be regarded as a believer. Not only must he be excluded from the fellowship of believers (which step Paul does not specifically mention here), he must not be afforded common social fellowship.[5] Paul says, "With such a man do not even eat." Harsh as it sounds, this means that there is to be no close association of any kind with the man.[6]

These people: the sexually immoral, the greedy, the idolaters, the slanderers, the drunkards, the swindlers, are open sinners and can be classified as renegades and traitors to the faith (Galatians 5:19-21; 1 Corinthians 6:9, 10).[7] Their lives openly, shamelessly, wickedly center in one or the other sin which, then, forces the conclusion that faith has been abandoned. These people are no longer under church discipline. They are out of the church and are continuing in their lives of open sin. To strike home to their hearts just how far they have removed themselves from Christ and his church, they are completely shunned as far as brotherly social contacts are concerned. The congregation's action of excluding the manifest and impenitent sinners is reinforced by the congregation's treatment of them, as though they have some odious, loathsome disease that can be caught. Not only is the isolating of manifest, impenitent sinners a logical testimony against their evil way of life that God abhors, it is a logical and necessary precaution to keep their life-style from spreading. Through their action of isolating manifest and impenitent sinners, the members of the congregation send up the red flag of warning to all who might tend to imitate them, and an additional warning to the sinners themselves to repent or perish. (See: 1 Thessalonians 5:14; 2 Thessalonians 3:6, 14-15; 2 Peter 2:20-22.)

THE BOARD OF ELDERS' INVOLVEMENT

What was said in our study of Matthew 18:15f. regarding the elders' involvement pertains here too. As they have opportunity to do so, the elders will continue their testimony against the sins of those who have been excommunicated. They will call on these people to repent and through clear testimony from Scripture do what they can to lead them back. The elders may have occasion to remind members of the congregation concerning the matter of the sinners' isolation and why this is necessary. The elders stand ready to guide the members in a responsible approach to the sinners' isolation on order to avoid undoing or watering down the action the congregation has had to take, lest the impression be given to the isolated sinners that their sins are not so bad after all and that Christians can live with them — or that the congregation is divided in its judgment over against their manifest sins and their state of blatant impenitence.

Scripture #5: Apostasy

... some have rejected these (i.e. faith and a good conscience) and so have shipwrecked their faith. Among them are Hymenaeus and Alexander, whom I have handed over to Satan to be taught not to blaspheme. (1 Timothy 1:19b-20)

Hymenaeus and Alexander had been members of the church of Ephesus before their exclusion. Final action had been taken in their case after it became evident to the apostle Paul during his discussions with them that they had truly apostatized. They persisted in the blasphemy they were teaching, thus remaining unrepentant. Their blasphemy did not consist only in doctrinal error but in denial of the gospel itself and the substituting of something else in its place. At one time they had been in possession of a good conscience for it was guided by the Word of God, which they believed. But they turned to false teachings that were diametrically opposed to the gospel. They successfully silenced their consciences thus allowing false teaching to take over more and more in their minds. And they spread these false teachings to others ("like gangrene" 2 Timothy 2:17). Finally, they lost their saving faith — they apostatized — for faith can't continue when the basis of faith, God's Word, which has trained the believer's conscience, is unconscionably set aside.

Discussions with the two men produced evidence that they were persistent in their false teachings, that they had shipwrecked their faith, that they were impenitent. Paul summarized the final action against the two men with the simple statement to Timothy: "... whom I have handed over to Satan."

We are not to conclude that Paul acted unilaterally — that he himself excluded Hymenaeus and Alexander from the congregation. 1 Corinthians 5:3-5 prevents us from drawing this conclusion. It is the congregation that excludes the impenitent sinners. The pastor casts his vote in the matter as a member of the congregation. And he certainly also gives much guidance in a case of excommunication, even advising and urging the congregation to take the action that will exclude the impenitent. The pastor can even make the motion for the congregation to do so. Paul's part in the congregation's action toward the two men enabled him to write to Timothy: "... whom I have handed over to Satan."

The remedial or reclaiming purpose in the excommnication of Hymenaeus and Alexander is brought out in Paul's words, "to be taught not to blaspheme." The two men were given occasion for serious soul-searching when they were informed that their failure to repent had put them in the same camp with Satan. Thus they were to be condemned and eternally punished along with him who was the very source of their blasphemy. They were also delivered into Satan's providence, which would result in ever-deepening guilt on their part. Perhaps such an extreme action would cause them to reconsider the teachings of God they had abandoned, and return to them. Thus they would be "taught not to blaspheme."

When blasphemy of the gospel rears its ugly head, it must be dealt with, and where its promoter(s) persists in his sin, refusing to repent, he must be excluded since he is no longer a believer. And this exclusion also constitutes a necessary public rejection by the congregation of this blasphemous doctrine. In a public action he is handed over, along with his doctrine(s), to Satan, to whom they both belong. That this action is necessary in order to prevent great harm within the congregation, we learn from Paul's words in his second letter to Timothy: "Their teaching will spread like gangrene" (2:17). Therefore it must be cut out of the congregation and rejected by expelling the ones who persist in teaching it.

THE BOARD OF ELDERS' INVOLVEMENT

Though all the members have the right and duty to watch over the doctrine that is being taught in a congregation, and to help guard against false doctrine (cf. the Bereans' example, Acts 17:11), the pastor and board of elders are *specifically* charged with this duty.

Scripture #6: Divisiveness

Warn a divisive person once, and then warn him a second time. After that, have nothing to do with him. You may be sure that such a man is warped and sinful; he is self-condemned. (Titus 3:10-11)

A divisive person — one who creates disunity — calls into question the congregation's doctrine and practice. And he does this by teaching ideas that forsake Scripture, or substitute for Scripture. What he teaches is the product of his own invention, and yet he regards it to be the truth. He regards as error everything that opposes his ideas. He may even be aggressive, promulgating his teachings in the congregation.

When a member of the congregation teaches something that isn't scriptural, division results: His teaching stands on the one side and the teaching of the Scripture stands on the other side. And his divisiveness may eventually reach into the congregation itself if he agitates among the members for acceptance of his views. Some will stand in danger of being drawn to his teaching.

Paul gave Titus the course to follow in the case of a divisive member and the rule still applies today: "Warn a divisive person once, and then warn him a second time." By calling for admonishment in the case of the divisive person, Paul laid down the rule that the church cannot close its eyes to error; it cannot allow a diversity of teaching within its midst. It cannot put up with those who call into question scripturally sound doctrine and practice. Doctrine and practice that are in agreement with Scripture must be maintained at all times, and each and every member of the congregation must subscribe to them.

Now then, Paul's strategy deliberately avoids a lengthy proceeding. Divisive behavior cannot be tolerated for long. An attempt is to be made to admonish the divisive person. He must be shown that he follows his own ideas or opinions — or someone else's — rather than God's Word. The object is to convince him that he must return to sound doctrine and practice. The counselors do not go to argue or debate but to let God be heard. And in doing so, they state the scriptural truths so clearly that there can be no doubt as to what God expects his people to believe and practice. The counselors show the divisive person where he errs from God's Word and warn him that he cannot hold to his views. They ask for a statement from him to the effect that he agrees with the teachings of the Scripture in the matter, that he agrees with the church's stand and no longer believes his own error. And, of course, they ask him also for a statement to the effect that he will no longer defend or promulgate the error(s) that he has held.

The first dose of correction may suffice. If not, the counselors will tell him that they will be seeing him again soon concerning the matter under discussion, and in the meantime to give serious thought to what has been told him. He is allowed a little time to search the Scripture and his own heart and conscience.

The second meeting is carried out like the first. Appropriate Scripture is offered for the person to accept. He is reminded that his views, being in error, cannot be tolerated under any circumstance, and that he cannot be allowed to undermine the spirit and unity of the congregation with his aberrant views.

The second dose of correction may suffice. If not, what then? The second meeting may not totally succeed, and yet it may give evidence that the person is softening, that his stubborness has begun to yield to the facts. In that case the admonishing should continue. But if it appears that the person is only "buying time," using the patience of the counselors as opportunity to strengthen his position in the congregation, the admonishing would have to be ended. At any rate, if the person disdains the counsel that is given him, so that he persists in his views, he is to be rejected along with whatever divisive teaching he clings to.

The reason for rejecting him is revealed by St. Paul — and this, of course, is God's own evaluation: "You may be sure that such a man is warped and sinful; he is self-condemned." The word "warped" has the meaning of "turned aside." He has been turned aside in his heart and mind from the truth. Since Satan is the father of lies (John 8:44), and since we have the warning that demons will teach false doctrine (1 Timothy 4:1), we can conclude that the powers of darkness have blinded the man's eyes to the truth, at least for the present.

Such a person sins. Clinging to error inspite of admonition from Scripture constitutes a sin that has become deeply ingrained. The divisive person has effectively silenced his conscience that once was trained to reject such views as he now clings to (1 Timothy 1:19) and has retrained his conscience to accept and even peddle error as truth. He stands "self-condemned." By his own stubborness, refusing to yield to Scripture, he shows that he cannot be regarded as a member of the congregation. He is of a different spirit. He condemns himself every time he opens his mouth to speak in defense of his unscriptural views. His false views condemn him, the church doesn't need to.

And so, in rejecting God's truth, which the congregation subscribes to and has pledged to uphold, the divisive person, by persisting in his error, places himself in the position of disassociating himself from the congregation. And he has to be helped to recognize this. Whether or not he finally does, the congregation is, nevertheless, called upon to take action. "After that, have nothing to do with him." Literally, "reject or dismiss him." He is to be rejected or dismissed also as a member of the congregation. After all, the error cannot be disowned by the congregation without the congregation disowning also the one who persists in it. In order to protect themselves from error and to maintain the truth — for false doctrine is a pervasive evil — the members have no alternative to terminating the person's membership. The errorist, to be true to his own convictions, will have to seek fellowship in a church which shares the same doctrine with him, or at least is tolerant of his error. The congregation, in announcing separation of the persistent errorist, is doing so both out of love to him and to the truth. (Consider also the following passages of the Scripture: Romans 16:17-18; 1 Timothy 6:3-5; Ephesians 4:13-15; 1 Timothy 1:3-7; 1 Timothy 4:1-2.)

Is the persistent errorist's rejection by the congregation the same as excommunication or exclusion? It can be, and then, again, it may not be. It depends upon the views that are being maintained. Are they views that deny fundamental doctrines of Scripture, that is, doctrines necessary for salvation? If so, he has denied the faith, and his rejection by the congregation also constitutes excommunication by which he is regarded as a pagan (one outside the faith) and a tax collector (one outside the church). If he still clings to the way of salvation set down in the Scripture, he is not to be excommunicated. After all, how can he in that case be regarded as unsaved?[8] But in being rejected as a confessional brother, he will be warned that his views — since they undermine God's Word — can eventually undermine the doctrine of salvation itself. Any false doctrine places a person's soul in jeopardy.

THE BOARD OF ELDERS' INVOLVEMENT

What part should the elders play in cases of divisiveness? When it is ascertained that there is some disagreement with the church's position — either in doctrine or practice — discussion time should be set up with the person, involving both the pastor and men from the board. The pastor and elders will serve as a team to admonish the divisive person. The team should be loving in its approach, and yet firm. The team must, in a clear and forthright manner, present the Scripture to the person so that the Holy Spirit can work in his heart to clear up his misunderstanding, doubts, confusion and false beliefs, and to turn him to the scriptural position. God must speak to the person with his own Word through the testimony of the pastor and elders. "All Scripture is God-breathed and is useful for teaching, rebuking, correcting and training in righteousness" (2 Timothy 3:16).

Consideration has to be given to the stage of spiritual growth and development that the member in question has reached. Is he a new convert? How thorough was his doctrinal instruction? The team has the opportunity and duty, now that difficulties have surfaced, to aid the member in his spiritual growth. If he is made to see his error and thus remains in the congregation, it might be well to require him to enroll in the pastor's adult class and review Christian doctrine. His attendance at the Sunday morning Bible class is in order too.

Sometimes divisive persons simply have an ax to grind and nothing is going to stop them. They stubbornly resist the facts; their minds are made up. They are convinced that they are right and that everyone who disagrees with them are wrong. They may even be church hoppers, who stay with a congregation only long enough to find out that they are not going to get their way, or be allowed to teach their error, or until the novelty of attending that particular congregation and listening to a pastor who is new to them wears off. These people cannot be allowed to rule the church or to upset the pastor and the other members. They have to be shown that their very action of "always keeping things stirred up," whereby they destroy peace and harmony in the congregation, is divisive and is itself sinful. And if they cannot be convinced of this, they then have to be shown that they are of a different spirit and cannot remain in the congregation to be a constant source of friction which can only result in demoralizing the congregation.[9] If they will not themselves take action by removing from the congregation, then the congregation will have to officially terminate the fellowship through action by the voters' assembly.[10] And this is done, of course, on the recommendation of the pastor and the board of elders.

† † † † † †

CHAPTER FIVE

THE ELDERS AT WORK: ADMONISHING THE OFFENDER

INTRODUCTION

The pastor's work includes admonishing manifest and impenitent sinners in the congregation, and the elders are elected to assist him. If these elders are chosen carefully, prayerfully and prudently, and given thorough, ungoing training, the pastor need not feel anxious or hesitant about using them in carrying out church discipline. Furthermore, laymen like being talked to by laymen.

The purpose of church discipline, that is, the purpose of admonishing offending members of the congregation on the basis of the Scripture, is to care for souls and to seek their salvation. By confronting the offending church member with scriptural admonition, the church seeks to bring him to repentance in order that his sins may be forgiven and his soul may be saved. A corrected life is, of course, the natural outcome of true repentance, and it, too, is the goal of discipline. Carried on with these purposes in mind, the work of admonishing offending church members is an extremely noble venture.

The proper tone of all admonition in discipline cases — whether by the pastor or by the elders, or by the pastor and elders as a team — is well stated in 1 Thessalonians in the words of St. Paul: "We were *gentle* among you, like a mother caring for her little children. We *loved you so much* that we were delighted to share with you not only the gospel of God but our lives as well, because *you had become so dear to us*" (1 Thessalonians 2:7). In Galations Paul wrote: "Brothers, if someone is caught in a sin, you who are spiritual should restore him *gently* (i.e. with humbleness that breeds gentleness and politeness)" (Galations 6:1).

As an elder-counselor you ought to approach all counseling sessions held with offending members of the congregation in the spirit of an evangelist who has been sent out to the community with the message of the law and the gospel.

> (The admonishing) of a sinner in the church is analogous to evangelism outside the church. As in evangelism repentance issues in forgiveness and fellowship, so in discipline response to the word of admonition issues in forgiveness and continued fellowship. Likewise, as in

evangelism, an individual's rejection of the gospel is respected and he is not incorporated into the body of Christ, so in discipline an individual's rejection of the word of admonition is respected and he is excluded from the body of Christ. The only difference is that admonition begins with a sinner in the church, whereas evangelism begins with one outside the church.[1]

For the sake of convenience, the words "counselor" and "counselee" are often used in this chapter to distinguish the two brothers involved in giving and receiving scriptural admonition.

What Admonishing the Offender Requires of the Elder-Counselor

1. **Admonishing the offender requires that you don't lose contact with God.** Depend on God to help you, to guide you, to counsel you with his Word and to bless your work. With constant prayer in your heart, prayer that began even while planning the meeting, and knowing that you have the Holy Spirit's help, concentrate on reproving, warning and encouraging the offender with appropriate Scripture.

2. **Admonishing the offender requires that you use utmost care to be true to Scripture.** It is important to keep in mind that you are going to the offender for the purpose of *leading his conscience*. You must do this with no other thing than God's Word, correctly interpreted and properly applied to him. Since you are leading another person's conscience you can afford no mistakes! In your face to face confrontation you are verbalizing God's Word; therefore, you are, in effect, bringing the offender face to face with what God has to say to him. You admonish the offender with *God's* admonition. You are only the humble instrument of the Holy Spirit — the divine Counselor — who works through the Word of God you use in order to effect the needed change in the individual under discipline.

3. **Admonishing the offender requires that you build rapport, cultivating friendship with him on the basis of genuine Christian love.** You are one sinner counseling another sinner and sharing the Savior's love with him. As his friend who loves him and who empathizes with him, you show him that you are deeply concerned by the hurt he is suffering, the loss he has incurred, the grief that weighs him down, the hardships that confront him. And always show him that you are vitally concerned about his eternal welfare. The impression you give as his

friend and one who dearly loves him should be: "I want you to be saved. If you should lose your salvation I would be heartbroken!" Building rapport will not only make your counseling session free of argumentation and rancor, it will leave the door open for future meetings, should they prove necessary.

4. **Admonishing the offender requires that you be gracious.** And to be gracious because you *truly are gracious in your heart*: "For out of the overflow of the heart the mouth speaks" (Matthew 12:34). Don't *ever* be discourteous and disrespectful. On your visits show that you recognize the individual and love him as a person irregardless of his problems and/or sins.

5. **Admonishing the offender requires that you be objective.** Don't make up your mind ahead of time concerning the person that you visit, or what you will encounter in your meeting. While you should be careful about the first impression *you* make on the person you visit, don't, on the other hand, make a great deal of the significance of your first impression of *him*. Christian love demands this (1 Corinthians 13:7; 16:14).

6. **Admonishing the offender requires that you use communication skills.** As you counsel the offender there is interaction between the two of you. The object is to keep this interaction under *your* control, guided by God's Word and the Holy Spirit. Using communication skills can help you do this. We will discuss this subject in a separate section of this chapter.

7. **Admonishing the offender requires that you allow the Holy Spirit time to work — that you don't rush him.** If you don't succeed right away, don't be discouraged. And be sure to try again soon. Be patient! We will discuss the matter of the Holy Spirit's working in the heart of the offender through the Scripture in another section of this chapter.

8. **Admonishing the offender requires that you be emotionally involved.** Your interaction with the offender in face to face confrontation involves you personally because your faith, your love for God, your love for God's Word, your love for the offender is involved. This in turn involves your emotions. St. Paul was not above shedding tears in dealing with people (Acts 20:31), or to let them know the distress he felt (2 Corinthians 2:4). In admonishing the offender, you,

the counselor, may appear shocked at what the counselee has said. You may reveal your feelings as these feelings have been programed by Scripture. You have the right to judge words and actions of the offender, the counselee, as being good or bad on the basis of whether they agree or disagree with the Scripture. In some worldly circles, counselors are advised to remain neutral. *You cannot be neutral*! The counselee's reaction to admonishment from the Scripture either agrees with, or strikes out at, what you know and believe to be the truth. You represent God through his Word so that what God hates you hate, and what he loves, you love. And you convey this to the counselee. You are not just a sounding board. You are admonishing the offender with the Word of God, which he needs to accept, believe and obey in order to be saved. His reaction to the Word of God effects you deeply because of your love for the Scripture and because of your love for him.

At times, anger may even be in place — anger at sin that has cropped up in the counseling session. However, anger must never be unjustified, and it must never go out of control. One must be angry, but not sin in his anger (Ephesians 4:26). To lose one's temper is to let one's anger get out of control, and that, then, is sin (Proverbs 14:29; 29:11). Remember that, "A hot-tempered man stirs up dissension, but a patient man calms a quarrel," and, "Better a patient man than a warrior, and a man who controls his temper than one who takes a city" (Proverbs 15:8; 16:32).

If the response by the offender is positive and scriptural, you ought, then, to register joy and enthusiasm. The angels do (Luke 15:10). Paul was joyful because the hurt, the sorrow his first letter caused the Corinthian congregation had led the members to repentance. He expressed this joy to them in his second letter (2 Corinthians 7:8-9).

And so, where the eternal destiny of precious souls is at stake, you cannot afford to be cold and unfeeling (mechanical) in your presentation, or aloof in your relationship. If you are, you only add to the confusion that already exists in the offender's mind and heart. If you are not emotional (responding with the correct emotions) you send mixed signals to the individual under discipline. Your emotional reactions to his answers and statements either reinforce or undermine (in his mind and conscience) what you are verbalizing.

Yes, you are emotionally involved *because you are spiritually involved.* And yet, you must keep your emotions always under control. Do not allow your emotions to cloud your judgment. Do not allow feelings to govern your actions. You must maintain the ability to think straight and to weigh things accurately even while being emotionally involved.

9. **Admonishing the offender requires that you demonstrate competence in getting your point across.** First, that you have a good grasp of the Scripture. Second, that you personally know and love God and, therefore, are speaking from genuine personal conviction. And third, that you have the ability to verbally confront people in such a way that they understand you. In getting the Scripture across from your heart to his, there is no substitute for the fitting word, clearly, boldly, and yet, kindly and courteously, spoken — "like apples of gold in settings of silver" (Proverbs 25:11-12).

10. **Admonishing the offender requires that you maintain control of the meeting.** You should strive to remain relaxed and natural in your presentation, and yet you must maintain control. You cannot allow the person under discipline to sidestep the issue, to change subjects, to keep you involved in superfluous conversation, to use delay tactics, to excuse his sinful conduct, or to pass the blame to someone else.

11. **Admonishing the offender requires that you not be moody.** You may have had a hard day — perhaps nothing seemed to go right — still you have no right to inject your personal frustrations into your visit. It can only do harm. You have asked him to meet with you to discuss what is wrong in *his* life, not what is wrong in *yours*.

12. **Admonishing the offender requires that you not be sarcastic.** Sarcasm often causes offense in a one-on-one situation and thus is destructive.[2] But don't overlook the meaning behind his sarcasm.

13. **Admonishing the offender requires that you keep control of your tongue.** Take care, then, not to argue, gossip, lose your temper (and thus become abusive), be impatient, be bitter or criticize the church or the pastor.

14. **Admonishing the offender requires that you protect the person under discipline, the offender, from the destruction of his reputation and from embarrassment if at all possible.** "Too much publicity and notoriety about discipline situations make it virtually impossible for the individual concerned to 'find his way back.' We have burned all his bridges. Let the congregation retain control of

discipline as it must biblically and let the Board of Lay Ministry (the elders) and the pastor seek quietly to win back who can be won. If some must be removed, their removal must be made public to avoid offense in the congregation; the 'choice' details need not be revealed unless the discipline itself is challenged."[3]

Using Communication Skills in Admonishing the Offender

While the use of communication skills is especially directed here to counseling sessions that are carried on for the purpose of admonishing offending church members, you will, of course, find applications for these skills in practically every meeting you hold with those under your spiritual care. Consider, then, the following basic communication skills[4] that you should use in the interaction occuring between you and the person being counseled:

OBSERVATION

This is simply your appraisal of the individual involved. You attune yourself to him, recognizing that he is a truly unique person. Appraising the individual and the situation will give an indication of the speed with which you should proceed, and the intensity with which you pursue the subject under discussion. When counseling offending church members there are occasions that require the "blitz" method: quick, firm confrontation. But there are other occasions when a slower, more deliberate, less intense approach is best. There are variables that come into play as you strive to maintain a Spirit-led and Spirit-blessed interaction with the counselee.

In making your appraisal you might ask such questions of yourself as these: Is the counselee weak in his faith and knowledge? Is he a recent convert, therefore an infant in the faith? Or is he an "old-time" church member? Does he seem to be enjoying the conversation or is he noticeably ill at ease, anxious, even fearful? Does he accept you, not only as a fellow-Christian but also in your official capacity? Is he friendly, open, gracious or does he give the impression of being hostile, resentful of this "interference" and "intrusion" in his life? Does his age and/or the deterioration of mental powers or his physical health interfer with his perception? And might these even determine the length of the counseling session? Is the counselee under pressure from others, perhaps intimidated by members of his family so that he is torn by the question of allegiance? Does he know his counselor well enough to place confidence in him, or is this an occasion when two strangers are meeting for the first time and have to get to know each other?

It is important, as was stated earlier, that the counselor be as objective as possible in making his appraisal of the individual he is to counsel. Things are often not as they seem on the surface. Like an iceberg, much of what a person really feels or thinks is hidden below the surface. Bear in mind that the shock — perhaps even embarrassment — of your first meeting may unsettle him to the point that he doesn't act like himself. It may be that he simply has to get used to you.

Body language can be of some help to the counselor in making his appraisal. Thus watch the individual's facial expression, eye contact and posture. These can give some indication of the degree to which you are being received and the amount of support that is being given your efforts to admonish him.

LISTENING

As the one doing the admonishing, you have the right to expect to be heard. After all, the offender, as a member of the congregation, has agreed to submit to Christian discipline when this become necessary. This is, in fact, one of the conditions of membership listed by the constitution. And the Scripture enjoins Christians to accept admonishment (Proverbs 13:8; 15:31; 9:8; Psalm 141:5; Ecclesiastes 7:5; 1 Timothy 5:20; 2 Timothy 4:2).

But don't do all the talking. The individual you are admonishing will soon grow weary and resentful. Undoubtedly he will not put up with your "preaching." He has the right of response. Therefore listen to what he has to say, for only by listening to him and observing him can you tell whether you are getting through. Listening, like observing, provides you with feedback. Feedback gives you direction as you continue to admonish him.

But a caution is in order: "Sometimes we should *not* listen. It is just as bad to listen when we should be speaking, as to speak when we should be listening."[5] Ask your Counselor, the Holy Spirit, for wisdom to know the difference.

Often the counselee's reaction to the counselor's words of admonition obscures his real problem. He may, for example, talk on many issues that do not touch on what really is wrong and, hence, what ought to be troubling his conscience. You not only have to listen, but then also help the counselee to speak about his sin and even to repent of it.[6]

Since what the counselee says may not be what the counselee means, you as elder-counselor would do well to listen with what is termed "the third ear." This means to listen to the tone in the individual's voice (betraying anxiety, hostility, sarcasm, etc.), to watch for body language (which may betray agitation, fear, relief, denial, agreement, sarcasm, etc.) and also to read between the lines. Sometimes you have to ask yourself: "What is he *really* saying to me?"

QUESTIONING

The questioning process is absolutely necessary in order to carry on effective interaction between counselor and counselee. The purpose of questioning is to uncover to the counselee himself what is really wrong so that he will see his error and make his heartfelt confession. The proper question, properly timed, helps the counselee express his guilt and, finally, his desire for forgiveness as well as his desire to change. The skill is to ask the right question at the right time. The answers given to proper, well-timed questions will, to a great extent, determine whether or not you are on course and are "getting through" or whether another tack is indicated.

Phrasing of questions is highly important. Questions should be simple, not complicated. They should be clearly stated and easily understood. Try to ask questions that require more than a yes or no answer — although these at times can be effective. Don't overwhelm the counselee with too many questions too quickly. A slower, deliberate pace is better. You thereby give the counselee time for thinking through his answers. You might deliberately ask for feedback with a question such as, "Do you understand the point I am making?" Or, "Do you agree with what I just said?"

In your questioning you are to determine for whom or for what the counselee has chosen to live . . . for himself or for God? Is he controlled and motivated by his sinful flesh, which continually receives impressions from the devil and the world, or is he motivated by the impressions which Christ's words make on his new man? It would be good to remind the counselee of Paul's words in his second letter to the Corinthians: "(Christ) died for all, that those who live should no longer live for themselves but for him who died for them and was raised again" (5:15). Ask him: "For whom are you living, Christ or yourself?"

It is best not to ask the question, "Why?" You already know why. The one you are confronting with scriptural admonition has sinned because he has a sinful nature, and he allowed his sinful nature to get out of hand. "What have you been doing?" is a meaningful question to ask. With it you are asking the individual under discipline to speak about his sin, to own up to it. Recall

Samuel's question to King Saul, who boasted that he had obeyed God when he really hadn't. The question left Saul with little choice. He had to own up to his disobedience (1 Samuel 15:12ff.).

Having heard the counselee's answer to the question, "What have you been doing?" — you as counselor know how to proceed. If the answer is one of owning up to sin, you can then determine how the counselee feels about his sin — with the purpose, of course, of finally granting him forgiveness. And when the counselee has been assured of forgiveness other questions are, then, in order. "What can be done about the situation?" "What does God in his Word tell you to do?" You ask quite frankly: "What are you going to do so that you live a holy life and do not repeat your sin in the future?" You then proceed to help him on the basis of Scripture.

RESPONDING

This is your reaction to the counselee's words and actions — your response to his response. Your goal is to use the answers, the statements, the excuses, the objections, the attempts to pass the blame, the questions he asks, and even the attitudes expressed and implied by the counselee, to guide the direction and intensity of further admonition. Your responses must always be aimed at facilitating the restoring process.

In your response you keep trying to get the offending church member to view himself as God views him so that he confesses his sin. "Confession is saying the same thing that God says about one's sin. It is to plead guilty to the charges made by conscience."[7] Your duty in responding to the offending church member who gives evidence of not yet being won over is to reinforce his conscience with the appropriate law-Scripture. And when he finally repents of his sin and confesses it, you are to respond with the gospel, pointing him to his perfect Savior who has paid for all sins, including that of the offender.

Confronting the Offender With his Sins

The church member has been termed an offender and placed under discipline because there is something wrong with him. Sin is being committed, or repentance over sin is being held back, because of something that needs to be changed in him. Therefore you have arranged a meeting for the purpose of straightening out the individual. You go to him (perhaps in the company of another elder and/or the pastor, if this is necessary) to confront him with his sin and to admonish him concerning it.

Two outstanding examples in the Bible of offenders confronted with their sins come to mind. There was King David who had been overtaken in the sin of lust and adultery, and even of murder. For a period of months David refused to confess his sin. Finally God sent Nathan to him, who stood toe to toe with David and admonished him. With a homely illustration right off the farm, Nathan showed David what he had done in taking his neighbor's wife. In his clever way of confronting David with his sin, Nathan got David to judge and condemn his own sin without suspecting it. When finally brought face to face with the terrible wrong he had done, David repented (2 Samuel 12:1-23). Then there was the apostle Peter. Having been warned by Jesus that he would disown his Lord three times, Peter, nevertheless, declared that he would never disown Jesus, even if he had to die with him. That very night Peter disowned his Lord those three times (Matthew 26:31-35). Later, on the shore of the Sea of Galilee, the risen Christ confronted his apostle early one morning and admonished him by asking him three times if he loved him — once for each denial. Peter was hurt because Jesus asked him the third time concerning his love. But Jesus had to wound Peter in order to heal him. He had to lead his conscience back to the wrong he had done (John 21:15ff.)

From these two illustrations out of the Scripture we see that when a person is admonished he must be confronted with what is wrong with him — what it is that needs to be changed — even though it causes hurt and embarrassment to do so. The hurting precedes the healing. When Eli confronted his sons who had committed gross wickedness, his words did not have the strength and intensity that were called for, and his insipid words of admonition finally accomplished nothing (1 Samuel 3:13).

The offender who is confronted with his sin may respond with excuses or objections. While listening to them you will not, however, accept them. Every member of the congregation is responsible to the congregation as well as to God for good behavior: godly conduct. It is expected of every professed believer that he live his faith. Christ wants each disciple to be disciplined in his behavior. When a member becomes involved in sin and fails to repent of it, he is acting irresponsibly. The church teaches responsibility to irresponsible members by responsible discipline. To accept excuses is not responsible discipline; it is not competent Christian counseling; it is not the way to confront an offender with his sin; it is not the way to admonish. Excuses must themselves be dealt with as sins, and as evidence of irresponsibility. The Christian counselor who accepts excuses ignores reality: the situation as it has developed with the offender, which has made this confrontation for the purpose of admonishing him necessary. Tolerating excuses simply circumvents the need for repentance, and negates the whole purpose of employing the Scripture to admonish the offender.

Bear in mind that the offender who makes excuses or states objections is hoping thereby to gain your sympathy. He reasons that if you accept his excuses or his objections you will thereby be giving God's stamp of approval to his sin. In other words, he is looking for you to reinforce his aberrant conduct by allowing his excuses to stand. He is even attempting to shift the responsibility for his actions from himself to you, and perhaps even to the congregation. This is something you simply dare not permit him to do.

As you confront the offender with his sin and reprove him for his impenitence, you will answer his excuses briefly from Scripture to show him the reality of his spiritual condition, which by his excuses he is trying to avoid. He is sinning, and there is no excuse for sinning. Sinning calls for one thing: repentance. Repentance, in turn, involves making confession (Proverbs 28:13; 1 John 1:9; Psalm 38:18; 32:5). Confession simply acknowledges that the sinner sees himself as God sees him, that he hates what he sees, and is ashamed and brokenhearted (Psalm 38:18; Ezra 9:6; Daniel 9:7f.; Luke 7:37ff.).

Admonishing the Offender Involves Giving Him Reproof, Warning, and Encouragement

In admonishing the offender you confront him with **WORDS OF REPROOF**. Jesus commanded: "If your brother sins, rebuke him (Luke 17:3). You state clearly, precisely, and without apology that his sin, followed by his failure to repent, has made your visit necessary. You show from Scripture that what he has done (and may still be doing) is sin and, therefore, unacceptable behavior. Paul had to take this action in the case of a fellow apostle. He reported in Galations: "When Peter came to Antioch, I opposed him to his face, because *he was in the wrong* (Galations 2:11). You also state what you hope to accomplish by your visit, namely, to win him over by bringing him to repentance. With that you then stress that God himself calls on him to repent — with all that this includes (contrition, making confession, asking forgiveness, receiving absolution, and living a corrected or amended life). See 2 Timothy 4:1-2.

In admonishing the offender you also use **WORDS OF WARNING**. You warn that unrepented sin results in damnation, for God cannot and will not tolerate impenitence. You warn him of the shame he should feel in his heart for having offended against his holy and good God. You warn him that he must understand the gravity of his present situation, which is the result of his own doing, with no one else to blame but himself. See 1 Thessalonians 5:14; Ezekiel 33:11; 3:18. If he doesn't repent he will, finally, be asked by God to pay in full for his sins in the eternal fires of hell. You and he are involved in a matter of utmost urgency. You must warn him of impending doom in hopes to save him.

Finally, in admonishing the offender you use **WORDS OF ENCOURAGEMENT**. You assure the offender that it is loving care for his soul that brought you to him, and that you hope he appreciates that. In calling on him to repent you hold out to him hope of God's mercy and forgiveness. Scripture is filled with God's words of encouragement to repentant sinners. Isaiah preached: "Let the wicked forsake his way and the evil man his thoughts. Let him turn to the Lord, and he will have mercy on him, and to our God, for he will freely pardon" (Isaiah 55:7; see Joel 2:13). Peter commanded the Jews of his day: "Repent, then, and turn to God, so that your sins may be wiped out, that times of refreshing may come from the Lord" (Acts 3:19; see 1 John 1:9). More will be said about the repentant offender later.

The Scripture is the Holy Spirit's Instrument to Work Change in the Offender

That the Scripture is the Holy Spirit's instrument to work in human hearts, Jesus clearly stated: "The Spirit gives life; the flesh counts for nothing. The words I have spoken to you are spirit and they are life" (John 6:63). Jesus again acknowledged the Scripture as the divine instrument of spiritual life and renewal when he prayed thus to his heavenly Father in behalf of his disciples: "Sanctify them by the truth, your word is truth" (John 17:17). St. Luke testified that the Holy Spirit worked in people's hearts through the spoken message of Peter, God's inspired apostle: "While Peter was still speaking these words, the Holy Spirit came on all who heard the message" (Acts 10:44). The Scripture is, indeed, the instrument of God to work change in the offender. It is "the sword of the Spirit" (Ephesians 6:17).

And so, Scripture must be used throughout the counseling and the Holy Spirit, who is the counselor's Counselor, counsels by it.[8] The Spirit must be allowed to do his work through his Word. What this finally means is that the counselor can rest assured — when he uses God's Word faithfully and accurately — that he does not counsel alone. Furthermore, the counselee can approach his need for change with the confidence that he does not change alone, but that the Holy Spirit works in his heart through the divine Word or Counsel to effect the needed change that he might bring forth "the fruits of the Spirit."[9]

It is sad but true that Christians often get into trouble because they forget God's Word — what it tells them to believe, and what it tells them to do and not to do — or they simply pay it no mind. Worse yet, they may stubbornly refuse to be governed by it any longer. One of the duties of the elder in admonishing the offender is to remind him of God's truth and at the same time remind him that his believing and obeying it is of utmost importance. "So I will always remind you of these things, even though you know them and are firmly established in the truth you now have. I think it is right to refresh your memory as long as I live in the tent of this body . . . And I will make every effort to see that after my departure you will always be able to remember these things" (2 Peter 1:12-15).

As a Counselor to the Offender, the Elder Needs to be Proficient in the Scripture

In restoring the offender by admonishing him face to face, there can be no substitute for the Scripture — for the divine truths of the Law and the Gospel — as the basis of what you, the elder, say to him. Human reasoning and clever notions will not do, no matter how attractive they may sound to the ear and the mind (1 Corinthians 2:12-13). The biggest favor that you can do the offender is to go to him in a spirit of loving concern and "level with him" from the Scripture, labeling sin as sin, telling him what God has to say about his particular sin, and confronting him with God's own admonition which counsels him to repent or perish. Harsh as this may sound, it is, nevertheless, an important and necessary part of the restoring process, for uncovering the sin and condemning it with God's Word, is preparatory to forgiving it. When the offender repents, you have the privilege of applying the gospel in all its sweetness and in all its power to comfort him and restore peace in his heart, and to correct what has been amiss in his life.

But there is no way that you, the elder-counselor, can be either truthful or effective in admonishing the offender if you do not know the Scripture and if you do not use it properly. You simply have no weapon with which to fight the devil and the offender's flesh, and no spiritual food to offer him to nourish his faith and promote spiritual growth, if you lack knowledge of the Word of God and the skill to handle it properly. As an elder you are called upon to admonish members of the church, and your admonition must be scriptural. Therefore *you* must be scriptural. That is, you must continually study God's Word, be filled with scriptural knowledge and use your knowledge wisely and properly.

In order to offer scriptural admonition to the offender, you as the elder-counselor must be proficient in the application of the law and the gospel. This is a fundamental matter. Confronting the offender for the purpose of restoring him is a ministry of both the law and the gospel. For your review a summary of the law and the gospel is given in Addendum Two.

In Order to be Restored, the Offender Needs to Accept the Scriptural Admonition Offered Him

As a confessed Christian and member of the church, the person who is being admonished should expect his counselor (pastor and/or elder) to speak to him from God's Word, and should willingly allow and accept — without excuse or objection — the admonition offered him. He needs to acknowledge the Scripture — what it has to say concerning his sin — regardless of how he feels. Also the elder's right to bind him to it. For example: The member may not feel like staying with his wife; he may feel that divorcing her is the right thing to do. But he needs to acknowledge that the truth of God's Word, aside from his personal feelings, is that walking out on his wife and filing for divorce is desertion, and marrying another woman is adultery in God's eyes. He must act on the basis of the Scripture and not on the basis of his personal desires, which in this case are influenced by his sinful flesh. Or take the case of a delinquent member who may stay away from church on the premise that he doesn't think that a person has to go to church in order to be a good Christian. His own thoughts aside, he must acknowledge that public worship, public preaching, public administration of baptism and the Lord's Supper is the scriptural way, and that the office of the pastoral ministry is a divine institution to serve them.

You may find, upon analyzing the offender's reaction, that he is not profiting from your verbal confrontation. Your disciplinary action toward him is not bearing fruit. This is so simply because he does not listen to you (nor to the Scripture you bear to him) with a humble heart full of repentance and faith. He may not be accepting your words with the same seriousness and earnestness with which you offer them. He may not recognize the gravity of the situation that has brought you to his door and into his living room. He may give the impression that he doesn't know what all the fuss is about. Or, he feels angry that you have intruded — and he may be embarrassed. His anger and embarrassment may hinder the restoring process. He may be a stubborn and quick-tempered individual. At any rate, he shows that he is tuning you out, and in tuning you out he is tuning out God's Word. His ears are hearing but his heart isn't receiving the message.

Of course, there is the possibility that you have failed to express the truth in such a way that he can understand what God says in his Word about sin. Whatever the reason for his being tuned out, more intensive admonition is in order in which you remind him of the authority of the Scripture in his life and of what God says concerning his sin. You again call on him to repent, since that is the message of the Scripture (God's message) to him in this situation. More prayer on your part is also in order.

If the offender insists on setting the Scripture aside, and thus will not allow himself to be admonished from it, the confrontation is at an impasse for he denies the only basis of it. By denying the authority of God's Word in his case, the offender ruins the power of God's Word to work spiritual restoration in his heart and life. Confronting the offending church member in order to admonish him precludes both the counselor's and the counselee's acceptance of the Bible as the inerrant Word of God and norm of faith and life.

When you are dealing as an elder with an offender who appears to be unable to comprehend your words of admonition, as though he is completely tuned out to what God's Word exhorts a Christian to do and to believe, it would be wise to proceed on the premise that he may very well not be converted. A return to the basics of what constitutes the Christian faith is, then, necessary. "How can one nurture a plant before it has taken root? How can one bring up a child that is not born?"[10] It would be in place for you to take through a presentation of God's plan of salvation with the member.

Forgiveness is Announced to the Repentant Offender and he is Admonished to Believe It

The offender's attitude toward sin *can be changed* even though this change seems slow in coming. But the only thing that can change his attitude is God's Word. You continue to confront him with the Scripture, with what God says about his sin and about impenitence. And it is also good to remind him that he is losing out on the joy of serving God with a steadfast heart and a responsible Christian life. You point out to him that by his actions he is showing himself to be an irresponsible person. He is going against God's will. That's lawlessness (1 John 3:4). Furthermore, he is in the process of destroying his Christian faith. That's damnation. And he is harming the spiritual life of his family and even of the church. That's offense. He must accept the responsibility of repenting of his sin and of living a good Christian life.

By God's grace you may be thrilled to hear the offender accept what you say to him and, repenting, ask for forgiveness. Well, then, the purpose of your disciplinary action toward him has been accomplished. Your loving concern that brought you to him has paid off, and you know a joy in your heart that is difficult to contain.

Upon hearing the offender's statement of repentance, you might lead him in the *General Confession*:

> O almighty God, Merciful Father, I, a poor, miserable sinner, confess unto you all my sins and iniquities with which I have ever offended you and justly deserved your temporal and eternal punishment. But I am heartily sorry for them and sincerely repent of them, and I pray you of your boundless mercy and for the sake of the holy, innocent, bitter sufferings and death of your beloved Son, Jesus Christ, to be gracious and merciful to me, a poor, sinful being. Amen.

In preparing to announce the absolution, you might address him with words patterned after those spoken by the pastor in the Confessional Service:

> I now ask you before God, Is this your sincere confession, that you from your heart repent of your sins, believe on Jesus Christ, and sincerely and earnestly intend, by the assistance of God the Holy Spirit, henceforth to amend your sinful life? Then declare it by saying: Yes.

Here, you are asking the repentant sinner: 1) to make this confession of sins his own, 2) to accept now with true, devout faith in Christ the absolution which is about to be given and 3) to be done with sin, and, in this case, to be done especially with the sin that made this disciplinary action necessary. Furthermore, in place of sin, to live a holy life.

Upon his affirmation, he must be given the forgiveness he has requested, no matter what sin he is guilty of. It isn't the kind or size of sin that matters, but the person's consciousness of it and his sorrow over it evidenced in his confessing and denouncing the sin, his seeking forgiveness for it and his stated desire to live an amended life free of sin. You have held the offender responsible for his sin and he has finally accepted responsibility, admitting full blame. Now then, there lies on you the blessed responsibility to forgive his sin(s). You might use the following words in absolving him, or similar ones:

> Upon hearing your confession, I, as your brother in Christ, announce the grace of God to you. In the name of God the Father, Son and Holy Spirit I forgive your sin(s). May our merciful God go with you to assist you in living your life to his glory. Amen.

Note well: Forgiveness of the offender's sin is not first enacted when he *proves* his repentance by a godly life subsequent to his repentance. No probation period dare be imposed to test the genuiness of his repentance before his sin is forgiven. Recall how the loving and merciful father dealt with his lost son, who came back home to make his confession (Luke 15:17-24). The father yearned for the moment his son would return so that he could forgive him. The father in the parable is none other than God, and what is pictured is God's instantaneous forgiveness of the sinner who repents. Therefore you tell the repentant sinner (no matter how great his sins, or what kind) that he is forgiven — washed clean of his sins — and you admonish him to believe it with all his heart. Up to this time you have been confronting the sinner with his sin and with the law of God, which both reveals and condemns sin. Now you confront the sinner with the unfathomable grace and mercy of God in Christ by which his sin is forgiven and he is justified: "If we confess our sins, he is faithful and just and will forgive us our sins and purify us from all unrighteousness" (1 John 1:9). "Whoever confesses and renounces them (his sins) finds mercy" (Proverbs 28:13; see Isaiah 1:18; Romans 3:28; 1 John 1:7, 2:2).

The Restored Offender is Admonished to Live a Restored Life

Your work of confronting the person under discipline with admonition from God's Word is, however, not over when you forgive his sin. After assuring him of God's forgiveness you then hold him responsible for living a changed life, not the same life; for living a renewed life, not the old life. His behavior will be different — must be different. A life that was of the flesh must give way to a life led by the Spirit of God.

The truly repentant individual will not only stop his sin (even an unbeliever can stop his sin), but stop it because he fears and loves God. And then he will live a changed, restored life out of the same fear and love of God. Zacchaeus not only stopped extorting money from people, he went on to show a heart liberated from greed and love for money, and filled with the power of God's love. He restored four times the amount he had stolen, and gave half his property to the poor (Luke 19:1-9).

That the renewed life not only involves stopping the sin but of actively living a righteous life is taught many times in Scripture. Paul, for example, urged: "He who has been stealing must steal no longer, but must work, doing something useful with his own hands, that he may have something to share with those in need" (Ephesians 4:28). In Titus, Paul wrote: "(Jesus) gave himself for us to redeem us from all wickedness and to purify for himself a people that are his very own, eager to do what is good" (2:14). Quoting Psalm 34, Peter reminds the Christian that "he must turn from evil and do good" (1 Peter 3:11).

In motivating the repentant offender to live a right life in the future so that he not only does not repeat his sin that brought on the discipline, but lives an active Christian life, he might well be reminded of his baptism. In being baptized he died to sin and became alive unto righteousness (Romans 6:4-5, 8, 11). He should be taught to pray that the Holy Spirit, who through baptism gave him faith to believe in the forgiveness of sins and put his old flesh to death, will keep dealing death to his old adam and keep spiritually renewing his new man. You assure the repentant offender that the Holy Spirit will aid him in living an amended life out of love to the Savior so that he can speak a deliberate no to sin and a resounding yes to righteousness. You might speak thus to the individual you have forgiven:

> With the Spirit's help die in your sinful flesh to sin and be alive in your new man. Live unto Christ. You know that sin is evil. You have confessed it and denounced it and received God's forgiveness for it. Now live in such a way that you show that you hate sin and turn from it, and that you love righteousness. Walk in the Spirit as God commands his people to do. Claim the life in the Spirit that Christ by his death on the cross wants to give you.

And so, you need to remind the repentant individual, whose faith in Christ you have heard him express, that he is alive spiritually. Therefore as a believer he is viable: he is capable of a spiritual life, capable of growing more and more into being the kind of person God desires him to be. After all, God rules in the lives of his believers with love and wisdom and power through the Holy Spirit. "Those who live in accordance with the Spirit have their minds set on what the Spirit desires . . . You . . . are controlled not by the sinful nature but by the Spirit, if the Spirit of God lives in you" (Romans 8:5, 9). "Live by the Spirit, and you will not gratify the desires of the sinful nature" (Galations 5:16). Though temptations will continue to assault the individual who has repented — as they do every Christian — he need not give in to them. God rescues his people, providing them with escapes from temptation. "God is faithful; he will not let you be tempted beyond what you can bear. But when you are tempted, he will also provide a way out so that you can stand up under it" (1 Corinthians 10:13; see Psalm 94:17-19; Psalm 23:4; 2 Timothy 4:18).

† † † † † †

CHAPTER SIX

THE ELDERS AT WORK: MINISTERING TO DELINQUENTS

INTRODUCTION

In any given year, the probability is high that the number of those who leave the church is similar to, and may even surpass, the number of new members received. How many of those who leave each year could have been kept in the flock and helped to grow spiritually had more diligent efforts been made to minister to the delinquents and others who were backsliders? Could a number of these have been restored if the pastor and board of elders had begun their work of admonishment soon after the member's problem or sin surfaced? Did the pastor and/or elders wait too long to begin, thus making the outcome of their efforts almost a foregone conclusion?

A few years ago a Lutheran pastor in Wisconsin sent out a questionnaire concerning *Delinquency and Excommunication*. The purpose was to determine the pattern of work being done with delinquents by pastors, elders and voting assemblies. The results were revealing. A total of forty-three pastors responded. To the question having to do with how frequently in the last five years delinquents began to be contacted, eleven indicated less than five times; ten indicated between five and ten times; five indicated between ten and twenty times and seventeen indicated more than twenty times. The author of the questionnaire concludes:

> One wonders whether ... there could be a great deal more concern when only seventeen have contacted more than twenty delinquents in a period of five years — and half of the congregations (according to the Statistical Report) have less than 50% of their members in church on the average. (Church attendance varies from 31-80%, with only two churches having better than 70% attendance.) There's no doubt that our delinquency efforts could stand some attention and upgrading. Consider also how many of us are working with people who haven't communed in over a year, and that the pastor is the person who initiates the majority of the contacts.[1]

Evaluating another part of the questionnaire that had to do with the terms used to categorize those members who leave the congregation (a variety of terms is being used), the author asks:

Do we have difficulty deciding whether members who leave our congregations are Christians? Is that why so many terms are used? Have we loved our members enough to stay in close contact with them, or don't we care and thus they slip away from us in all sorts of ways? Note that only seven pastors checked that the majority of their delinquents leave their congregations by transfer, presumably to become active again elsewhere ... Thirty-three of us usually get no further in disciplinary cases than speaking to the offender privately ... The most frequent response (is) that the offender asks to be deleted from our membership ... Most of us are unsuccessful in regaining the straying. There are ninety-seven check marks ... saying we speak to our delinquents, but only twenty of them say that the offender usually repents.[2]

Congregations ought to be deeply concerned over cases of delinquency, for chronic absence from church services and from the communion table is a serious sin. Delinquents in effect turn their backs on the meal of divine grace that God serves up in church to feed their souls so that their faith may grow, and that they might be strengthened against sin. It has been pointed out that despising the means of grace is a greater sin than most people imagine because it is a sin against the remedy (i.e. for sin) itself.[3] "Delinquents are despising the means of grace, and that involves the very tools of the Holy Spirit for bringing about repentance."[4]

Scripture shows us that God's people, as a matter of course, meet together at God's house to worship him, to hear his Word expounded and to partake of the Lord's Supper. (See Addendum Four: *Scripture Topics Index*: **Church and Communion Attendance; Word of God, hearing the; Word of God, preaching the; Worship, Public; Pastoral Office; Offerings, church.**) The practice of church fellowship (attending church) with other Christians is closely bound to the Christian's confession of Christ, and, indeed, is an important part of his confession. When Christians worship together, making common confession of their faith, they carry on what has been termed, "a mutual edification society."[5] Everyone benefits. Participating in public worship is God's will. It is not God's will that Christians be loners, holding themselves aloof from the church as it gathers to enjoy the Word and the Sacraments (Matthew 18:20; Hebrews 10:23-25; 1 Corinthians 10:17; Psalm 22:22; Acts 2:46-47; Colossians 3:16).

And so, delinquency is not only serious sin (soul-destroying sin) but also a blight on the congregation. Christians detract from the spirit of fellowship by their absence from the worship service and the communion table. Their absence erodes the morale of other Christians, having a negative spiritual impact on their faith. A little bit of yeast causes the lump of dough to be leavened (1 Corinthians 5:6). Delinquency robs the Lord of financial resources for his gospel ministry. It makes outreach into the community with the gospel even more difficult, and certainly dampens the pastor's enthusiasm for his work.

The members of the congregation who neglect Word and Sacrament are sinning, and they must be admonished for their sin of neglect, just as we must admonish them for any other sin. After all, the salvation of their soul is jeopardized.

Who is to do the admonishing? Certainly the pastor and the elders are charged with the duty of admonishing the neglecter of Word and Sacrament. And yet, this duty is not in their hands alone. Each and every member of the congregation has a duty over against every other member of the congregation: to help deliver his soul from sin. Each of us is our brother's keeper. Many times, more good can be accomplished when a man's best friend goes to him to admonish him concerning a sin, than when he receives an "official" visit from the pastor and/or the board of elders. Brotherly love tenderly administered, along with scriptural admonition, can do much to sway the heart to do the right thing.

Finally, the work of elders in ministering to delinquents can be classified as sort of a "closed-circuit" evangelism, for it is work performed in the church to win back to Christ those who have backslid but are still counted among the church's membership. And this form of evangelism ought not be overlooked or minimized, for while the church has an obligation to the unchurched, it has an even greater obligation to the members who are in the church but are in grave danger of leaving it by losing their faith. They are in danger of losing their faith through their neglect of Word and Sacrament. Those who are in the church (at least their names appear on the membership roll), and yet distance themselves from it, are in sore need of help.

SCRIPTURE'S WITNESS AGAINST DELINQUENCY OR INACTIVE CHURCH MEMBERSHIP

1. **God wants his believers to receive spiritual care from faithful pastors, whose duty it is to watch over their souls. Since the founding of the New Testament church, Christ's ministers have used the public worship service as an important means to provide instruction in God's Word and spiritual care to the believers under their charge.**

> *It was he who gave some to be apostles, some to be prophets, some to be evangelists, and some to be pastors and teachers, to prepare God's people for works of service. (Ephesians 4:11)*

> *Guard yourselves and all the flock of which the Holy Spirit has made you overseers. Be shepherds of the church of God, which he bought with his own blood. (Acts 20:28; see also 1 Peter 5:2)*

> *Remember your leaders, who spoke the Word of God to you. (Hebrews 13:7; see also 1 Timothy 4:16; 2 Corinthians 5:18, 20)*

> *Obey your leaders and submit to their authority. They keep watch over you as men who must give an account. (Hebrews 13:17; Acts 1:15, 2:42-47, 20:20; Romans 16:5)*

2. **God wants his Word to be preached and the Sacraments to be administered.**

> *Preach the Word; be prepared in season and out of season; correct, rebuke and encourage — with great patience and careful instruction. (2 Timothy 4:2; see also 1 Peter 1:25)*

> *This cup is the new covenant in my blood; do this, whenever (Greek: as often as) you drink it, in remembrance of me. (1 Corinthians 11:25)*

3. **God wants his believers to hear his Word as it is preached and taught. He does not want his Word to be despised or neglected. Furthermore, God wants his believers to put his Word into practice. God also wants the Lord's Supper to be received over and over, yes, on a regular basis.**

> *Blessed . . . are those who hear the Word of God and obey it. (Luke 11:28; see also Matthew 13:23; 1 Timothy 4:1)*

> *And we have the word of the prophets made more certain, and you will do well to pay attention to it. (2 Peter 1:19)*

> *He who belongs to God hears what God says. (John 8:47)*

> *Humbly accept the Word planted in you, which can save you. Do not merely listen to the Word, and so deceive yourselves. Do what it says. (James 1:21a-22)*

Whenever you eat this bread and drink this cup, you proclaim the Lord's death until he comes. (1 Corinthians 11:26)

4. **God wants his church to the end of time to carry on public worship of him, and Christian fellowship with one another. The Scripture provides many examples of public worship and fellowship. We have, furthermore, the example set by the Savior in worshiping regularly at the temple in Jerusalem and at the local synagogue.**

In the congregation will I praise you. (Psalm 22:22)

Where two or three come together in my name, there I am with them. (Matthew 18:20)

Guard your steps when you go to the house of God. Go near to listen. (Ecclesiastes 5:1)

Let us consider how we may spur one another on toward love and good deeds. Let us not give up meeting together, as some are in the habit of doing, but let us encourage one another — and all the more as you see the Day approaching. (Hebrews 10:24-25)

Let the Word of Christ dwell in you richly as you teach and admonish one another with all wisdom, and as you sing psalms, hymns and spiritual songs with gratitude in your hearts to God. (Colossians 3:16)

They devoted themselves to the apostles' teaching and to the fellowship, to the breaking of bread and to prayer. (Acts 2:42)

(Jesus) went to Nazareth, where he had been brought up, and on the Sabbath day he went into the synagogue, as was his custom. (Luke 4:16; see also Matthew 26:55)

5. **God wants his church to receive offerings; he wants his Christians to give regularly and cheerfully in proportion to their income.**

Jesus sat down opposite the place where the offerings were put and watched the crowd putting their money into the temple treasury. (Mark 12:41)

Each man should give what he has decided in his heart to give, not

> *reluctantly or under compulsion, for God loves a cheerful giver. (2 Corinthians 9:7)*
>
> *On the first day of every week, each one of you should set aside a sum of money in keeping with his income. (1 Corinthians 16:2)*

WHY DO CHURCH MEMBERS BECOME DELINQUENT?

Listed below are some of the reasons church members become delinquent. No pretension is made that the list is complete. It does, however, cover some of the main problem areas in church membership leading up to delinquency. In counseling the delinquent, look for the "disease," not just the symptoms. What is it that is *really* bothering the delinquent and turning him off toward Word and Sacrament and Christian fellowship? The following list should at least help make you aware of things to look for in counseling the delinquent and less content to accept superficial responses to your queries.

Members May Become Delinquent . . .

1. **Because their needs are not being met.** Oh, their need for the Word of God is being met insofar as this need can be supplied by the pulpit. The pastor preaches faithfully and scripturally. (Of course, it may happen that a member may become inactive because he objects to the message of a "liberal" pastor, but this is another matter.) Many people go to church not only to worship God and hear his Word preached, but for the fulfillment of social needs as well. One of the foremost social needs is to love and be loved. Thus they want to build a closeness, a bond of loving fellowship with other Christians in the church. They aim at establishing rapport with others. But when they attend church, they fail to find the closeness they yearn. They hear frequent talk from the pulpit how Christians are to love one another, and yet they do not experience this love from their worship group — or at least they think that they don't. They see — or they imagine that they see — a basic tenant of their Christian religion hardly in evidence and are confused as a result. They wonder if there is not more to church than the preaching done by the pastor, which preaching few seem to put into practice. They may feel rejected, and they may also feel bitter. They may remove from the church to avoid the pain they feel, the pain of loneliness and of rejection. They don't appear to be loved and accepted by other members of the congregation; therefore, they tell

themselves that they really don't need the church. They don't enjoy being around people that seem to reject them; neither do they want to continue a fellowship that has proved to be fruitless. When they are asked the reason for their withdrawal from the spiritual community they may complain that it is a "cold congregation" or that they don't "feel comfortable in it."

This type of "hurt" which the member is experiencing may be more widespread among delinquents than we realize. From his extensive study, John Savage concludes that the inactive church member is *basically* a screened-out member, one whom the congregation doesn't want (or at least he is given that impression — probably inadvertently). His cries for help are not being answered. Savage points out that the screened-out member (bear in mind that the congregation is probably not even aware that it has screened him out) probably will become angry and strike out either at the congregation or himself. The inactive member who is angry at the congregation thus blames the situation on the environment or others. He vents his anger externally on objects or people. "I'm just as good a Christian as the ones who are going to church!" he might be heard to say. The one who is angry with himself maintains his anger internally. He blames himself, minimizing his proficiency in Scripture, his personal worth, etc. The process of disassociation will commence if the congregation continues to ignore the cries for help issuing from this inactive member who feels that he has been screened-out: ignored, not accepted, not given love, isolated. The screened-out member, who has already begun to be inactive as far as the church service is concerned, will commence to pull out of committees, choir, programs, church school. Finally, if this action doesn't bring results he will tender a letter of resignation.

He seals off the pain he has been experiencing as a screened-out member by his inactivity as a member and, finally, by being a non-member. Once he has become inactive, he feels comfortable again. How often hasn't the pastor and/or the elders heard the complaint: "I just don't feel comfortable in "your" church, or "that" church. (Note: not "my" church, or "our" church.) By not attending church, and perhaps by even disassociating completely from the church, the member who feels that his needs are not being met, feels comfortable again and begins to reinvest his time and money in other pursuits.[6]

There is much work to be done by the counselor to help this type of fallen-away member to heal the hurt that has caused the pain, which, up to this time, has simply been sealed off. And if the congregation has helped to bring it on, the congregation will have to do some changing on its part to help heal the hurts it has caused, even though inadvertently. Has the congregation failed to supply outlets for the individual's talents and willingness to work? Is the congregation cliquish, cold and indifferent toward people? Is the congregation so set in its ways that it will not even permit an exchange of ideas? "We've *never* done it *that* way!" The church is *people*, and people have needs. People should care *about,* and care *for* people. Too often the church doesn't. And when it doesn't, the isolation and rejection of certain members results. The consequence of all this? In effect, the church is being restrictive in the matter of membership. The church that doesn't carefully integrate new members into the life of the church, and strive to keep *all* members integrated so that no one feels isolated and rejected, is pathetically ignoring its responsibility. It is not enough to get a person's name on the membership roll. It is everyone's responsibility to help keep it there, to see that the new member has no reason ever to feel isolated, unneeded and unloved.

It is a real tragedy whenever the church, though set on a course of perpetuating itself by gaining new members, fails to meet the needs of the individual member by failing, for example, to integrate him and make him feel accepted.[7]

2) **Because they are not willing, finally, to accept the responsibility of church membership.** Indeed, they might not show a responsible attitude generally. They are simply what we might term "irresponsible individuals." Church membership is more than the simple act of joining a congregation. It very much involves shouldering responsibility. Church membership is not a spectator sport; it's a hands-on experience that calls for active participation.

3) **Because they no longer agree with the church's position in some matters.** Rather than make an issue, they fade quietly into the distance.

4) **Because of outright unbelief.** They no longer accept the Christian religion for themselves. Therefore they no longer make the confession of faith involved in attending church with those who, to all appearance, are believers.

5) **Because they are "cold" toward the Word of God.** They lack a hunger and thirst for the means of grace, mainly for the reason that worldly activities now consume their thinking, their time, their energy and even a goodly portion of their means.

6) **Because of sins that particularly bother their conscience and embarrass them.** For example, they may be living in fornication. They know very well that they are not living up to their membership requirements. They feel that they would be acting hypocritically if they came to church and worshipped with the congregation under the circumstances. Also, attending church services would serve to remind them of their sin, since they would be closely associated with God's Word there. And they fear that sooner or later the pastor is bound to hit on their sin in his sermon.

7) **Because of laziness: physical and spiritual.** They can't get up and get going on Sunday mornings for they lack the necessary motivation. Getting up and getting dressed and getting to church on time simply requires too much effort. Still they make it to work on time all during the week. In that particular pursuit there is sufficient motivation: a paycheck.

8) **Because of self-righteousness and work-righteousness.** Attending church is a work they feel that they don't really need. They can be good Christians, they reason, without going to church. They define a Christian simply as one who lives a decent life, one who keeps the law outwardly — not one who trusts in Jesus Christ for salvation.

9) **Because they lack love and concern for their fellow Christians.** Brotherly love is the main distinguishing mark of the believer. Yet they have no desire to come to church to encourage others in the faith, to help lift the spirits of others, to pray for others and with others, to partake of the Lord's body and blood in the Sacrament together with others, and to give their financial support to the work of preaching the gospel so that souls can be saved.

10) **Because of work conflicts.** They have a work schedule that does not permit them to attend public worship on Sunday morning. This may or may not be of their own choosing. Some work on Sunday just for the extra money, but are not required to do so. Thus, materialism may enter the picture.

11) **Because they allow their sinful flesh to rule them,** and thus don't get anything out of the service. Their sinful flesh is bored, and because they listen to their flesh they reach the conclusion that church is unessential and a waste of time. They put nothing into the church

service and get nothing out. They seek thrills for the flesh, not theology for the spirit. There are other things they would rather be doing.

12) **Because of peer pressure.** Much of the time they may be around people who are unchurched and who ridicule church-goers. Children and adults can both experience this. At school, at play, or at work, they find much opposition to religion — especially to attending church. In weakness they resolve not to appear "odd" by taking church membership seriously.

13) **Because of hurt feelings, anger and frustration over something that was said or done by the pastor or a member of the church.** And it may have been something ever so slight. It may even have been a simple misunderstanding. Or perhaps they didn't get their way over something. They either can't or won't come to grips with the situation.

14) **Because of personality clashes** with people in the congregation, especially with the pastor.

15) **Because of disagreement with the way the church is run.** They want to have more of a voice — perhaps even an office — but since that is impossible, they show their discontentment by dropping away.

16) **Because they may not have been ready for confirmation.** Their heart wasn't in it. They went ahead with it simply to make their spouse, or their parents happy. They feel that they have fulfilled their obligation by being confirmed, and now they see their obligation ended. They have no further desire toward the church, or need of the pastor, until, of course, they want to get married or some calamity enters their life.

17) **Because of negativism and rebellion:** they don't feel that they "have to attend church." They will come to church when they have the desire, and at the present time they are without the desire.

18) **Because of mixed-marriage difficulties.** Husband and wife keep arguing about whose church is right, which church the children should be brought up in, and so forth. They also feel lonely when they go to church since their spouse, and perhaps their children, aren't with them. They see other families attend church together. They might even be thinking of searching for a third (neutral) church to join.

19) **Because of greed or miserliness.** They do not want to give, and resent being confronted with the offering plate, or with references to giving in the sermon and bulletins.

20) **Because they may not perceive the body and blood of the Lord in the Lord's Supper** (1 Corinthians 11:29). Therefore they find no reason to partake of Communion. Or they are not alarmed by their sins and therefore feel no urgent need to receive the assurance of forgiveness bestowed on the believer in the Lord's Supper.

21) **Because the devil has robbed them of their faith** (Luke 22:31; 1 Peter 5:8).

22) **Because they have become captivated by worries, cares and worldly desires, which destroy the good effect of God's Word on them.** Materialism, desire for personal pleasure, has so engrossed them, or a particular sin has so entwined itself around their heart, that they have lost their appetite for spiritual food. They have lost their zeal for the priceless treasure of Christ and salvation.

23) **Because of family problems.** Problems with raising the children, money problems, friction between family members, disagreements, hurt feelings, etc., occupy their attention and dampen their enthusiasm for spiritual matters.

24) **Because of health problems:** physical, mental, emotional.

25) **Because when they do come to church, they let the devil perch on their shoulder,** who then robs them of God's Word, and no reason remains for them to put forth the effort to attend church.

26) **Because they feel sorry for themselves** — they work hard all week and feel that they must have one day to do just what they want to do. "Sunday is the only day I have to myself." "Sunday is the only day that the family is all together."

27) **Because they don't get anything out of the sermon.** They feel that the pastor lacks relevancy to the times.

28) **Because they don't like such things as the hymns and the liturgy and they refuse to adjust.**

29) **Because it's too much bother to bring their young children to**

church. They don't get anything out of the service because they are so busy trying to keep the children quiet. They may complain that the church doesn't provide a nursery school which their little ones could attend during the service. The simple fact may be that they don't have their children under control.

PREVENTING DELINQUENCY

Making Their Responsibilities Clear to Prospective Members

Ministering to delinquents, neglecters of Word and Sacrament, is a time-consuming work, and a difficult one. It is possibly the most difficult work the elder will engage in. No doubt some delinquency could be prevented if the new members were properly integrated into the congregation. All new members should be given a clear picture of their responsibilities and of what the congregation's procedure will be if they don't act responsibly: if they don't measure up in fulfilling their membership duties. The church must teach responsibility to its membership from the very beginning. If the pastor and board of elders took more time with new members to carefully instruct them on the duties and privileges of church membership, no doubt less time would have to be devoted later on to keeping their membership intact.

The pastor and elders must make crystal clear to all newcomers what the membership requirements are as imposed both by Scripture and the governing constitution. This is true whether they are newly confirmed, received by transfer or accepted on their profession of faith. Thus the one who is to be received into membership at the voters' meeting should be made aware that his failure to attend services will not be overlooked, nor will neglect of Word and Sacrament be allowed to go on for any length of time before there is a visit by the pastor/elders. Only if the prospective member is willing to abide by the Scripture and the constitution, thus to conduct himself responsibly, should he be received into membership.

Certainly no one should be received into membership who was listed as a neglecter of Word and Sacrament at the time he left his previous congregation and applied for membership in the new congregation. The simple fact is that people can transfer their inactivity from place to place.[8] Neither should one be accepted who has proved himself delinquent prior to the time of confirmation. First, such delinquents must set their spiritual house in order so that they can give a profession of faith that has substance. To grant membership to chronic delinquents gives a clouded testimony as to what responsibilities come with membership. Chronic delinquents received into membership in the congregation would have to have their names immediately placed on the delinquency list. It would be difficult to understand the logic of such a move. The congregation has every right to expect people applying for membership to display sincerety. Thus their stated willingness to assume the responsibilities of membership ought to be matched by performance.

Signs of Impending Delinquency

From a study conducted over a period of years, Lutheran pastor and author Donald A. Abdon lists five signs of impending spiritual delinquency to watch for:

1) The individual does not worship every Sunday. (Thus, absent by choice, not on account of work; but frequent absence on account of work can certainly lead to spiritual disaster also.)

2) The individual does not commune every time Holy Communion is offered ... The more frequently a person communes, the less apt he is to become delinquent.

3) The individual is not involved in any kind of Bible study and has not been, usually since confirmation.

4) The individual is not involved in any kind of Christian fellowship or service ... "Loners" get "picked off" by the Forces of Darkness rather quickly.

5) The individual comes from a "divided home," i.e. the individual is a member of the congregation but the husband or wife does not attend at all (i.e. is inactive or totally uncommitted) ... [9]

Now then, if these negative factors in the member's life are the signs of oncoming delinquency, reversing these negative factors ought to contribute to healthy, responsible, sustained membership. Thus every member of the congregation, in order to prevent falling prey to delinquency, ought to:

1. be regular in his church attendance,
2. be regular in communing at the Lord's Table (as frequently as possible),
3. carry on regular, diligent Bible study at home and attend regularly a Bible study course at the church.

4. participate in Christian fellowship and works of Christian service,
5. be united with his spouse not only in marriage, but united also in Christ, so that husband and wife worship together at home and at church.

Note that the first three on the list directly involve the members with the means of grace, the gospel in Word and Sacrament. The Holy Spirit is active in the heart of the Christian through the gospel to strengthen and preserve his faith.

The elders should, with the help of the pastor and elder assistants (if the church has them), continually take the spiritual "pulse" of each member of the congregation with the divine purpose of *preventing* delinquency from occuring. In larger congregations the elders, by welcoming people to church, can more easily determine who among those entrusted to their individual care are absent from the service. Each elder should pay particular attention on a Sunday morning to those members who are his spiritual responsibility. The individual communion record can be used in taking the member's spiritual pulse for it not only shows his communing habits but presents a fairly accurate record of his church attendance as well. A time should be regularly set aside in board meetings to assess the delinquency situation, during which the elders can compare notes and accurately determine the list of members for whom concern needs to be shown.

How Soon Should the Initial Contact be Made With a Member Who Appears to be Headed for Delinquency?

It is a sad but real fact of life that many pastors and boards wait much too long before making their initial contact. Every so often the notion occurs to them that it is "time to cut timber," to "get rid of the dead wood." It would appear that their main concern, finally, is not the salvation of souls but the updating of the membership list. If this is true, it is also tragic. By the time they make their initial contact with those who have been absent from worship, the chance of restoring the straying sheep are minimal or even nonexistent. The tardiness of their action has allowed the individual's problem of delinquency to become severe.[10] By the time the pastor and elders act, the delinquent member may be well entrenched in his sin.

The pastor and elders should not allow much time to lapse before the initial contact is made when it becomes evident that a member is beginning to neglect Word and Sacrament. The sooner the problem is dealt with the more one can hope for a good response on the part of the member. The farther removed a person gets from the preaching of God's Word, the more difficult it is to bring him back.

> Working with those who have lost interest may be one of the toughest assignments in the pastoral ministry of church officers. The seeds which sprang up quickly have withered now. If at all possible, this growth must be revived.
>
> The main matter is to get there quickly when the flower *begins* to fade. Too often we let it dry up until even the most thorough waterings cannot bring it back.[11]

How quickly, then, should the first contact be made? Suggestions vary. It is the conclusion of this writer that no more than four Sundays should transpire in the period of inactivity before the member is contacted. Any member who can purposely stay away for a period of a whole month is already in a dangerous way. Of course, it may happen that the member has a valid reason for not having attended the past few worship services and, therefore, no spiritual problem exists. But this will not be known unless contact is made.

If the board of elders is properly organized and trained, there should be little problem getting to the member soon after his delinquency is noticed. The individual elders should set aside time each week, especially in larger congregations, for visiting members. If an elder is not willing (or is unable) to donate adequate time to the visits he must make to the members assigned to his care, he should not accept the office. The work of an elder is time-consuming work and let no one be mistaken about this. On the other hand, the rewards of this work are great, both for the elder and for the congregation. It is a proven fact that frequent contacts with the membership by the pastor and elders result in high spiritual gain for the congregation.

What about the Lord's Supper? How frequently should the membership be expected to attend? When does a member become guilty of neglecting (perhaps even of despising) the Sacrament? Unless there are extenuating circumstances, why shouldn't the member plan to commune each time the Lord's Supper is offered? What if the Lord's Supper is offered once a month, and the member communes only every other month? In that case it would be in order to ask the question: Why not commune each time? Why shouldn't the entire congregation, that is, the whole number of communicants who are present on communion Sunday, commune together? Why should some remain in their pews? An exception is the member under discipline who is asked not to commune until the matter of his sin is cleared up. If there appears to be a pattern of non-communing, it would be in order to find out the reason for it. Perhaps the member may even be laboring under the false impression that it is improper for him to commune each time.

Regarding the question of how often a Christian should commune, Martin Luther urged that professing Christians should prepare often to receive the Lord's Supper. At the same time he spoke ill of the practice of allowing a year or two or three, or an even longer time to elapse without communing. He even drew the conclusion that people who stand aloof and abstain from the Lord's Supper for a long time ought not be considered Christians. Luther urged that Christians are not to treat the Lord's Supper as a mere spectacle but are to follow Christ's command to eat and drink and in this way remember him.[12]

ADMONISHING THE DELINQUENTS

Delinquency Must be Treated as Sin

Delinquency is a sin against the tool which the Holy Spirit uses to work in the heart and life of the believer. Visits to delinquents are discipline calls. What was said in a previous chapter in regards to confronting sinners with scriptural admonition applies to visits made by the elders to members who have become inactive. As to the methods that should be used in counseling neglecters of Word and Sacrament, these have been touched upon already in a previous chapter. There are, however, some special considerations to be given to the counseling of delinquents and these are brought out here.

The main thing to bear in mind is that you as elder are attempting, with God's help, to reverse the delinquent's present course which is taking him away from God's Word and Sacrament, away from the warmth of Christian fellowship and away from important opportunities for Christian service. You must realize that the defeat of his faith is a very real possibility. How very much the delinquent needs you! He needs your demonstration of loving concern; he needs your scriptural admonition; he needs your patience and understanding, and he needs your prayers.

You may not particularly enjoy going to the inactive member's home to confront and admonish him. But that's beside the point. Whether it brings you pain or pleasure is all the same; it is work that is vital to the spiritual welfare of the individual involved, and to his church. Until you go to the delinquent and speak with him you cannot begin to understand the cause of his action, or afford him the spiritual help that he so desperately needs. There are other calls that you probably would sooner make, e.g. to the sick or the elderly, but none need your attention more than the neglecter of Word and Sacrament!

> Calls on delinquents are usually the most difficult to make. In the first place, elders are somewhat annoyed by the fact that these people are causing extra work. They are apt to be a little bitter because delinquents wilfully and carelessly stray from the fold. The sick man may not be at fault for his illness. The delinquent could come to church and grow in the faith if he wanted to.
>
> But this is just the point. Perhaps Satan is attacking him with doubts and with unbelief. In any case, he is in danger of falling from grace. If you felt like he did, perhaps you would not come to church either. He may be just as much in need of your sympathy and understanding as one who is physically ill.[13]

Questions the Elder May Ask the Delinquent

1) Tell me about your faith. What do you believe? I am especially interested to hear from you how it is that you hope to be saved.

2) How would you describe your spiritual growth this past year? Are you becoming stronger or weaker?

3) Do you think that your faith is being helped by your absence from God's house?

4) Do you pray daily for your faith to grow and be preserved, and to show itself in Christian works? Do you feel that your absence from church has any effect on your Christian growth and your doing good works?

5) Don't you have any sins to confess together with the congregation?

6) Does the absolution spoken by the pastor to the congregation no longer thrill you?

7) When was the last time you were in God's house?

8) When was the last time you received the Lord's Supper?

9) Don't you need God anymore?

10) Don't you love God and his Word anymore?

11) Don't you love the brotherhood of saints, the congregation, anymore?

12) Have you been attending another church?

13) Is your remaining away from God's house and the Lord's Supper something you presently have no control over (e.g. working hours)? Would you be there if you could?

14) Is your remaining away from God's house and the Lord's Supper a matter of choice?

15) What are you doing on Sunday morning that is more important to you than worshipping God with the congregation and hearing God's Word preached?

16) Can you name just one change in your life, which if you made it, would bring you back to church?

17) Does whatever it is that keeps you from God's house on Sunday, keep you from work on Monday?

18) When you were confirmed you promised God, the pastor and the congregation that you would faithfully use the Word and Sacrament. What happened that caused you not to keep your promise?

19) Do you believe that God has failed you, and that this is the reason you are turning your back on him?

20) Do you feel that your fellow Christians in the congregation have failed you?

21) Do you think the congregation misses you? Do you miss the congregation?

22) Do you still consider yourself a part of the congregation, a sheep of the flock, or are you straying away and want to stay away?

23) How would you feel if you prepared a fine meal and the invited guests failed to come, even though they promised to?

24) Though you have been absent from church, have you continued to contribute to the Lord's work carried on by the congregation and its pastor? Are your church envelopes up to date? Do you believe that God holds us responsible for good stewardship?

25) What must your unchurched neighbors think when they take note of your staying at home Sunday after Sunday instead of attending church? That you are one of *them* instead of one of *us*? What message are you giving? Is it: "Look at me, neighbors! I don't go to church. Church isn't necessary. You don't have to go to church to be a Christian"?

26) Would you want God to treat you as you have been treating him and his Word: with neglect?

27) Do you regard your neglect of God's Word and the Sacrament a sin?

28) Are you willing to repent of this sin, willing also to give it up and come back to God's house, to the Word and Sacrament? Do you want forgiveness?

29) Is there some spiritual problem that either I or the pastor can help you with?

30) What is the message you wish to send to God by your continual absence from his house of worship and your continual neglect of his Word and Sacrament?

Pitfalls to Avoid in Ministering to the Delinquents

1) Don't operate on the assumption that those who have strayed away will someway and someday stray back all by themselves.[14] More likely that they will stay away. Spiritual weakness took them away, and spiritual weakness — resulting, finally, in spiritual death — will keep them away.

2) Don't take the delinquent's faith for granted. Just because a person has been confirmed, and has even come to church for a number of years, is no reason to take for granted that he understands God's plan of salvation. It should be your primary concern to uncover what his understanding of sin and grace is, and what he believes concerning the crucial question: "How can I be saved?" Donald A. Abdon, after making hundreds of calls on fallen away members, lists as a major reason the church is not reaching those who are backsliding, that the church is working with the wrong set of assumptions. He concludes that most delinquents are no longer Christians.[15] Abdon found that almost inevitably the fallen away member does not understand the doctrine of justification (forgiveness of sins) by grace through faith. In other words, they have fallen prey to Satan's lie that man can save himself by his good works.

3) Don't let many Sundays go by before inquiring into the reasons for a member's absence from church. To wait until the end of the year to determine who hasn't been coming or communing is inexcusable. To wait even a few months is the wrong thing to do. By that time much damage has been done. The person has had too much time to become accustomed to absenting himself from God's house, too much time to cool off toward Christian fellowship and the means of grace, too much time to retrain his conscience. Have on ongoing, accurate soul-accounting procedure, and **use** it!

4) Don't limit yourself to one meeting. You may have to visit the delinquent several times (and perhaps in the presence of another person). Don't try to accomplish too much in one hour on your visit. It may take several, perhaps many visits to his home, and months of patient counseling for the Holy Spirit to regain the straying by rekindling the spiritual life (faith) that has been slowly dying over a long period of time; indeed, may already be dead.

5) You must find out as soon as possible in the counseling session why the person absents himself from church. This is a "must" if you are to treat the disease and not the symptoms. You must help him remove what is wrong in his life, in his heart, before you can get him back to church and the Lord's Supper. Thus don't put overmuch stress on church and communion attendance at the beginning. *Put stress on treating the disease.* The symptoms — neglect of Word and Sacrament, and failure to return thank-offering to the Lord — give evidence of the disease. If he is absenting himself because of a quarrel with the pastor or another member, then, before church attendance can be stressed, he must first be reconciled to his brother — and you must help him do this. If the delinquent is being "screened-out" by the congregation, this process itself will have to be reversed before the delinquent can be expected to feel at home in church. It may be that he is once again a slave to his flesh. In fact, he may no longer be a believer. You will have to deal with him accordingly.

6) Don't minimize the importance of God's Word in solving the delinquent's problems. He is forgetting, or at least ignoring, what God's Word says to him. The cure is the Word of God clearly and comprehensively applied to him by which the Holy Spirit can work on his heart. He needs, then, to be reminded what God says to him,

especially in his present spiritual situation and condition. If a thorough review of Christian doctrine in the pastor's adult class is called for, prescribe it; insist on it. Adult Bible class on Sunday morning may very well be part of the cure too.

7) In counseling the delinquent, listen for his cries for help and then help him. Don't confuse cries for help with trivial excuses or objections. He may, for example, be suffering some emotional trauma that has not only effected his church attendance, but his entire life as well. His family may be suffering and his job may be suffering from it. Yes, it just may seem to him as though the world has turned upside down on him. Listen to him. Help him. Pray for him and with him. Be supportive and understanding. Be loving.

8) Beware of excuses or objections. Since the delinquent may again be in bondage to his flesh — a strong possibility — and since the flesh schemes and connives against God, the person for this reason may not want to talk about his relationship to God and, therefore, will attempt to put the elder or pastor on the defensive by voicing objections or excuses.[16] These must be handled as quickly and briefly as possible, but you must not let the delinquent sidetrack the discussion. You must get him back on the main track, which is to talk about his faith and his sin of neglecting Word and Sacrament. Be careful to determine if the person has a genuine excuse or merely a crutch that can't hold him up. Mild or trivial excuses are simply polite ways to say: "I really don't want to do this." The cause of these excuses or objections is thus weakness of faith (perhaps even lack of faith) and sin. The delinquent is allowing his sinful flesh to rule in his life, and his faith is dying. Indeed, it may have already expired. He may well be a cold spiritual corpse in which the rigor mortis of stubborn resistance to the Holy Spirit's pleadings has set in. However, there may yet be hope for him. Keep him on track in the counseling sessions and faithfully present God's Word, law and gospel, to him. The subject of excuses will be brought up again later.

9) Avoid thinking that the delinquent is necessarily telling you what is really eating away at him just because he has decided to sit and talk with you. Don't jump to conclusions. Be patient and display loving concern. Let him talk. At first he may be posturing. But when he really has a chance to talk it out, he may level with you and reveal what his real spiritual problem is. It may be a quarrel he has had with a member of the congregation. It may be a hurt that he has suffered in a meeting, when

he didn't get his own way. It may be that members of the congregation, with whom he wanted closer fellowship, have screened him out or isolated him. Don't be gullible, thinking that everything lies right out there on the surface. But do be tactful.

11) Don't neglect to help the delinquent with his spiritual problems that you may uncover in the course of your conversations with him, even those you weren't prepared for. Where it is necessary to refer him with his problem(s) to the pastor, do so.

11) Avoid a better-than-thou attitude when dealing with the delinquent. You are a sinner too. But by the grace of God you would be walking in his shoes. Pray God that you never share his sin. And pray that he will overcome his.

12) Remember your primary concern: It is not the relationship of the person to the local congregation, but his personal relationship to God. For out of this relationship comes the person's relationship with the congregation, and the use he makes of Word and Sacrament. And so, be careful not to consider membership in the local congregation more important than membership in the invisible Christian Church. Your primary purpose is to save a soul that may have begun to stray from the Lord, not to keep the person as a member of the congregation.

13) Don't equate initial neglect of Word and Sacrament with defiance or indifference toward the Word. Work at finding the root cause of the neglect. What it is may truly surprise you. Thus it is important to visit the delinquent early on in his absence from church. The longer the matter goes on, the greater the danger that the delinquent's attitude will change to one of defiance and belligerance.

14) If you uncover the fact that the counselee views things differently in some areas than the church does, be careful. Don't equate doctrinal indifference with outright unbelief. A person who does not agree with the church on all points of doctrine is not for that reason to be regarded as a pagan or a tax collector (one outside the faith and the church: Matthew 18). If he denies saving doctrine, it is, of course, a different matter. Denial of any teaching fundamental to salvation is unbelief.

15) Don't come at the delinquent like a steamroller. "Steamroller" tactics make the person feel threatened, resentful, and place him on the defensive. You must be careful that your action does not push the

delinquent completely away from the church and, finally, from the Savior. Use Christian sanctified common sense, and try to be all things to all people, putting yourself as much as possible in the counselee's shoes. Have empathy. You should speak to the delinquent in such a manner that he knows you love him, that your heart is reaching out to him, and that it is aching over his present problem or sin.

16) Be careful of wrong motivation. Your goal is to lead all people to eternal life rather than to have "clean membership lists." (In mission congregations, be careful not to let the level of fiscal responsibility set by the Mission Board, and based on the number of members, determine how you deal with delinquents.)

17) Don't neglect to pray for the delinquent and yourself. Pray for a successful meeting with him. Pray in his behalf for a change of heart. Pray that the Lord will give you the words with which to testify to him.

18) Do not think that letters, even when they are personalized, can take the place of face-to-face confrontation. Letters have their place, but must be used carefully. They are not a substitute for personal contact, but serve to reinforce your testimony. Sometimes letters addressed to the whole congregation can be helpful in getting a message across to those who tend to be delinquent. A duplicated form letter should *never* be used in dealing with delinquents. (See the separate chapter as well as the addendum that deal with letters.)

19) Don't frustrate people by refusing to take their questions or doubts seriously. Try to furnish the answers. When it concerns matters of policy (such as that which prohibits Lodge membership), the pastor should be brought in.

20) Avoid unnecessary judging. Be charitable. Don't go to the delinquent with the purpose of finding fault. How would Jesus deal with the sinner?

21) Avoid using the law (e.g. the Sabbath Commandment) to bring about church attendance. You may get the delinquent to come back to church with the threat of the law, but it is gospel motivation that will keep him coming. Emphasize the Savior's love for him, the wonderful saving message of the gospel (which he should desire to hear). Emphasize that the worship service is the place where grateful hearts praise God and bring thank offerings to him. This is not to say that the law is not to be used. What the delinquent is doing is sin. He is absenting

himself from the Christian fellowship provided through the congregation, and he is neglecting Word and Sacrament. He must be called to repentance.

22) Don't let the delinquent put you in the middle. Never let him inveigh against the pastor or against other members of the congregation. God's Word requires the one who has a complaint to go to his brother and tell him his fault privately, and endeavor to clear up the matter. So does the church constitution.

23) If an impasse is reached, don't be discouraged. Don't threaten excommunication. You've testified enough for one time. Make an appointment to come back, and then bring another member (need not be, can be an elder) with you. If you can make use of a good friend of the delinquent to accompany you as a witness, so much the better. Someone the delinquent trusts and respects.

24) Just because the member comes a few Sundays to church after he has been visited, is not cause enough to regard him now as penitent. He may be coming to church simply for the reason that he feels he has no other choice. To spare himself further embarrassment and admonishment, he may have agreed to come back. But if his heart is not in it he will drop away again. When he finally comes to church without being prodded, you can better conclude that your admonishing him has borne fruit.

25) Avoid the "easy solution" to a delinquency problem: simply removing the inactive person's name from the membership list. If you accept this solution, you have done nothing to help his soul.

The Significance of Excuses or Objections

The person who wants his name kept on the church roll but does not want to join in the worship services or partake of the Lord's Supper or give his offerings to maintain the church and its work or in other ways participate in the Lord's work, and makes trivial excuses for his backsliding, is a truly pathetic character! This person gives evidence of believing that he is saved by having joined the church organization. As long as he maintains his name on the church roll he feels eternally safe; yet he has no time for the church itself. His absenteeism clearly demonstrates his disinterest. However, in order to discourage the church from removing his name from the rolls, he makes excuses for his disinterest, hoping the church will be satisfied and leave him alone to carry on as he has been doing. This isn't always the case, of course, for some delinquents by their excuses are actually daring the church to remove their names from the rolls.

While giving brief attention to excuses or objections, it is important that you, the counselor, remember that there are probably deeper spiritual problems that lie hidden beneath the surface and are the real cause of the delinquent's inactivity. Excuses or objections are symptoms of a faith problem. Matters that wouldn't keep many other Christians out of church are, nevertheless, keeping the delinquent from God's house. He has used excuses as a wall to isolate and insulate himself from the Christian community and any action the community might wish to take regarding his membership. By making trivial excuses or objections the delinquent betrays a faith that is dying or is already dead. There are good reasons to believe that most delinquents are no longer Christians. If they are Christians, they are weak ones in the process of backsliding.

While excuses or objections must be heard and dealt with as speedily as possible, they cannot be accepted without doing further damage to an already weak faith or without minimizing the chances of a dead faith being rekindled. A person who cannot attend the church services has a legitimate reason that will, of course, be accepted. In his case the pastor, perhaps with the help of the elders, will do what he can to serve him with Word and Sacrament.

Handling a delinquent's excuses or objections should not be considered a "defensive" maneuver. Certainly you are always struggling for the truth of Holy Scripture to be heard, but you must bear in mind that you are not on the defensive. When the delinquent makes an excuse or states an objection he is going outside the Scripture, yes, even working against it; and you must hold him responsible. Sometimes the delinquent will attempt to put the pastor and/or the congregation in a bad light. He is simply attempting to transfer guilt so as to appear justified in his absence from church and in his failure to keep up his offerings. You do not accept his behavior for it is sinful, even though you do accept his statement for the purpose of commenting on it and leading him to the truth. You are the one with the message from God, a message you boldly, hopefully, but also lovingly and tactfully take to the delinquent as you handle his excuses or objections through counseling. Bear in mind that the proper handling of excuses or objections is an attempt on your part to save a soul. In Addendum Three you will find a thorough presentation of the more common excuses offered by delinquents and how to respond to them.

BRINGING THINGS TO A HEAD

How Many Times Should the Delinquent be Visited?

In dealing with the neglecter of Word and Sacrament, you may soon find that one visit to his home will not be sufficient. Follow-up visits will be necessary if . . .

1) the first visit doesn't succeed in bringing the delinquent to repentance. He maintains that he is doing no wrong by separating himself from Christian fellowship in the congregation, yes, even demands the right to do so. Still he wants to remain a member.

2) the first visit does not succeed in moving the delinquent to attend church soon afterwards. The member in question has agreed with you that he should be in church on Sunday mornings, and has even promised to come. In spite of that, Sunday after Sunday goes by and he still hasn't attended a service. We would have to conclude that his repentance was very shallow. The facts have to be presented to him again, and he has to be reminded of promises that he has made that are still unfulfilled.

3) the first visit succeeds only temporarily in moving the delinquent to attend worship services. It often happens that the person will attend several worship services and subsequently revert to his old ways. His repentance is shallow. He has to receive additional admonishment as soon as possible.

4) the first visit uncovered differences with the church's policy or doctrine. It is important to take the pastor along to present as clearly as possible the correct scriptural teachings on the points in controversy.

In every visit that is made subsequent to the first one, it would be wise to take along one or two people to help with the discussion and serve as witnesses to the delinquent's response. Whether or not these should be elders will have to be determined by the circumstances.

How many visits should be made, and over what length of time? About the best answer that can be given to this question is: as long as it is prudent to do so. Your purpose is to gain the brother, not to "cleanse the membership list." Indeed, it may take several visits to him before he really opens up and tells you what is gnawing at him and keeping him from God's house of worship. While much love and patience is to be used in dealing with the delinquent as succeeding visits are made, he must always be told that his failure to attend services and to partake of the Lord's Supper are serious sins, and that he is giving public offence.

Final Action

The delinquent may at any time during the discussion simply request that his name be removed from the congregation's membership list. He may or may not give reasons for this request. In effect he cuts himself off from further admonishment and disassociates himself from the congregation. Of course, he must be warned that he has sinfully severed his connection with the congregation, and the voters' assembly must declare the same. The person who at this point (i.e. during discussions with the elder(s) disassociates himself, is not to be excommunicated. By no longer claiming membership in the church, by withdrawing from fellowship (even if it is done to evade church discipline) he has removed himself from the responsibility of the congregation. However, he is to be warned of the spiritual consequences of his action: the spiritual consequences of his impenitence.[17]

If all admonition is fruitless, the neglecter of Word and Sacrament must be called to a meeting of the congregation's voters' assembly (in the event he has not withdrawn from membership). If he appears at this meeting, and the admonition that is offered him bears fruit, he should make his confession and be granted absolution.

However, if the neglecter of Word and Sacrament not only persistently refuses to heed the admonition offered by those who visit him at his home, but also refuses to heed repeated summons to appear before the church, he is to be excommunicated. His refusal of this overture of loving brotherly concern is the evidence of his impenitence, which (impenitence) becomes, then, the basis of the excommunication. He has refused to "listen even to the church" (Matthew 18).

If the member, after being summoned before the church at a voters' assembly, sends word that he will not appear and wants his name removed from the church roll, he is to be recontacted. Finally, if he does not change his position in the matter, he is to be excommunicated. The affair reached "the church," but he refused to appear before the voters' assembly. This action, along with his seeking to avoid possible excommunication with the request to have his name removed from the membership list, must be read as refusal to repent, yes, as refusal to "listen to the church."

It goes without saying that if the member in question, after obeying a summons to appear before the church (in this case: voters' assembly), remains unrepentant, he is to be excommunicated (Matthew 18:17). He is, however, not excommunicated for the sin of neglecting or despising the means of grace, for had he repented that sin would have been forgiven him. He is excommunicated for impenitence.

Members Who Have Moved Away

Included in our highly mobile society of today are many church members. The pastor and board of elders will, of course, do all that they can to help the removed church member to find a new church home. (Note: Addendum Three which provides sample letters to be sent to removed members.) However, as it all too frequently happens, church members move without leaving a forwarding address. Sometimes these members simply cannot be followed up. All contact with them is lost.

> If people move away from the church, or are gone for such a long time as to lose all contact, it ought to be clear that removing the names of such people from the rolls is simply an accomodation to reality, and not an accusation of sin. These people can no longer be classed as members of the church, nor can they be treated according to the steps of Matthew 18. We might indeed be disappointed that these people do not consider their relationship to their church in a more responsible manner and do something meaningful about it. But we have no realistic way of judging their spiritual condition.[18]

Helping the Former Delinquent With the Problem That Caused the Delinquency

Don't think that your work as elder is done when you have heard a confession of sin from the delinquent, and the delinquent promises to be back in church. The sin of delinquency may be confessed and forgiveness for it pronounced — the guilt thus removed — but basically nothing may be changed. The following example is offered by way of illustrating to you the need for not only dealing with the delinquency itself, but also with the problem or sin that caused it. If it is not dealt with and overcome, delinquency may again occur.

There is the case of the woman who, failing to be elected to office in the women's auxiliary, lashes out at the other women in the congregation, accusing them of showing favoritism and insenitivites to her qualifications. Deeply hurt, she stays away from church. The elder visits her and helps her see her sin of unwarranted anger and bitterness against the other women in the congregation. She repents and is assured of forgiveness. Still, she feels uncomfortable about coming to church. Thus her basic problem still exists and needs to be dealt with.

She has equated being an officer in the women's auxiliary with being accepted by the ladies and the church, and also with her worth as a Christian. She has to be shown that she is needlessly anxious about acceptance. First of all, she really doesn't have to be accepted by the ladies in the sense that they entrust her with a position of ruling over them through an office in the auxiliary. She should be satisfied with simply being accepted as a fellow Christian and co-worker of Christ. Even if she were not "accepted" by her peer group, she still is accepted by her Savior who died for her and forgives her. Through faith in Jesus she is God's child. She is his servant and can do many wonderful things for her Lord, thereby achieving a feeling of personal worth without being an officer of the women's auxiliary. There are many forms of Christian service she can do that are not dependent upon election by her peer group to an office.

When she is helped to see this truth, and helped to joyfully serve her Lord and her fellow Christians by *every* opportunity of service with which she is challenged (no matter how seemingly small and unimportant), and to see her worth as a child of God whom God loves, then her situation will be turned around. She will not only repent of her bitterness and unwarranted hurt feelings, she will have an active and fulfilling role in her church, and regular participation in the Bible class and worship service as well.

Her needs are to feel accepted and to feel worthwhile. Her needs are met when she sees every opportunity of Christian service as an opportunity to feel worthwhile. She will also be content with being accepted by her peers simply as a fellow Christian: a fellow saint with whom they share a common faith and are united in the bond of Christian love.

And so, don't overlook the problem or sin that caused the delinquency, and don't neglect to help the member recognize it and treat it. You'll gain a much more solid member when you do, one who is far better adjusted spiritually and emotionally to his individual role in God's kingdom and the local church of which he is a member.

† † † † † †

CHAPTER SEVEN

THE ELDERS AT WORK: WRITING LETTERS

CAUTION MUST BE EXERCISED IN THE USE OF LETTERS

Rarely Can Letters Take The Place of Personal Contacts

Letters have their place in the work of the board of elders, and this chapter recognizes that fact. Letters *can* be helpful, but they can also cause harm if they are not properly composed and managed. Letters don't take much time, especially if one can be pulled from the files and fired off to whomever is in need of receiving one: the delinquent, for example. And for that reason, especially, pastors and elders are tempted to take the easy way out and depend on letters in place of personal visits to the member in trouble. Letters are sometimes used to avoid footwork. But how unfortunate! Rarely can a letter take the place of a personal visit. Pastors and elders must exercise extreme caution in the use of letters and not allow them to take the place of personal contact. "Church discipline requires personal involvement and concern because the gospel is always a personal appeal."[1] Letters simply do not provide the means of interaction, of dialogue, that is so necessary to enable the counselor to understand the person and properly deal with his problem (sin).

Resorting to the use of letters to avoid footwork and to save time and effort doesn't make sense. When it takes so much time and effort to win a soul for Christ in the first place, and to get the person into the church, why should we be unwilling to spend even a great deal of time and effort to keep that soul with Christ and retain him as a member of the congregation? Letters can only take the place of a personal visit if the visit is impossible to make (e.g. when several attempts to make personal contact have failed and a letter is used to request a meeting and to express concern), or if the desirable impact would best be achieved by a letter. A gentle letter may sometimes appear as less threatening to the person than a visit from the elder. A letter may be used to acquaint the member with the elder who has him under his watch care, and to inform the member of an impending visit.

Waiting a long time to tackle the problem of a member's delinquency tends to lump all the delinquents together as a group, thus approaching the problem en masse with a single form letter sent out to everyone. Where, then, is the individual care that should be expected from the pastor and the elders?

Each member, active and inactive, is a unique individual who should be personally approached and dealt with as such.

The Board May Be Tempted to Resort to Letters When the Work Piles Up

When a letter to a delinquent begins: "Our records show that you have not attended church for a long time (sometimes the statement reads, 'for a year or more')," we know immediately that something is wrong with the system. Not only is the delinquent guilty of inactivity, so is the pastor and the board of elders! When the pastor and elders let names pile up on the delinquency list until, out of sheer desperation, they feel compelled to resort to letters, incompetence is simply added to neglect. The very fact that the member's inactivity was allowed to go on for a long time without his being admonished shows a lack of watch care, and it shows neglect of a serious duty.

The Board May Be Tempted to Resort to Letters to Update the Membership List

No letter to a delinquent member should begin: "Our congregation is endeavoring to get its membership list up-to-date...." This is a dead giveaway of the elders' neglect to do their work. They haven't been visiting the delinquent members to admonish them, or they haven't been seeing the visits through to a conclusion. It also gives the impression that the church's primary concern is the congregational list and the delinquent's relationship to it, instead of concern for his personal relationship to Jesus Christ. And, when that is indeed the case, what a pity!

Letters Can't Properly Deal with Unbelief

Keep in mind that in many cases of delinquency, especially the long-standing ones, the members who are involved may no longer be Christians. How is one to deal properly and adequately with the condition of unbelief in a letter? If these members are possibly no longer believers, they will have to be dealt with face-to-face, patiently and lovingly, in repeated attempts to bring them back to the Savior's love.

Letters, at Times, Tend to Be Threatening When They Shouldn't Be

Letters, especially those that are written after the delinquent has failed to respond favorably to overtures, tend to be threatening. They threaten the person with a meeting at the church if there is continued inactivity and, finally, with excommunication itself. But members of the congregation should never be threatened with being called to a meeting. Immediately they feel intimidated. And rightly so! They are given the impression that being called to a meeting is some sort of punishment to be avoided at all costs. Any meeting held with a member of the congregation is, ideally, held for the purpose of showing him loving concern. If this purpose is conveyed to the person he will have little cause to be frightened off from attending the meeting. Thus instead of threatening the member with being called to a meeting if he doesn't do so and so, the impression should rather be given: "We want to meet with you because we love you and want to help you. We want to help you see that what you have been doing is a sin to be repented of. We hope that you do repent. We stand ready to forgive you in God's name, and to help you set a course in life that will be pleasing to God."

Be Careful With Letters Stressing Communion Attendance

Letters stressing communion attendance after a long absence are really out of place. They convey the impression that all it takes for the delinquent member to shape up is to come to communion. Communion attendance becomes, then, the work that is supposed to make amends for all the inactivity of the past, whether the heart feels repentant or not. But if the delinquent, after a long absence from worship and the Lord's Supper, suddenly appears at the altar simply because he is urged to do so — having been given the impression that he will be considered a member in good standing if he communes — what really is accomplished?

Much harm is done if the delinquent comes to communion without having properly examined himself to see if his heart is truly repentant and believing. Much harm is done if nothing is changed in his attitudes. Much harm is done if he comes to communion simply to obey a church rule and make the elders and pastor happy, and not because he, a sinner, desires the Lord's Supper as means of grace. To say it simply: if the person is no longer a Christian — a very real possibility — then communion, chiefly to fulfill an obligation of membership, is disastrous to his soul. Communion attendance in the case of a long absence from the Sacrament should not even be urged upon the person. First he has to be reinstructed in the plan of salvation. He has to confess his sins and his Savior. When he finally does celebrate the Sacrament with the congregation, it must be as a worthy communicant.

You have the privilege of using letters to encourage communion attendance generally. Don't abuse this privilege by directing letters stressing communion attendance, to long-standing delinquents.

LETTERS TO THOSE WHO HAVE MOVED OUTSIDE THE VISITING AREA

When Does Contact by Letter Become Necessary?

As soon as it is known that a member is planning to move from the area and will be unable to continue attending his church, an elder should visit him. The elder should discuss at length with the removing member what is expected of him when he settles in at his new location, and also the matter of transfer. He should be given a list of sister-churches in the new area along with the pastors' names and phone numbers. The removing member should be informed that he is expected to report back just as soon as possible concerning his new church home — within a month at the most. And he should be informed that the elders will follow up after a month if no contact has been made. The removing member should be asked for his new address and phone number if he already has that information. When the address and the time of arrival of the removing member are known ahead of time, this information should be forwarded to the pastor or pastors in the area.

In case the removed member does not contact the home church and ask for a transfer, the pastor and elders will have to contact him by letter. A *series* of letters encouraging transfer to a sister congregation may have to be sent. A pastor in the removed member's new area may have to be called in to give him counsel. Many people are lost from the church each year because they do not find their way into a congregation in the area to which they have removed. And their home church does not put out enough effort to lead them into a new relationship. Why is this? Is it for the reason that the pastor and elders feel a lack of responsibility for the member once he has moved outside the visitation area? Who is to blame when the member becomes lost in transit? Certainly the member himself is to blame. But often the home congregation must share his blame:

> The blame for the loss of members through removal must in most cases be placed upon the home congregation, which permits its members to become lost in transit. The duty of a congregation to the removed member does not end until that member has definitely joined a sister congregation. We repeat for emphasis that the responsibility of a home congregation to its members does not cease through the removal of a member. It ceases when that removed member has been received into membership in a sister congregation.[2]

Letters of Transfer

What information should the letters of transfer of removed members contain? Should the wording of transfers be specific, informing the other congregation of the member's status at the time of his removal? Should letters of transfer inform the other congregation of spiritual problems if such problems existed? Should the other congregation be apprised, at least to some extent, of outstanding weaknesses and strengths? Or isn't it any of the other congregation's business how the removing member conducted himself in his former church?

> In dismissing church members from one congregation to another, our congregations grant so-called releases, or letters of transfer. These letters of transfer are in many cases too vague. Charity, of course, is a Christian virtue, but when charity does not concern itself primarily with the spiritual welfare of a fellow Christian, it is not the right kind of charity. When a letter of transfer endorses a person as a member "in good standing," that person should be worthy of that designation. "In good standing" means that a member is faithful in his attendance at the house of God and at the Lord's Table and in the financial support of his church. To designate a member as one "in good standing" who does not come up to this standard is a misrepresentation of facts. Sometimes the releases are accompanied by explanatory letters, expressive of the hope that the member will become a better Christian in his new surroundings.[3]

Letters of transfer should not be vague, misleading or dishonest. On the other hand, they should avoid too much detail. We would suggest that the following matters be included in letters of transfer: 1) A report on the regularity with which the member worshipped in his own congregation (whether every Sunday, every other Sunday, once a month or even less frequently. 2) A report on the member's communion attendance (how often he communed in the past year). 3) The faithfulness and seriousness with which the member responded to the scriptural concept of regular, proportionate giving (without stating amounts). 4) The offices held by the man in the congregation; the offices held by the woman in the Women's Auxiliary. 5) Specific talents and interests that might serve the other congregation:

> We may feel that it is none of the business of a sister congregation to receive all this information. But we are our brother's keepers, and this

information is necessary if the new member is to profit spiritually. It is a disappointment when a member supposedly "in good standing" is added to the congregation and turns out to be anything but that. The sister congregation may as well know from the start that the removed member has been lax in attendance and support. Such a member may be made to understand at once that good attendance and good support are expected in his new surroundings.

Every member who removes should understand that his removal does not break the tie with the home congregation and that the home congregation has a right to know his whereabouts and what efforts he is making to affiliate with a sister congregation.[4]

The board of elders at its monthly meetings should be kept up-to-date on the status of removed members. Letters of admonishment should be sent out as necessary from the pastor and the board. A copy of letters to removed members should be sent to the nearest pastor of the Synod in the member's area, along with further information, when this pastor's help is solicited.

INDIVIDUAL LETTERS ARE CALLED FOR

Letters to individual members should never be duplicated. If the letter is so addressed that the recipient is being singled out for attention, the letter itself must be *personalized*: written or typed specifically for him (even when a sample letter is used as a guide). Letters addressed to the entire congregation will of necessity have to be mass produced.

Various occasions arise in a congregation that may be noted with letters from the board of elders. For example: a letter to each communicant on the first anniversary of his confirmation, a letter to a couple celebrating their 25th, 40th or 50th Wedding Anniversary, a letter of commendation for services rendered the church, and so forth. Needless to say, copies of all letters dealing with individual members should be kept on file. (NOTE: See Addendum Five for samples of letters.)

† † † † † †

ADDENDUM ONE

A PRESENTATION OF GOD'S PLAN FOR OUR SALVATION

When you as an elder make a call on a delinquent member of the congregation — or for that matter, on any member of the congregation who is under discipline — your primary concern is his personal relationship to Jesus Christ. Before you can proceed with your testimony to him concerning the scriptural validity of church and communion attendance, before you can counsel with him concerning his sin, you must ascertain his understanding of God's plan of salvation. Does he know the gospel? Does he profess to be saved by God's grace through faith in Jesus Christ? The following brief outline should prove helpful.

ELDER: One night a Roman prison guard came trembling to Paul and Silas and threw himself down in front of them. He was terribly frightened. His conscience told him that the God of these apostles was angry with him. He pleaded with Paul and Silas: *"Men, what must I do to be saved?"* Do you know the answer to this all-important question? Yes, how can you, a sinner like myself, be saved from God's wrath and punishment so that you can go to heaven? (WAIT FOR ANSWER)

(NOTE: If the person proceeds to give an accurate rendition of the true doctrine of salvation, indicating that he is saved by God's grace through faith in Christ, you should express joy and thankfulness over the fact that he knows and trusts his Savior. You might make the following point as a quick review of the plan of salvation:)

ELDER: Many who once knew Christ have fallen away from the Savior, no longer trusting that they are saved by God's grace alone, through faith alone. Instead of trusting that Jesus' blood cleanses away their sins, they trust their own good works to save them. Of course, whoever trusts in his own good works is not saved for his sins condemn him. No one is perfect.

> *All who rely on observing the law are under a curse, for it is written: "Cursed is everyone who does not continue to do everything written in the Book of the Law." (Galations 3:10)*

Instead of telling us that we are perfect, the law shows us how sinful we are; it shows up every one of our sins.

> *Therefore no one will be declared righteous in his sight by observing the law; rather, through the law we become conscious of sin. (Romans 3:20)*

We are saved only through faith in Jesus Christ, for God gave his Son to be our Savior from sin and asks that we believe in him.

> *For God so loved the world that he gave his one and only Son, that whoever believes in him shall not perish but have eternal life. For God did not send his Son into the world to condemn the world, but to save the world through him. Whoever believes in him is not condemned, but whoever does not believe stands condemned already because he has not believed in the name of God's one and only Son. (John 3:16-18)*

Instead of trusting in our good works to save us, we are to confess our sins to God and ask him to forgive us for Jesus' sake, fully believing that he does.

> *If we confess our sins, he is faithful and just and will forgive us our sins and purify us from all unrighteousness. (1 John 1:9)*

> *But now a righteousness from God, apart from law, has been made known...*

> *This righteousness from God comes through faith in Jesus Christ to all who believe... We maintain that a man is justified (i.e. declared innocent, forgiven) by faith apart from observing the law. (Romans 3:21-22, 27)*

(NOTE: You might continue your conversation by expressing your surprise that the delinquent's knowledge and faith has allowed him to slip away from the church and the preaching of salvation:)

ELDER: As sinners who are redeemed by Christ, we should desire to hear over and over the wonderful message that Jesus came to save sinners like us. We should desire also to attend the Lord's Supper where Christ gives us the wonderful seal of God's forgiveness through receiving his body and blood with bread and wine. In the Lord's Supper we recall the sacrifice Christ made for us.

When we Christians fail to hear the preaching of the law and the gospel, we can easily become unrepentant and self-righteous. No longer hearing the pastor preach the law, which reveals our sins to us, we can forget that we are sinners very much in need of saving. Indeed we can convince ourselves that we live decent enough lives to **earn** a place in heaven. Furthermore, we need the gospel preached to us by our pastor in order to be reminded that Christ suffered and died for us. The simple fact is that we need the law and the gospel preached to us continually in order that we keep confessing our sins and keep believing in Christ alone for salvation.

(NOTE: At this point in dealing with a delinquent who confesses faith in Christ, you would proceed to discuss the scriptural reasons for regular church attendance and frequent communing, as well as the scriptural basis for public preaching, worship etc.) (See: *The Scripture Topics Index*, the appropriate headings.)

In the event the delinquent shows ignorance of the scriptural teaching of salvation . . . .

If the delinquent's answer to the above question ("What must I do to be saved?") indicates that he is not clear regarding the way of salvation, and in fact shows that he trusts in his good works to take him to heaven, a review of the Bible teaching of sin and grace is in order. The following outline-presentation should be helpful, especially if you commit it more or less to memory. (Copies of it could also be made, and presented to the person to follow.)

ELDER: We dare not trust in ourselves — in our good works — for salvation. We are guilty of sin, and sin earns punishment from God. Even one sin is enought to damn the sinner.

Surely I have been a sinner from birth, sinful from the time my mother conceived me. (Psalm 51:5)

There is not a righteous man on earth who does what is right and never sins. (Ecclesiastes 7:20)

All have sinned and fall short of the glory of God. (Romans 3:23)

Like the rest, we were by nature the objects of wrath. (Ephesians 2:3)

Whoever keeps the whole law and yet stumbles at just one point is guilty of breaking all of it. (James 2:10)

ELDER: Out of great love for us, God had his Son Jesus Christ come to earth to suffer and die on the cross for our sins.

For God so loved the world that he gave his one and only Son, that whoever believes in him shall not perish but have eternal life. (John 3:16)

(Jesus Christ) is the atoning sacrifice for our sins. (1 John 2:2)

He was pierced for our transgressions, he was crushed for our iniquities. (Isaiah 53:5)

God demonstrated his own love for us in this: While we were still sinners Christ died for us ... we have now been justified (i.e. declared innocent, forgiven) by his blood. (Romans 5:8-9)

ELDER: God does not want us to trust in our good works to save us, but calls on us to repent, that is, to look with sorrow upon our sins and to confess them, trusting in Jesus Christ as our personal Savior. We are saved from our sins by God's grace through our faith in Christ, not by our good works.

If we confess our sins, he is faithful and just and will forgive us our sins. (1 John 1:9)

Repent, then, and turn to God, so that your sins may be wiped out. (Acts 3:19)

Believe in the Lord Jesus, and you will be saved. (Acts 16:31)

For it is by grace you have been saved, through faith — and this not from yourselves, it is the gift of God — not by works, so that no one can boast. (Ephesians 2:8-9)

A man is justified by faith apart from observing the law. (Romans 3:28)

ELDER: No, we are not saved by our good works, but only through faith which trusts fully in the merits of Jesus Christ. We do good works as believers, not to be saved, but BECAUSE we are saved. Our good works, even though they are not perfect, testify of the love we have for God, who saved us through Jesus. They are the evidence, the proof of faith — the natural fruit of being justified by grace through faith.

Christ's love compels us ... he died for all, that those who live should no longer live for themselves but for him who died for them and was raised again. (2 Corinthians 5:14-15)

Faith by itself, if not accompanied by action, is dead. (James 2:17)

That you may live a life worthy of the Lord and may please him in every way: bearing fruit in every good work. (Colossians 1:10)

ELDER: Do you confess your sins? Will you put away all trust in your good works and trust alone in Jesus Christ for salvation? (EXPECT AN ANSWER)

NOTE: In the event the person remains unsure of his personal relationship with Jesus Christ and remains self-righteous, the following additional references can be used in presenting the law and the gospel:

Luke 13:1-8 Repent or perish.

Luke 15 The Lost Sheep – The Lost Coin – The Lost Son – Joy over the Repentant.

Luke 18:9-14 The Pharisee and the Tax Collector.

John 3:14-18 The world has a Savior. Faith saves. Unbelief damns.

1 John 1:8-2:2 Telling the truth about ourselves. Believing the truth about Jesus.

Romans 3:19-28 All have sinned. Redemption comes by Christ through faith.

Psalms 32, 51, 103, 130 Penitence and forgiveness.

ADDENDUM TWO

THE LAW AND THE GOSPEL

Because the law and the gospel, together with their proper use, are so fundamental to admonishing the offender, space is devoted here to a brief summary of these basic teachings of the Scripture. The suggestion is in order that you carefully review this section before each counseling session.

1. The LAW commands us to do and not to do . . . The GOSPEL announces what God did and still does for us.

    A. **The LAW is that Word of God which commands us to be holy, telling us what we are and are not to do, commanding the things that please God and forbidding the things that displease him. The LAW also threatens punishment to the sinner.**

    Be sure to keep the commands of the Lord your God and the stipulations and decrees he has given you. Do what is right and good in the Lord's sight, so that it may go well with you. (Deuteronomy 6:17; see Exodus 20:1-3, 7-8, 12-17; Leviticus 19:2)

    Cursed is everyone who does not continue to do everything written in the Book of the Law. (Galations 3:10b; see Deuteronomy 27:6)

    B. **The GOSPEL is that Word of God which especially declares what God has done and still does to save us sinners from our sins: from guilt and punishment. And so, the GOSPEL is good news announcing God's grace and mercy in Christ Jesus, giving forgiveness of sins, yes, eternal life and salvation to all who hear and believe it.**

    For God so loved the world that he gave his one and only Son, that whoever believes in him shall not perish but have eternal life. (John 3:16)

    I am not ashamed of the gospel, because it is the power of God for the salvation of everyone who believes. (Romans 1:16)

> ... *to give his people the knowledge of salvation through the forgiveness of their sins, because of the tender mercy of our God. (Luke 1:77-78)*

2. The LAW **demands** righteousness of us ... The GOSPEL **imputes** righteousness to us.

   A. **The LAW demands perfect righteousness of us by demanding perfect obedience to God — which, we, in fact, cannot render. The LAW pronounces the righteous man (the man who has not sinned) righteous. Righteousness by the LAW is earned righteousness. Therefore it is righteousness which none of us have nor can ever acquire since we are sinners.**

   > *The Lord commanded us to obey all these decrees and to fear the Lord our God, so that we might always prosper and be kept alive as is the case today. And if we are careful to obey all this law before the Lord our God, as he has commanded us, that will be our righteousness. (Deuteronomy 6:24-25)*

   > *Be holy because I, the Lord, your God am holy. (Leviticus 19:2)*

   > *There is not a righteous man on earth who does what is right and never sins. (Ecclesiastes 7:20)*

   > *There is no difference, for all have sinned and fall short of the glory of God. (Romans 3:22b-23; see Daniel 9:4-5, 7; Isaiah 64:6)*

   B. **The GOSPEL does not demand righteousness of us but covers us who are unrighteous with the righteousness of Christ: the forgiveness of sins he won for us by keeping the law in our stead and by suffering our punishment for us, even bleeding and dying in our place. The righteousness offered by the GOSPEL is righteousness imputed to us sinners by grace through our faith: righteousness given to us believers free of charge to take the place of our guilt and to save us from punishment.**

   > *"Come now, let us reason together," says the Lord. "Though your sins are like scarlet, they shall be white as snow; though they are red as crimson, they shall be like wool." (Isaiah 1:18)*

> *God made him (Christ) who had no sin to be sin for us so that in him we might become the righteousness of God. (2 Corinthians 5:21)*
>
> *Through the obedience of the one man (Christ) the many will be made righteous. (Romans 5:19)*
>
> *To the man who does not work (i.e. who doesn't trust his deeds to save him) but trusts God who justifies the wicked, his faith is credited as righteousness. (Romans 4:5; see Romans 5:8-9)*

3. The LAW awards eternal life to those who earn it by perfect obedience . . . The GOSPEL promises eternal life as a gift to us sinners who believe.

   A. **The LAW awards eternal life** conditionally, **that is, on the condition that we obey the LAW perfectly. And so, the LAW cannot be the means for us to be saved, for we cannot keep it perfectly. We sin.**

   > *The law is not based on faith; on the contrary, "The man who does these things will live by them. (Galations 3:12; see Luke 10:25-28)*
   >
   > *For whoever keeps the whole law and yet stumbles at just one point is guilty of breaking all of it. (James 2:10; see Romans 3:20)*

   The GOSPEL promises eternal life absolutely free, as an unmerited gift of God's grace through Jesus Christ. This gift of God's grace is accepted by us sinners through faith.

   > *For it is by grace (i.e. a gift) you have been saved, through faith . . . not by works, so that no one can boast. (Ephesians 2:8-9; see Romans 3:21, 24)*
   >
   > *Whoever believes in the Son has eternal life. (John 3:36a)*

4. The LAW reveals our sins . . . The GOSPEL reveals our Savior from sin.

   A. **The LAW reveals our sins to us, thereby revealing our utter inability to render perfect obedience to God.**

   > *Now we know that whatever the law says, it says to those who are under the law, so that every mouth may be silenced and the whole world held accountable to God. Therefore no one will be declared*

righteous in his sight by observing the law; rather, through the law we become conscious of sin. (Romans 3:19-20; see Romans 7:7)

B. **The GOSPEL reveals our Savior Jesus Christ to us, urging us to place all our trust and hope in him, for he suffered and died and rose again for us.**

"Men, what must I do to be saved?" They replied, "Believe in the Lord Jesus, and you will be saved — you and your household." (Acts 16:30-31)

... also for us, to whom God will credit righteousness — for us who believe in him who raised Jesus our Lord from the dead. He was delivered over to death for our sins and was raised to life for our justification. (Romans 4:24-25)

5. The LAW terrorizes us . . . The GOSPEL comforts us.

   A. **The LAW strikes fear and terror into our hearts convincing us that we are sinful, lost, and damned; filling us with sorrow and shame that we have sinned. The LAW works repentance.**

   But the tax collector stood at a distance. He would not even look up to heaven, but beat his breast and said, "God, have mercy on me, a sinner." (Luke 18:13)

   We have sinned and done wrong. We have been wicked and have rebelled; we have turned away from your commands and laws . . . O Lord, we . . . are covered with shame because we have sinned against you. (Daniel 9:5; see Acts 2:22-23, 36-38)

   B. **The GOSPEL comforts and gives peace and joy to us sinners who place our trust in Christ, and the GOSPEL actually works this saving faith in our hearts.**

   Take heart, son; your sins are forgiven. (Matthew 9:2)

   Therefore, since we have been justified through faith, we have peace with God through our Lord Jesus Christ . . . And we rejoice in the hope of the glory of God. (Romans 5:1-2; see Acts 8:26-39)

   He called you to this through our gospel, that you might share in the glory of our Lord Jesus Christ. (2 Thessalonians 2:14; see Romans 10:17)

6. The LAW cannot furnish us the power and incentive to do good ... The GOSPEL is the cause of our doing good.

   A. **The LAW does not supply the will or the spiritual strength to comply with its precepts. The LAW by its demands actually turns us off toward keeping it, and stirs up anger and resentment in our sinful flesh, as experience shows.**

   The law was powerless ... in that it was weakened by the sinful nature. (Romans 8:3)

   B. **The GOSPEL imparts spiritual life to us, filling our hearts with faith and also with love for God, who loved us first and saved us through Christ. Thus it gives us the will (inspires us) and the spiritual strength, through the Holy Spirit, to walk pleasing to God.**

   Christ's love compels us ... he died for all, that those who live should no longer live for themselves but for him who died for them and was raised again. (2 Corinthians 5:14-15)

   In view of God's mercy ... offer your bodies as living sacrifices holy and pleasing to God — which is your spiritual worship. (Romans 12:1; see Romans 7:22)

7. The LAW is to be preached especially to the impenitent ... The GOSPEL is to be preached to the penitent.

   A. **The LAW is to be preached especially to the impenitent, or secure sinners: sinners who are not alarmed concerning their sins, who do not sorrow over them and thus do not turn away from them.**

   Scripture Reference: *2 Samuel 12:1-9* The law was preached to impenitent David.

   B. **The GOSPEL is to be preached to sinners who are alarmed over their sins, who repent and thus confess their sins.**

   Then David said to Nathan, "I have sinned against the Lord." Nathan replied, "The Lord has taken away your sin. You are not going to die." (2 Samuel 12:13; see Luke 7:37-38)

THE THREE USES OF THE LAW

1. **The law serves us believers as a CURB. Since we still have our old adam or sinful flesh, which wars against our new man, the law must then continue to be preached to us in order to curb (even terrorize) our old adam and thus keep it in check.**

   For the sinful nature desires what is contrary to the Spirit. (Galations 5:17)

   My flesh trembles in fear of you; I stand in awe of your laws. (Psalm 119:120)

2. **The law serves us believers as a MIRROR. Though we are converted, we continue to sin every day. We need the law to show us our sins lest we become smug and deny our sinfulness. When we are reminded by the law of our sinfulness we are driven again and again to seek the comfort of forgiveness from the gospel.**

   Through the law we become conscious of sin. (Romans 3:20)

   Wash away all my iniquity and cleanse me from my sin. For I know my transgressions, and my sin is always before me. (Psalm 51:2-3)

3. **The law serves us believers also as a RULE or GUIDE. We need to be reminded of what the law demands and forbids in order that we might be guided to live in accordance with God's holy will and thus live sanctified lives. It is God's love, believed by the heart, that compels us to live by the law — which simply shows us what avenues our love for God should take.**

   How can a young man keep his way pure? By living according to your Word. I seek you with all my heart; do not let me stray from your commands. I have hidden your Word in my heart that I might not sin against you. (Psalm 119:9-11; see Joshua 1:8)

   If you love me, you will obey what I command. (John 14:15)

ADDENDUM THREE

RESPONDING TO EXCUSES OR OBJECTIONS

INTRODUCTION

The material that follows should be of some help to you, the elder or counselor, in meeting the excuses or objections offered by the fallen-away member. It can at least give you some ideas for your approach to him as you focus on the scriptural and spiritual issues that are involved. One important way that this material can be used is in follow-up letters to the person you are counseling. After visiting the counselee — especially when the visit has not produced the desired results — you may want to write him a letter reinforcing the testimony given to him in the meeting. This material can thus be used as an important source (together with the Scripture Topics Index) in formulating such a letter.

In dealing with excuses or objections offered by the counselee, there are certain things that you, the counselor, should keep in mind. First, there is the strong possibility that the fallen-away member with whom you are conversing is no longer a Christian. He may very well be back under the control of his sinful flesh, and his excuses or objections reflect this. Also, if he is no longer a Christian he may be deceitful and not tell you what he really thinks and feels. Excuses or objections may be smoke screens thrown up by the counselee to obscure far more serious soul matters that are disturbing him and robbing him of his faith. Therefore be prepared to press the issues to determine the real problem(s).

The delinquent may use excuses or objections to sidetrack the conversation for various reasons. Don't spend much time on detours; get back as quickly as possible to the subject at hand. Remember that the main subject — the reason you came to counsel the fallen-away member or delinquent — is his faith, his relationship with God and the Savior. His present way of life, including his absence from church services and the communion table, indicate that his faith has begun to fail. In fact, it may be dead already. And by his absence from the preached Word and the Sacrament — the gospel — he is sinning against the cure for unbelief. For the Holy Spirit operates only through the Word and the Sacrament to keep faith alive. Therefore always return the counselee to a discussion of his personal faith, his personal relationship with God. Continually emphasize, too, the importance of God's Word and the Lord's Supper to his faith.

In your answers to the counselee's excuses or objections you will strive to lead him into a self-examination of his conscience as well as his heart. You will impress upon his conscience the seriousness of sin. Thus you will see to it that the law has its part, showing the counselee the sins that are the cause of his excuses or objections. And you will remind him that his backsliding is itself a most serious sin. Furthermore you will impress upon him that you are eager to hear him talk about his personal relationship with Jesus; and where this relationship is lacking, you are eager to help bring him closer to the Savior. At every opportunity you will remind the counselee of the sacrifice on the cross which Jesus made for all sins and every sinner, and urge him to return in faith to it as the only way for him to be saved. Be prepared at all times to take the counselee through a review of God's Plan of Salvation.

PART ONE: The delinquent passes the blame to others, or places the blame on particular circumstances or conditions.

1. I don't get anything out of the sermon. (And another that is similar to it: I don't get anything out of church.)

COUNSELOR: I suppose we all feel this way at one time or another. But is it the pastor's fault ... or our own? Certainly the pastor must prepare to preach. But have you ever stopped to consider that we who sit in the pews need to prepare to listen to what our pastor has to say? And his message for us is of tremendous importance: he preaches God's Word, which includes the saving message of Jesus Christ. He speaks of life and death matters in the eternal sense. We should get proper sleep on Saturday night and prepare mind, heart and body for God's message. And we ought to earnestly pray to the Holy Spirit, asking him to help us receive God's message with an open heart and thus enable us to understand, appreciate and believe what we hear.

We come to church to worship our God: to sing and speak his praise. We come to hear his Word, which shows us our sins and tells us we have a wonderful Savior from sin. But to properly prepare to worship God and to hear and appreciate his Word, we need to rid ourselves of all distractions as we enter the sanctuary. And we need to come to church with humility: like an empty vessel that is ready to be filled up. Yes, we ought to be eager to hear what God has to say to us in the Scripture. What is it that you expect to get out of the sermon and the service? (WAIT FOR ANSWER) Jesus said, "Blessed ...

are those who hear the Word of God and obey it" (Luke 11:28). The apostle James also gives us some timely words of advice about hearing the Word of God: "Therefore, get rid of all moral filth and the evil that is so prevalent, and humbly accept the Word planted in you, which can save you. Do not merely listen to the Word, and so deceive yourselves. Do what it says" (James 1:21-22). That includes believing it. Tell me about your personal relationship with Jesus Christ. What do you believe? (WAIT FOR ANSWER AND RESPOND ACCORDINGLY)

2. I was sick and nobody visited me, not even the pastor.

COUNSELOR: I'm sorry that you were ill. How long ago was this? (WAIT FOR ANSWER) I hope that you are now enjoying good health. Christ certainly wants us to visit our suffering fellow Christians to comfort and encourage them, and to pray for them. Our Christian love should move us to do so. It is sad when God's people fail this labor of love. Did you inform the pastor that you were ill? (WAIT FOR ANSWER) Quite often people take for granted that the pastor somehow knows or in some way hears about the ill or injured members. Perhaps the pastor never received word of your condition.

Love demands that we put the best construction on everything, including this situation that is disturbing you so, and not accuse anyone of wilfully neglecting their duty. Furthermore, because you do not feel loved is no reason to withdraw from the fellowship of the congregation. You should still love your fellow Christians and want to be with them. The basis of your love toward others is not their love toward you but the love of Christ which he demonstrated when he died for your sins on the cross. As St. John points out: "We love because he first loved us" (1 John 4:19). Do you not find it easy to love and forgive others when you consider how much God loves you and forgives you? (WAIT FOR ANSWER) Do you make it a point to visit the ill and injured in the congregation? (WAIT FOR ANSWER)

3. A friend of mine was married in the church, but the pastor wouldn't let her have the music she wanted. It was her wedding; she was paying for it. Her feelings were hurt. If this is the way people are treated by the pastor and the church I want no part of it.

COUNSELOR: I wonder if you have full knowledge of the situation. Have you gone to the pastor to hear his side? (WAIT FOR ANSWER) It is the pastor's responsibility to make judgments regarding wedding music: what is, and what is not acceptable for a church wedding. St. Paul has given the rule that everything is to be done "in a fitting and orderly way" (1 Corinthians 14:40). This broad rule must certainly govern the selection of music that will be presented in a worship setting. The same rules that govern a Sunday service, and the same standards that determine what is appropriate in music for a Sunday service apply for the public wedding service, no matter when it is held. You do realize, don't you, that a public wedding held in the church is a worship service? (WAIT FOR ANSWER)

The pastor does not act arbitrarily in the matter of determining what is acceptable in wedding music. He weighs everything according to the standards of God's Word and good, sound Lutheran custom and practice. Do not resent the pastor for doing his job. Love him for faithfully teaching you about Jesus your Savior and for doing things in a fitting and orderly way. I will make arrangements with the pastor for you and me to speak to him about this matter. What time would be best for you to meet with him? (WAIT FOR ANSWER)

4. **The pastor refused to conduct the funeral for _____. I know that he wasn't a member of the church, but that shouldn't make any difference. He was a good man, a well-liked man. Everyone has the right to a Christian funeral. The pastor should not have refused to bury him. Furthermore, we have no right to judge anyone.**

COUNSELOR: The church not only has the right but also the duty to judge a person in such a case. The church does not afford Christian burial indiscriminately. Christian burial is just what the term implies and thus is reserved for professing Christians. The church must judge on the basis of the person's own testimony and the person's own actions whether or not to afford him a Christian burial. If the person in question was not a professed believer in Christ, to give him a Christian burial is to deny that salvation comes to the sinner alone through repentance and faith. The purpose of Christian burial is to comfort those who mourn. The comfort is this: because the person was a believer in Christ while he lived, his soul is now in heaven with God, having attained the salvation which was the goal of his faith. Furthermore, his body awaits Christ's command on the last day to rise from the grave and stand in glory at Christ's right hand. These comforting sentiments are expressed throughout the Christian burial service: in Scripture readings, in hymns, in prayers and in the sermon.

But what a sham to express these sentiments on the occasion of the death of a person who did not profess faith in Christ. Even though he lived an outwardly moral life, if he was without repentance and faith he was lost from God while he lived and remains eternally lost now that he has died. No one has the right to ask a pastor to go against the church's spiritual principles and his own conscience to afford Christian burial to the person who has given the clear impression of not being a believer in Christ. And this holds true no matter how much the deceased person meant to certain members of the flock. Jesus himself advised: "Let the dead (that is, spiritually dead or unbelievers) bury their own dead (that is, those among them who have suffered physical death)" (Matthew 8:23). Jesus also said: "Whoever believes in him is not condemned, but whoever does not believe stands condemned already because he has not believed in the name of God's one and only Son" (John 3:18).

The pastor is obligated to afford Christian burial only to those who are members of his flock as well as to others who, though they may not have acquired membership, nevertheless accepted his ministry and as a result were brought to repentance and faith before they died. But to demand Christian burial for a professed unbeliever, for one who never accepted the pastor's message or his ministry, is most unreasonable. On the other hand, to choose Christian burial for a dead unbeliever (who is unable to voice his protest) is, to say the least, unfair to him. To involve a church and a pastor which the person shunned while he was alive is surely a betrayal of his wishes. Do you understand what I am saying? (WAIT FOR ANSWER) And now I would like to ask you: upon what do you base your own hope of going to heaven when you die? (WAIT FOR ANSWER AND RESPOND ACCORDINGLY)

5. I don't like the minister.

COUNSELOR: I'm sorry to hear that. I suppose that's a complaint that is heard in every congregation. Even St. Paul, the Lord's first-rate apostle and minister, found that he was not popular with everyone. But whether or not you like the minister is beside the point. Whether or not he is faithful to his calling, preaching the Word of God in its truth and purity, finally determines his qualifications as your pastor. Remember that the pastor is bound by our Lord to teach you to obey everything that he has commanded (Matthew 28:20). Our pastor preaches God's Word, law and gospel, in every sermon. When we go to church, we don't go to hear the man but to hear what the man has to say from God's Word. Don't let personal feelings or personality conflicts rob you of hearing God's message that is needed so desperately by all of us sinful human beings. Jesus said to his ministers: "He who listens to you listens to me; he who rejects you rejects me" (Luke 10:16).

Finally, you owe it to the pastor to go and speak with him about anything that he has said or done that has offended you. The Lord requires this of us. Thus he tells us: "If your brother sins, rebuke him, and if he repents, forgive him" (Luke 17:3). Ask God to help straighten the matter out. You are sinning if you are holding a grudge. If this **is** the case, then repent and seek God's forgiveness. Let me remind you how you can show that you hold no grudge against the pastor: Come to church and hear God's Word that he faithfully preaches, and also speak with him about whatever it is that is bothering you. Are you willing to do this? (WAIT FOR ANSWER AND RESPOND ACCORDINGLY)

6. Members of my family don't go to church. I don't like to go alone.

COUNSELOR: Our own repentance and faith, our own obligations to God and our church do not depend on what the other person does or doesn't do. If all around us our friends, our neighbors and even our family choose to remain in sin and despise Christ and his Word, what has that to do with us as far as our attending church and worshipping God is concerned? (WAIT FOR ANSWER) Can we refuse to serve our dear Lord with a believing heart because no one else in the house does? (WAIT FOR ANSWER) Recall that Jesus said: "Anyone who loves his father or mother more than me is not worthy of me; anyone who loves his son or daughter more than me is not worthy of me; and anyone who does not take his cross and follow me is not worthy of me" (Matthew 10:37-38). Ultimately, what should motivate you to go to church is Christ's love for you that caused him to sacrifice himself on the cross for your sins. Isn't that so? (WAIT FOR ANSWER)

Bear in mind that if just one person in the family believes in Christ and worships him, both at home and in church, the Word of God is thereby present in the family, and others have a chance to hear and be converted. We can bear Christ's testimony to the unchurched members of our family only by practicing our religion. By our attending church regularly, by reading our Bibles at home we can get the message across to them how much Jesus means to us, and how much he should also mean to them. Tell me: what does Jesus mean to you? (WAIT FOR ANSWER) I would like to speak to the other members of your family about Jesus and also invite them to visit our church. When would it be convenient for me to do this? (WAIT FOR ANSWER)

7. I feel bitter concerning a bad experience that I had with someone in the church. I was treated unfairly. I am deeply hurt.

COUNSELOR: By whom were you treated unfairly? Who caused you to be deeply hurt? Was it God? I'm certain that you do not want to accuse God of treating you unfairly or of causing you hurt. Wasn't it instead a fellow human being who, like ourselves, is a sinner? So then, why punish God by staying away from his house? Do you not agree? (WAIT FOR ANSWER)

With the Holy Spirit's help and guidance you ought to deal with the situation and straighten things out between you and your Christian brother or sister. If you don't succeed, don't give up. Call on another Christian brother or sister to help you. Remember what Scripture says on the subject. "Be completely humble and gentle; be patient, bearing with one another in love. Make every effort to keep the unity of the Spirit through the bond of peace" (Ephesians 4:2-3). "If your brother sins, rebuke him, and if he repents, forgive him" (Luke 17:3). "Get rid of all bitterness, rage and anger, brawling and slander, along with every form of malice. Be kind and compassionate to one another, forgiving each other, just as in Christ God forgave you" (Ephesians 4:31-32). Since God forgives all your sins shouldn't you be willing to forgive your brother or sister who sins against you? (WAIT FOR ANSWER) Do you want forgiveness from God for your own sins? (WAIT FOR ANSWER) Will you not go to the person who has offended you and straighten out the matter? (WAIT FOR ANSWER AND RESPOND ACCORDINGLY)

8. I have no money to give to the church.

COUNSELOR: If that's so, don't be concerned; the church doesn't charge admission. An offering is received from the people present, but each gives according to his ability. If a person has no money, none can be expected from him. God wants to give you something that is absolutely free: the forgiveness of sins and eternal life in heaven, which is something we should not be without. This gift was purchased for us with Jesus' precious blood and promised in the gospel. We learn about God's gift each time our pastor preaches to us. Remember, no cost to you is involved.

But to say that you have no money to give to the church for the Lord's work may be saying it a bit too strongly. You probably mean that you do not have a large enough income at present to give the amount you would like to give. But that should not stop you from giving something. It is the proportion that counts, not the amount. Also the spirit with which the offering is given. One day Jesus saw a widow give her offering to God. Jesus pointed out that her offering, tiny though it was in actual money, was great in proportion to what she had. Indeed, it was *all* she had. Always remember that you need something from the church far more than the church needs your money from you. Do you know what it is? (WAIT FOR ANSWER AND RESPOND ACCORDINGLY)

9. All the church wants is my money / The church keeps asking for money.

COUNSELOR: What the church wants, and what Jesus himself wants, is your whole life (you and everything you have: time, talents and treasure) dedicated to God. Everything that we have belongs to God. He lends it to us. But God gave us something far more precious than money or anything else that we have. He gave us the gift of his one and only Son (John 3:16), whom he sent here to be our Savior from sin. And Jesus gave his very life for us on the cross. He purchased our salvation with his own blood that we might live for him and serve him in every way, and with everything. Tell me: what does Jesus mean to you? (WAIT FOR ANSWER)

You resent giving money to the church. When you give to the church you are giving to the Lord, and what you give helps to carry on the Lord's work. St. Paul gave the general rule for giving in the church when he wrote: "On the first day of every week, each one of you should set aside a sum of money in keeping with his income" (1 Corinthians 16:2). And again, when he wrote: "Each man should give what he has decided in his heart to give, not reluctantly or under compulsion, for God loves a cheerful giver" (2 Corinthians 9:7).

Of course we get back what we give so that we can give again, for Jesus promised: "Give, and it will be given to you" (Luke 6:38). Are you willing to take Jesus at his word and give cheerfully, proportionately of your blessings — first of all, giving yourself to him? (WAIT FOR ANSWER AND RESPOND AS NECESSARY)

10. I can't tolerate being in a crowd.

COUNSELOR: And yet you drive or ride in a car on a crowded highway, and go shopping in a crowded store and sit in a crowded reception room waiting to see the doctor! Perhaps you are simply too self-conscious when you come to church. The problem may be that you are thinking too much on yourself and not concentrating on worshipping our precious Lord. You may think that all eyes are on you. But don't you suppose that the other people sitting in church are there, not to stare at you, but to direct their thoughts in worship to God?

God wants us to go to church to fellowship with others, but especially to hear his Word preached, and to otherwise worship him. Since this is something God wants us to do, we should trust him to help us carry it on. Please ask God to help you overcome your fears that everyone is looking at you. Ask him to give you the spiritual and emotional strength to attend public worship with your fellow Christians. He will help you. Recall St. Paul's words: "I can do everything through him who gives me strength" (Philippians 4:13). Allow me to lead you in prayer right now concerning this matter. (HAVE A BRIEF PRAYER WITH THE MEMBER)

11. I never feel good in the morning.

COUNSELOR: Perhaps you should retire earlier the night before. Are you careful about eating a good, nutritious breakfast? Have you seen your doctor about this? Perhaps you have a physical condition that needs correcting, or perhaps a change in your diet. (WAIT FOR ANSWER) Going to church on Sunday morning and worshipping God together with the congregation is such a wonderful and uplifting experience I personally do not see how anyone can be without it. Recall the words of the Psalmist: "I rejoiced with those who said to me, 'Let us go to the house of the Lord'" (Psalm 122:1). Commit this matter of your not feeling good in the morning to the Lord. Ask him to help you. Not just to make you feel better, but to give you the courage and zeal to go to church even when you are not feeling up to it. In fact, allow me to lead you in prayer concerning this matter right now. (HAVE A BRIEF PRAYER WITH THE MEMBER)

PART TWO: The Delinquent Shows Lack of Commitment, Motivation and Understanding

12. I work so hard during the week that I'm simply too tired when Sunday comes. I have to have my rest. I simply collapse on week ends.

COUNSELOR: Tell me: who doesn't work hard? Who doesn't need their rest? Do you really think that your situation is so different? (WAIT FOR ANSWER) If everyone were excused from God's house on Sunday morning for the reason you give, his house would be nearly empty of worshippers. Even the children work hard in school all week, and they have their homework to do. The fact is that the Holy Spirit moves many hardworking men, women and children to come to God's house to worship him and hear his Word every Sunday. Thank God for this! Tell me: what does Jesus Christ and the church mean to you? (WAIT FOR ANSWER)

Have you ever stopped to consider that God's house affords the rest you and I need the most: rest for our spirits in his holy gospel. We sinners can come with our burden of sin and know that our hearts will find sweet peace, our consciences rest. We will be told of God's forgiveness through Jesus

Christ. Jesus has invited us saying: "Come to me, all you who are weary and burdened, and I will give you rest" (Matthew 11:28). Come to church to hear the sweet message that Jesus died for your sins. It's a message I personally love to hear. Hear it together with me and the rest of the congregation. Won't you put out every effort, with God's help, to do this? (WAIT FOR ANSWER)

13. I really want to come to church, but I just can't seem to get started on Sunday morning. I have a tendency to sleep in.

COUNSELOR: No doubt most of us would like to sleep in on Sunday morning. But then we also like to go to God's house and worship him. No doubt you feel that you can sleep in on Sunday morning because others will be on hand to go on with the service. You don't feel that the church really needs to count on you. But that thinking is wrong. Every congregation is made up of individuals like yourself. Each one is important to the whole. A church succeeds or fails because of the attitudes and actions of individuals just like yourself.

What you are really admitting to is laziness. Physical laziness? Yes, but something even worse: spiritual laziness. You have begun to backslide and perhaps you don't even realize it. If you really had a deep enough desire to be in God's house you would put out a far greater effort to get up and get going on Sunday morning. Stop and think about what you are missing. Consider the reason you personally need to hear the Word of God, and why you need the fellowship of other Christians. Think of the great spiritual benefits that derive from taking part in the service. Can you list some of these benefits that you are now missing because you don't put out the extra effort to be in God's house on Sunday morning? (WAIT FOR ANSWER AND COMMENT AS NEEDED) The Psalmist was aware of these spiritual benefits he enjoyed in church and therefore he looked forward to each church service. He wrote: "I rejoiced with those who said to me, 'Let us go to the house of the Lord'" (Psalm 122:1). Consider once again your personal relationship to Jesus Christ. Tell me what you think: is it what it really should be? (WAIT FOR ANSWER AND RESPOND ACCORDINGLY)

14. I can worship God in my own home; I can be close to him there. I don't need to go to church.

COUNSELOR: God expects us who believe in him to worship him in our own houses and to be close to him always, wherever we are. In fact, worshiping God in **your** house in private ought to incite you to worship God publicly in **his** house. Worshiping God alone at home was never meant to take the place of worshiping God in his house with other believers. Surely, your study of the Bible ought to convince you of this. Your attitude, however, is that you want to "go it alone." Your attitude seems to be that you can provide adequately for your soul's welfare, and for the souls' welfare of the members of your family ALL ALONE. You know that you can't. Willfully absenting yourself and your family from God's house: the preaching of his Word, the Lord's Supper, the fellowship of the saints, and the public worship of his holy Name invites fearful consequences to your soul and the souls of the members of your family. Letting your worship of God at home take the place of assembling with other believers for public worship is the opposite of what God intends for you and his other believers. It is an undeniable fact that God's people in Bible times gathered for public worship. Furthermore, Jesus himself set the example for us when he was on earth. While, on the one hand, he sometimes sought solitude up in the hills and on the mountains where he prayed alone, yet the Gospels record Jesus' custom of going regularly to the temple in Jerusalem and to the local synagogue. And don't forget the warning given by the writer of Hebrews: "Let us not give up meeting together, as some are in the habit of doing, but let us encourage one another — and all the more as you see the Day approaching" (Hebrews 10:25). You do want to follow God's Word in this matter, don't you? (WAIT FOR ANSWER AND RESPOND ACCORDINGLY.)

15. I just don't see the good of going to church every Sunday. Actually, church kind of bores me.

COUNSELOR: That's sad. The benefits the Christian receives in church are so wonderful that the Christian should desire to receive them frequently. If they are desirable on one Sunday, they ought to be desirable on every Sunday. Who can say he ever gets enough of God's Word? Does God's Word bore you? (WAIT FOR ANSWERS) Furthermore, in church we worship God: we adore him, thank him and praise him. Bear in mind that much of our time in heaven will be spent worshipping God. Do you really consider it a boring experience to worship God? (WAIT FOR ANSWER)

There is a practical aspect to regular church attendance. To skip even one Sunday is to weaken a good habit. Church attendance is a good habit, but if we can purposely stay away from church one Sunday it is easy to stay away two. Finally our flesh convinces us that we can get along without church entirely. Wouldn't you say that it is your sinful flesh that has convinced you that church is boring? (WAIT FOR ANSWER) The reason your sinful flesh can convince you that you are bored is that you probably lack understanding and appreciation of God's Word, especially the gospel that tells us about Jesus and how he saved us from our sins. It appears to me that you need a thorough restudy of Bible truths and I am suggesting that you enroll in the pastor's adult doctrine review class. Tell me: do you love Jesus? (WAIT FOR ANSWER) Do you love God's Word that tells you of Jesus? (WAIT FOR ANSWER AND RESPOND AS NEEDED)

16. **I guess you're right — I should go to church. From now on I'll try to be there.** *(Comment: Watch out for confession or remorse that is not genuine, that is merely an attempt to get rid of the counselor. The counselee is perhaps only telling you what he knows you want to hear.)*

COUNSELOR: The fact that you have stayed away from church for some time has made my visit necessary. But do not think that the main emphasis of my visit is to get you back in church? I am concerned that you correct any faith-problems you might have, that has resulted in your staying away from God's house for so long. Also that you are truly sorry for this sin and that you ask the Lord's forgiveness. Nothing would make me happier than to see you give evidence of possessing a genuine, faith-filled relationship with the Lord. An important evidence of this would be regular attendance at the worship services. I am happy that you are willing to come back to God's house. But would you tell me what has caused you to volunteer to be active again? What has changed? (WAIT FOR ANSWER) Let me explain why we should desire to come regularly to church and to the communion table. (GIVE BRIEF EXPLANATION) Tell me: do you understand what I just said? Do you agree? (WAIT FOR ANSWER) Allow me to lead you in prayer, so that together we can ask God the Holy Spirit to help you fulfill your intention to attend the worship services and the Lord's Supper. (LEAD THE MEMBER IN A BRIEF PRAYER)

PART THREE: The Delinquent Gives Evidence Of Rebellion Against God And His Word And the Church, And He Gives Evidence Of Self-righteousness / Work-righteousness And Lack Of Remorse

17. **The church demands too much of me. The church is too strict with its members. I really am not ready to settle down and be the kind of Christian that's asked of me.**

COUNSELOR: Then you have changed! At your confirmation you vowed that you were ready to be faithful to the Bible and to God to the death and promised to live a righteous life. What you have just said indicates that you are backsliding from God and his Word. The Bible in no uncertain terms condemns the backslider for his return to unbelief and sin. For example, the Book of Proverbs warns: "The faithless will be fully repaid for their ways" (Proverbs 14:14). The Book of Hebrews warns that those who shrink back from faith will be destroyed (Hebrews 10:39). The Second Epistle of Peter warns against becoming entangled again in the corruption of the world (2 Peter 2:20, 22). Your words indicate that you have started on a path away from God that leads to destruction. Don't you see this? (WAIT FOR ANSWER)

The Bible tells us that we are to *love* the Lord with all our heart and soul and strength (Deuteronomy 6:5). It also tells us to *serve* the Lord with all our heart (1 Samuel 12:20) and to *serve* him with gladness (Psalm 100:2). What has caused you to lose your love for God and his Word that you once confessed before the church? (WAIT FOR ANSWER). Recall those pointed words of Joshua to the Children of Israel in his time: "But if serving the Lord seems undesirable to you, then choose for yourselves this day whom you will serve . . . But as for me and my household, we will serve the Lord" (Joshua 24:15).

The church asks of its members no more than God asks of all his believers: that they believe in him with a steadfast faith and live a righteous life to the honor of his name. I beg you to turn to Jesus with all your heart. Bring your sins to him for forgiveness and then serve him with a holy life out of love for him. Think how he loves you and even gave himself for you. Won't you count yourself dead to sin, but alive to God in Christ Jesus? (Romans 6:11). Are you willing to do this? (WAIT FOR ANSWER AND RESPOND AS IS NECESSARY)

18. I don't think it is a sin not to go to church.

COUNSELOR: We all recognize that our physical life is sacred. God gave us our life and expects us to protect and preserve it. As Christians has he not also given us spiritual life by regenerating us through the Holy Spirit? Our faith, our spiritual life is most precious and God expects us to protect and preserve it with the Holy Spirit's help. The Spirit works on our faith through God's Word and the Lord's Supper. If we cut ourselves off from God's Word and Sacrament we allow our faith to die. Wouldn't you agree that this would be a terrible tragedy as well as a great sin? (WAIT FOR ANSWER) In church God feeds our spiritual life with wonderful spiritual food and we ought to always hunger for it. Recall the apostle Peter's words: "Like new born babies, crave pure spiritual milk, so that by it you may grow up in your salvation" (1 Peter 2:2). Jesus himself said: "Blessed . . . are those who hear the Word of God and obey it" (Luke 11:28).

To despise the preaching of God's Word is a grave sin for it is a sin against the cure for unbelief, for sin, for weakness of faith. God's Word is the cure; you realize that don't you? (WAIT FOR ANSWER) Recall that Jesus prayed to his Father in behalf of his disciples: to sanctify them through the Father's Word, which Jesus called the truth (John 17:17). There isn't a verse of Scripture that you can point to that tells God's people that it isn't necessary for them to gather at God's house to share God's Word together. On the contrary the Book of Hebrews gives us this exhortation: "Let us not give up meeting together, as some are in the habit of doing, but let us encourage one another — and all the more as you see the Day approaching" (Hebrews 10:25).

Next to the family, the basic unit of society for God's people in Bible times was the congregation meeting in regular assembly for worship. I am afraid that your negativism toward church indicates that you have a faith problem. May I ask you: what does Jesus Christ mean to you? What does the Bible mean to you? What do your fellow church members mean to you? (WAIT FOR ANSWER AND RESPOND ACCORDINGLY)

19. There are too many hypocrites in the church! That turns me off.

COUNSELOR: The sad fact is that there have always been and always will be hypocrites in the church on this side of heaven. I guess we should be surprised if there weren't. Even Jesus had to contend with a hypocrite among the apostles. His name was Judas. But the presence of a hypocrite didn't cause Jesus to love the others any less. In time hypocrites often show their true colors, just as Judas did, and the church is able to deal with them accordingly.

But when you use the term "hypocrite" you perhaps are referring to the imperfect life lived by members of the congregation. Their "hypocrisy" is that they don't always live up fully to what they profess. On this side of heaven none of us are perfect in our actions or speech. But remember this: the Word of God that imperfect Christians hear in God's house is the one thing that can change them into better Christians. While those whom you criticize for their so-called "hypocrisy" may be coming regularly to God's house to hear his Word that can change their hearts and their lives, you are staying away. Self-righteousness is no less an evil than hypocrisy, wouldn't you agree? (WAIT FOR ANSWER) I really didn't come to talk to you about the possible insincerety or the imperfection of others. I have come to talk to *you* about *your* faith, about *your* personal relationship to Jesus Christ. Tell me: what do *you* personally believe concerning Jesus? (WAIT FOR ANSWER AND RESPOND ACCORDINGLY)

20. Church just doesn't seem to me to be that important. I feel that I can come when I want to come, and nobody has the right to tell me that I have to come. When I feel like it, I'll be there. The church will have to take me as I am. I refuse to commit myself and tell you that I will come every Sunday.

COUNSELOR: How would we like it if God were so noncommittal toward us? Where would we be if God ruled our lives with such cold indifference? How would we like it if God said regarding our prayers: "I'm sorry, but I can't promise you an answer"? Do you recall the day you confessed your faith publicly and were received into the church? (WAIT FOR ANSWER) At that time you promised to come to church regularly, and to partake of the Lord's Supper with diligence. Now you say that you won't promise to do what you already promised, yes, before God himself and the church! You really don't want to break this promise, this covenant you made with God and the church, do you? Don't you think that your fellow Christians should hold you to your promise — both for your own good and for theirs? (WAIT FOR ANSWER)

Your problem is, first of all, a faith problem. I fear that Christ and his heavenly kingdom and his holy Word do not mean to you what they did when you first became a Christian and a member of the church. It sounds like you are beginning to waver in your love and in your trust toward God. Your zeal is growing cold. Tell me in all honesty and frankness: what does Jesus Christ mean to you? (WAIT FOR ANSWER AND RESPOND ACCORDINGLY) You are a sinner like me who needs God's rich grace to forgive your sins. You need to come to God's house confessing your sins; you need to listen with a joyful heart to the gospel telling you that your sins are forgiven. And you need to do this on a regular basis so that your love for God and his Word will not grow cold. Also, that your faith can be built up. St. Paul reminds us: "Faith comes from hearing the message, and the message is heard through the Word of Christ" (Romans 10:17). Don't listen to your sinful flesh that tells you to stay away from God's house. Listen instead to Jesus who said, "Blessed . . . are those who hear the Word of God and obey it" (Luke 11:28).

The hours you spend in church hearing that Jesus died for your sins and rose again are tremendously important for they will prepare you to spend eternity in heaven. One of the things that will make heaven such a joy is praising our God there with all the other saints and the angels. Isn't it a joy right now, while we live in this world, to praise God in his house together with our fellow Christians? (WAIT FOR ANSWER) Instead of being resentful toward your fellow church members for encouraging you to come regularly to God's house to worship with them, let the joyful enthusiasm of the Psalmist guide your heart and your actions. He exhorts us: "Come, let us sing for joy to the Lord; let us shout aloud to the Rock of our salvation. Let us come before him with thanksgiving and extol him with music and song . . . Come, let us bow down in worship, let us kneel before the Lord our Maker; for he is our God and we are the people of his pasture, the flock under his care" (Psalm 95:1-2, 6-7). I would like to lead you in a prayer, asking the Holy Spirit to fill you with a joyful desire to come regularly to God's house for worship and instruction. (HAVE A BRIEF PRAYER WITH THE COUNSELEE)

21. I don't want to be told that I have to go to church, or that I have to give or that I have to do other things.

COUNSELOR: It is unfortunate that you have taken on such a negative attitude. You shouldn't even have to be told to go to God's house, or to support the Lord's work with your gifts, or to do deeds of service for the Lord. True faith in Christ produces love in the heart for the Savior, as well as for the brother, and that love will compel the Christian to attend God's house regularly, to give generously, and to willingly do acts of loving service. St. John wrote that "we love because he first loved us" (1 John 4:19). And Jesus said: "If anyone loves me, he will obey my teaching" (John 14:23).

The fact that you resent being told to attend church services indicates that you really don't enjoy sitting through a worship service. That means that you don't enjoy the singing, the praying, the preaching, the praising of God, the fellowship of other Christians that makes up a worship service. And that you don't care for the instruction, guidance and comfort that God's Word gives. You don't enjoy the Lord's presence. Jesus promised: "Where two or three come together in my name, there am I with them" (Matthew 18:20). Is there really any difference between your attitude and that of the unregenerated person, the unbeliever? Are you certain that you are a Christian? (WAIT FOR ANSWER) Please tell me what you personally believe about Jesus Christ? (WAIT FOR ANSWER) Would you agree that you have allowed your sinful nature to gain the upper hand, instead of having the Holy Spirit guide and bless you? (WAIT FOR ANSWER) Will you repent of your sinful attitude? (WAIT FOR ANSWER AND DEAL APPROPRIATELY WITH IT)

22. I don't have to go to church to be a Christian. / I don't have to go to church to be a good Christian.

COUNSELOR: What do you mean by a "Christian"? I would gues that you think of a Christian in terms of someone who lives a decent, law-abiding, morally upright life. Certainly, there are those who never set foot in church who are outwardly very respectable people. This, however, is not the definition of the word "Christian" that fits the discussion you and I are having. Rather, a Christian is one who believes in Jesus Christ as his personal Lord and Savior, and makes public confession of his faith. A "good" Christian — to use the term you used — is one who is serious about his faith and carries it out, that is, demonstrates it, in his every day life.

Now then, attending church and humbly paying attention to the Word of God that is preached and taught there, most definitely helps a person to be a "good" Christian. Jesus himself said that the believers are sanctified by God's Word of truth (John 17:17). By saying that you don't have to go to church to be a Christian, you are in effect saying that the Word of God taught in God's house does not make the Christian grow in his faith and Christian life or preserve him as a believer. You are saying that a Christian can get along without the Word of God. The very opposite is true. St. Paul wrote: "The Word of God . . . is at work in you who believe" (1 Thessalonians 2:13). St. Peter urged: "Like newborn babies, crave pure spiritual milk, so that by it you may grow up in your salvation" (1 Peter 2:2). St. Paul said: "I commit you to God and to the Word of his grace, which can build you up and give you an inheritance among all those who are sanctified" (Acts 20:32).

Finally, why do we Christians go to church, to God's house? Is it merely to perform a good work that would classify us as "good" Christians? Don't we rather go to God's house because we have sins to confess and to be forgiven, a faith to be strengthened, a heart to be comforted, a Christian life to be guided and a precious God and Savior to be worshipped and praised? And isn't the preaching and teaching of God's Word at the center of it all? (WAIT FOR ANSWER) Tell me: do you count yourself as a sinner who needs Jesus Christ as your Savior? (WAIT FOR ANSWER) Do you love the Word of God that you hear in church? (WAIT FOR ANSWER AND GIVE THE PROPER RESPONSE)

23. It's none of your business whether or not I come to church!

COUNSELOR: You once confessed your faith publicly, and asked to be received as a member of our Christian congregation. You said you would abide by the rules of the congregation and carry out the privileges and duties of membership. All that made you *my* brother (sister) in a spiritual sense. And now as *your* brother it is my duty to counsel you in loving concern for your soul. Please regard me as one who loves you deeply in the Lord. Accept me and what I have to say to you in Christ's name. He is actually warning and encouraging you through me. I represent the Lord; I have not come on my own. To turn me away with the rebuff that it's none of my business is to turn the Lord away. Christ told his disciples engaged in the work of testifying his name and gospel to others: "He that hears you, hears me, and he that despises you despises me, and he that despises me, despises him that sent me" (Luke 10:16). Do not despise Jesus Christ. Hear me out, I have come in the Savior's name. He loves you, and so do I. Please permit me to ask you a very important question: what does Jesus Christ mean to you personally? (WAIT FOR ANSWER)

24. Why don't you pick on someone else? I know a lot of people in the church who are worse than I am. I used to be very active!

COUNSELOR: The board of elders is committed to help *all* who are in spiritual trouble. I am not here to pick on you but to help you, just as I go to other members of the congregation to offer my help to them. Our Savior has taught us that even one sheep is precious to him, and when that sheep is straying he wants the church to use every means at its disposal to reclaim it. I am here in your house because our Savior is concerned about you personally. And your fellow church members are concerned about you, as he wants us to be. Would you mind expressing to me what you believe your relationship to Jesus Christ is? (WAIT FOR ANSWER AND CONTINUE ON THE BASIS OF IT)

25. I'll take my chances.

COUNSELOR: Years ago when two successful vaccines for polio were discovered and marketed, free vaccination clinics were set up in convenient locations throughout the United States. Everyone was urged to visit a clinic to receive the vaccine. If a person, especially a young person, did not make use of the clinic but took his chances instead, he gambled, quite literally, with his life, taking the chance that polio would never strike him. The same is true today with people: they either accept the vaccine or "take their chance." What would we say of the attitude: "I won't be vaccinated; I'll take my chances"? A response like that is foolish, and you know it.

God forbids any of us to take our chances when he tells us throughout the Bible to repent of our sins and believe the gospel. Salvation isn't a matter of "taking your chances;" it is a matter of trusting in Christ and of being absolutely certain. "He that believes and is baptized *shall* be saved" (Mark 16:16). "Whoever believes in the Son *has* eternal life" (John 3:36). If one "takes his chances" he will be damned, for he is trusting in himself, his own works to get him by — and that trust can only damn. Recall St. Paul's words to the Galations: "All who rely on observing the law are under a curse, for it is written: 'Cursed is everyone who does not continue to do everything written in the Book of the Law" (Galations 3:10). Really, there is no such thing as "taking your chance." All of us deserve damnation, for we are sinners. God sent Christ to save sinners like us, who had no chance. Salvation is by God's grace through faith in Christ (Ephesians 2:8). Tell me: upon what do you base your hope of eternal life? (CONTINUE ON THE BASIS OF THE RESPONSE THAT IS GIVEN. A BRIEF REVIEW OF GOD'S PLAN OF SALVATION MAY BE IN ORDER)

26. My money is all mine, and no one has the right to tell me what to do with it, not even the church.

COUNSELOR: The wealth of the church lies in the wealth of the individual Christians. The church as a whole can only undertake what the individual Christians in it are willing, with cheerful heart and generous spirit, to undertake. The Scripture emphasizes that each Christian "should give what he has decided in his heart to give, not reluctantly or under compulsion, for God loves a cheerful giver" (2 Corinthians 9:7). Giving is a good work. Love for God and for those in need will move Christians to give, for love produces good works. But love for money, and also selfishness, will keep a person from giving. The Scripture warns: "Keep your lives free from the love of money" (Hebrews 13:5).

Once the love of money takes over in the heart it rules like a tyrant. The person begins to measure security, happiness, power and success in terms of dollars and cents. Jesus warns that if a person is a slave to money, if a person loves money (and being tight-fisted with money indicates a love for it) then he is not a servant of God, nor is a believing heart found in him. A person either serves God with good works such as giving, or he serves money — using it only for his own pleasure and benefit. Jesus warned: "You cannot serve both God and money," and the reason is that "no servant can serve two masters" (Luke 16:10, 13).

What you and I think of wealth — earthly possessions — will determine the use we make of it. If we think of it as belonging only to us, and love it, we will spend it only on ourselves and selfishly refuse to share it with others. If, on the other hand, we consider that wealth really belongs to God (as the Scripture clearly says that it does), we will use our wealth not only on ourselves but also give a portion of it to the church and to charity to benefit others. And this is the God-pleasing way, as the writer to the Hebrews points out when he urges us: "Do not forget to do good and to share with others, for with such sacrifices God is pleased" (Hebrews 13:16).

You seem to think a great deal of your earthly wealth, but isn't there a wealth God gives us that is far more precious than such things as money? Isn't the greatest treasure that we can possibly own, the forgiveness of sins and everlasting life that God offers sinners like us through Jesus Christ? (WAIT FOR ANSWER) How much does Jesus Christ and his salvation mean to you? (WAIT FOR ANSWER) Won't you admit that your attitude toward your money and toward the Christian good work of giving has been wrong up to now, and that you have shown a lack of appreciation of Christ and his salvation? (WAIT FOR ANSWER AND PROCEED ACCORDINGLY)

PART FOUR: The Delinquent Gives Evidence Of Being Preoccupied With Other Matters.

27. I haven't the time to come to church. I'm involved in so many activities that I have to use Sundays to catch up.

COUNSELOR: It's really a matter of establishing priorities isn't it? None of us are able to do everything we would really like to do. We have to do the things of greatest importance first: things that have to do with preserving our faith, worshipping God, learning his Word and fellowshipping with our fellow Christians. It seems, however, that you have set aside the most important for the less important. If we take care of spiritual matters first, God will see to it that the other things fall into place in our lives. But we must trust him. Be careful not to set your heart on worldly matters. Be careful not to forget God. Remember that of all things that we have, and of all things that we do, only our faith and the works that we do for Christ will survive the destruction that is coming on the world on the Last Day. Jesus exhorts us to seek first the kingdom of God and his righteousness (Matthew 6:33). "Seeking the kingdom of God and his righteousness" means to pay undivided attention to God's Word that tells us our sins are forgiven for Jesus' sake. Tell me: what is the most important thing in your life? (WAIT FOR ANSWER AND RESPOND ACCORDINGLY). *(Note: Other Scripture references: Luke 21:34; Mark 4:19; 1 Corinthians 15:58; 2 Peter 3:1-14)*

28. Right now my life is all messed up. I've got to have time to get things straightened out.

COUNSELOR: I'm sorry to hear that you have hit some rough spots in your life. If your life needs straightening out you must recognize that the only one who can help you do it is God's Holy Spirit. He is the divine Counselor whom Christ has given to his church. He guides us and helps us and heals our emotional wounds, and he also forgives our sins — all through the counsel of his divine Word. The Psalmist confessed to God: "Your word is a lamp to my feet and a light for my path" (Psalm 119:105). St. Paul, too, points out the wonderful uses a Christian can make of God's Word: "All Scripture is God-breathed and is useful for teaching, rebuking, correcting and training in righteousness, so that the man of God may be thoroughly equipped for every good work" (2 Timothy 3:16-17). Tell me: isn't it God's Word that you receive in the church service and in Bible Class? (WAIT FOR ANSWER) Don't neglect the one thing that can help you get your life straightened out and then keep it on the right course.

And if you have serious problems in your life, recognize that sin is somehow the cause. God's remedy for sin — both its guilt and power — is Jesus Christ, who is presented faithfully to the people by the pastor in his teaching and preaching. You need Jesus Christ now, as much as you have ever needed him. Jesus wants to be your Savior and Friend; don't turn him away. Tell me about your personal relationship with Jesus Christ. (WAIT FOR ANSWER)

I hope that you agree that staying away from God's house and neglecting to hear God's Word can only harm your efforts to straighten your life out; that you will only add to your problems and find it harder to cope with temptations and troubles. By the way, the pastor is ready to give you additional counseling in private to help you straighten out your life. Have you spoken to him lately about your problem? (WAIT FOR ANSWER. BE WILLING TO HELP THE COUNSELEE TO MAKE AN APPOINTMENT TO MEET WITH THE PASTOR)

29. I have to work on Sundays.

Comment: Each situation here is different and has to be dealt with accordingly. The following questions may prove helpful to the counselor in judging the merit of the counselee's excuse.

1. How long have you been working on Sundays?
2. Is this something your employer requires, or is it a matter of choice?
3. Do you work **every** Sunday?
4. Have you been keeping up with your Christian giving, though unable to be in the services?
5. Do you feel that you are missing out on something important?
6. How much longer do you anticipate working on Sundays?

7. Have you made arrangements with the pastor to receive private communion and to hear the sermon on tape?
8. Do you now attend the evening services provided for persons like yourself? (Or: would you attend evening services if they were provided?)
9. Do other members of your family who don't work on Sundays attend Sunday worship services?

ADDENDUM FOUR

SCRIPTURE TOPICS INDEX

INTRODUCTION

When you, an elder, counsel others, you counsel on the basis of God's Word. It is God's Word alone that can bring about the needed change in the person you are admonishing. The place of God's Word, the Scripture, in counseling has well been stated in St. Paul's Second Letter to Timothy: "All Scripture is God-breathed and is useful for teaching, rebuking, correcting and training in righteousness, so that the man of God may be thoroughly equipped for every good work" (3:16).

If you would do God's work, you must use God's tool, his holy Word, so that the Holy Spirit may work through it to win the person back from sin as well as from doubt and unbelief; but also to comfort, guide and encourage him. The purpose of the following *SCRIPTURE TOPICS INDEX* is to provide you with a basic list of Scripture verses to apply to various situations that you may encounter in counseling sessions; as a resource to aid you in composing letters, and as a resource to which you can refer in elder, council and congregation meetings. We would suggest that you thoroughly familiarize yourself with this index of Scripture verses. You might even take this handbook along on your visits and, as occasion requires it, refer to it. However, it would be most effective to use this handbook only for reference and to do the actual reading of appropriate Scripture verses from the Bible itself.

As you study your Bible and Catechism you will no doubt find other Scripture references that you can add to what is presented here. Always be ready to share your finds with the pastor and other elders. This list does not, of course, cover everything. In addition to the *SCRIPTURE TOPICS INDEX* there are the many references presented throughout the book covering a variety of subjects. Equip yourself also with these.

The Holy Spirit is the counselor's Counselor. Depend on him to help you remember and apply the appropriate Scripture in a counseling situation. Thus diligent prayer for his help and blessings is always in order.

    O Holy Spirit,

        A trusty weapon is Thy Word,

Thy Church's buckler, shield, and sword.
Oh, let us in its power confide
That we may seek no other guide. Amen (TLH 292:8)

Abortion   (God's witness against killing that which must be regarded as a human being)

Listen to me, O house of Jacob, all you who remain of the house of Israel, you whom I have upheld since you were conceived, and have carried since your birth. Even to your old age and gray hairs I am he, I am he who will sustain you. I have made you and I will carry you; I will sustain you and I will rescue you. (Isaiah 46:3-4)

Before I formed you in the womb I knew you, before you were born I set you apart; I appointed you as a prophet to the nations. (Jeremiah 1:5)

Your hands shaped me and made me. Will you now turn and destroy me? Remember that you molded me like clay. Will you now turn me to dust again? Did you not ... clothe me with skin and flesh and knit me together with bones and sinews? You gave me life and showed me kindness, and in your providence watched over my spirit. (Job 10:8-12)

Surely I have been a sinner from birth, sinful from the time my mother conceived me. (Psalm 51:5)

He (i.e. John the Baptist) will be a joy and delight to you, and many will rejoice because of his birth, for he will be great in the sight of the Lord ... and he will be filled with the Holy Spirit even from birth (or, from his mother's womb) ... Even Elizabeth your relative is going to have a child (literally: has herself also conceived a son) in her old age, and she who was said to be barren is in her sixth month. For nothing is impossible with God ... When Elizabeth heard Mary's greeting, the baby leaped in her womb, and Elizabeth was filled with the Holy Spirit ... But why am I so favored, that the mother of my Lord should come to me? As soon as the sound of your greeting reached my ears, the baby in my womb leaped for joy. (Luke 1:14-15, 36, 41, 43-44)

You shall not murder. (Exodus 20:13)

   Also: Psalm 139:13ff.

Admonishment   (One Christian of another)   (See also: Reproof of Sin)

If your brother sins, rebuke him, and if he repents, forgive him. (Luke 17:3)

If your brother sins against you, go and show him his fault, just between the two of you. (Matthew 18:15)

Brothers, if someone is caught in a sin, you who are spiritual should restore him gently. (Galatians 6:1)

Let the Word of Christ dwell in you richly as you teach and admonish one another with all wisdom. (Colossians 3:16)

Warn a divisive person once, and then warn him a second time. After that, have nothing to do with him. (Titus 3:10)

And let us consider how we may spur one another on toward love and good deeds. (Hebrews 10:24)

Adultery   (Sixth Commandment)   (See also: Sexual Immorality)

You shall not commit adultery. (Exodus 20:14)

My master has withheld nothing from me except you, because you are his wife. How then could I do such a wicked thing and sin against God? (Genesis 39:9)

You have heard that it was said, "Do not commit adultery." But I tell you that anyone who looks at a woman lustfully has already committed adultery with her in his heart. (Matthew 5:27, 28)

For out of the heart come evil thoughts, murder, adultery ... (Matthew 15:19)

Do you not know that the wicked will not inherit the kingdom of God? Do not be deceived: neither the sexually immoral nor idolaters nor adulterers ... will inherit the kingdom of God and that is what some of you were. But you were washed, you were sanctified, you were justified in the name of the Lord Jesus Christ and by the Spirit of our God. (1 Corinthians 6:9-11)

I tell you that anyone who divorces his wife, except for marital unfaithfulness, and marries another woman commits adultery. (Matthew 19:9)

Therefore, I tell you, her many sins have been forgiven — for she loved much. But he who has been forgiven little, loves little." Then Jesus said to her, "Your sins are forgiven." — Jesus said to the woman, "Your faith has saved you; go in peace." (Luke 7:47-48)

    Also: Proverbs 2:16-18a   The adulteress and the destruction she causes. Provers 5:3, 4, 8

Alcoholism   (See: Drunkeness)

Anger, God's

God is a righteous judge, a God who expresses his wrath every day. (Psalm 7:11)

O Lord, do not rebuke me in your anger or discipline me in your wrath. (Psalm 6:1)

For the Lord your God is a consuming fire, a jealous God. (Deuteronomy 4:24)

It is a dreadful thing to fall into the hands of the living God. (Hebrews 10:31)

Like the rest, we were by nature objects of wrath. (Ephesians 2:3)

The Lord is compassionate and gracious, slow to anger, abounding in love. (Psalm 103:8)

Anger, Man's (Temper, Fifth Commandment)   (See also: Self-control)

You shall not murder. (Exodus 20:13)

A quick tempered man does foolish things, and a crafty man is hated . . . A patient man has great understanding, but a quick-tempered man displays folly. (Proverbs 14:17, 29)

A fool gives full vent to his anger, but a wise man keeps himself under control. (Proverbs 14:17)

But I tell you that anyone who is angry with his brother will be subject to judgment. (Matthew 5:22)

In your anger do not sin: Do not let the sun go down while you are still angry . . . Get rid of all bitterness, rage and anger, brawling and slander, along with every form of malice. Be kind and compassionate to one another, forgiving each other, just as in Christ God forgave you. (Ephesians 4:26, 31)

But now you must rid yourselves of all such as these: anger, rage, malice, slander, and filthy language from your lips. (Colossians 3:8)

    Also: *James 1:19, 20*   Slow to become angry.
               Proverbs 16:32   The hot-tempered man/The patient man.
               Proverbs 22:24-25

Anxiety   (See: Worry)

Apostasy   (See: Backsliding)

Backsliding   (Apostasy)

The faithless will be fully repaid for their ways, and the good man rewarded for his. (Proverbs 14:14)

"Return, faithless Israel," declares the Lord, "I will frown on you no longer, for I am

merciful," says the Lord, "I will not be angry for ever." (Jeremiah 3:12)

"But my righteous one will live by faith. And if he shrinks back, I will not be pleased with him." But we are not of those who shrink back and are destroyed, but of those who believe and are saved. (Hebrews 10:39)

Yet I hold this against you: You have forsaken your first love. Remember the height from which you have fallen! Repent and do the things you did at first. (Revelation 2:4, 5)

    Also: 2 Peter 2:20, 22   Entangled again in the corruption of the world.

Blame Shifting

The man said, "The woman you put here with me — she gave me some fruit from the tree, and I ate it." Then the Lord God said to the woman, "What is this that you have done?" The woman said, "The serpent deceived me, and I ate." (Genesis 3:12, 13)

A man's own folly ruins his life, yet his heart rages against the Lord. (Proverbs 19:3)

But each one is tempted when, by his own evil desire, he is dragged away and enticed. (James 1:14)

Body   (For God's glory)

Therefore, I urge you, brothers, in view of God's mercy, to offer your bodies as living sacrifices, holy and pleasing to God — which is your spiritual worship. (Romans 12:2)

Do you not know that your body is a temple of the Holy Spirit, which is in you, whom you have received from God? You are not your own; you were bought at a price. Therefore honor God with your body. (1 Corinthians 6:19, 20)

Brotherliness   (See: Love, Christian)

Causing Offense

But if anyone causes one of these little ones who believe in me to sin, it would be better for him to have a large mill stone hung around his neck and be drowned in the depths of the sea. Woe to the world because of the things that cause people to sin! Such things must come, but woe to the man through whom they come! (Matthew 18:6)

If your brother is distressed because of what you eat, you are no longer acting in love. Do not by your eating destroy your brother for whom Christ died. . . . Do not destroy the work of God for the sake of food. All food is clean, but it is wrong for a man to eat anything that causes someone else to stumble. It is better not to eat meat or to drink wine or to do anything else that will cause your brother to fall. (Romans 14:15, 20, 21)

Child/Parent   (Fourth Commandment)

"Honor your father and mother" — which is the first commandment with a promise "that it may go well with you and that you may enjoy long life on the earth." (Ephesians 6:2, 3)

Sons are a heritage from the Lord, children a reward from him." (Psalm 127:3)

Remember not the sins of my youth and my rebellious ways; according to your love remember me, for you are good, O Lord. (Psalm 25:7)

Listen to your father, who gave you life, and do not despise your mother when she is old. (Proverbs 23:22)

Children, obey your parents in the Lord, for this is right. "Honor your father and your mother." (Ephesians 6:1, 2)

    Also: *Colossians 3:20*   Pleasing God with obedience to parents.
              1 Timothy 5:4   Repaying parents and grandparents.

Christian Life, The   (See also: Love, Christian; New Man; Body)

I am the vine; you are the branches. If a man remains in me and I in him, he will bear much fruit; apart from me you can do nothing. (John 15:5)

And he died for all, that those who live should no longer live for themselves but for him who died for them and was raised again ... Therefore, if anyone is in Christ, he is a new creation; the old has gone, the new has come! (2 Corinthians 5:15)

So I say, live by the Spirit, and you will not gratify the desires of the sinful nature ... Those who belong to Christ Jesus have crucified the sinful nature with its passions and desires. Since we live by the Spirit, let us keep in step with the Spirit. (Galations 5:16, 24-25)

For we are God's workmanship, created in Christ Jesus to do good works, which God prepared in advance for us to do. (Ephesians 2:10)

And we pray this in order that you may live a life worthy of the Lord and may please him in every way: bearing fruit in every good work, growing in the knowledge of God. (Colossians 1:10)

Since everything will be destroyed in this way, what kind of people ought you to be? You ought to live holy and godly lives as you look forward to the day of God and speed its coming. (1 Peter 3:11-12a)

What good is it, my brothers, if a man claims to have faith but has no deeds? Can such faith save him? ... Faith by itself, if it is not accompanied by action (i.e. good works), is dead. (James 2:14, 17)

Also: *Titus 2:11-15* "No" to ungodliness. Live self-controlled, upright lives.
Acts 9:36-39 Dorcas, a woman full of good works.
Matthew 5:13-16 Let your light shine before men, that they may see your good works.

Church and Communion Attendance (See also: Giving, Christian; Offerings, Church; Word of God, Hearing and Obeying the; Word of God, Preaching the; Word of God Works in the Christian; Worship, Public)

They devoted themselves to the apostles' teaching and to the fellowship, to the breaking of bread and to prayer ... Every day they continued to meet together in the temple courts. They broke bread in their homes and ate together. (Acts 2:42, 46)

Guard your steps when you go to the house of God. Go near to listen. (Ecclesiastes 5:1)

One thing I ask of the Lord, this is what I seek: that I may dwell in the house of the Lord all the days of my life, to gaze upon the beauty of the Lord and to seek him in his temple. (Psalm 27:4)

I love the house where you live, O Lord, the place where your glory dwells. (Psalm 26:8)

In the congregation will I praise you. (Psalm 22:22)

I rejoiced with those who said to me, "Let us go to the house of the Lord." (Psalm 122:1)

How lovely is your dwelling place, O Lord Almighty! My soul yearns, even faints for the courts of the Lord ... Blessed are those who dwell in your house; they are ever praising you ... Better is one day in your courts than a thousand elsewhere; I would rather be a doorkeeper in the house of my God than dwell in the tents of the wicked. (Psalm 84:1-2, 4, 10)

Let us hold unswervingly to the hope we profess, for he who promised is faithful. And let us consider how we may spur one another on toward love and good deeds. Let us not give up meeting together, as some are in the habit of doing, but let us encourage one another — and all the more as you see the Day approaching. (Hebrews 10:23-25)

For where two or three come together in my name, there am I with them. (Matthew 18:20)

(Jesus) went to Nazareth, where he had been brought up, and on the Sabbath day he went into the synagogue, as was his custom. (Luke 4:16)

Every day I sat in the temple courts teaching. (Matthew 25:55)

For whenever you eat this bread and drink this cup, you proclaim the Lord's death until he comes. (1. Corinthians 11:26).

Because there is one loaf, we, who are many, are one body, for we all partake of the one loaf. (1 Corinthians 10:17)

Commitment of Faith

Now fear the Lord and serve him with all faithfulness. Throw away the gods your forefathers worshiped beyond the River and in Egypt, and serve the Lord. But if serving the Lord seems undesirable to you, then choose for yourselves this day whom you will serve, whether the gods your forefathers served beyond the River, or the gods of the Amorites, in whose land you are living. But as for me and my household, we will serve the Lord. (Joshua 24:14-15)

Yet (Abraham) did not waver through unbelief regarding the promise of God, but was strengthened in his faith and gave glory to God, being fully persuaded that God had power to do what he had promised. (Romans 4:20-21)

Therefore, my dear brothers, stand firm. Let nothing move you. (1 Corinthians 15:58a)

I have fought the good fight, I have finished the race, I have kept the faith. Now there is in store for me the crown of righteousness. (2 Timothy 4:7-8a)

Now faith is being sure of what we hope for and certain of what we do not see. (Hebrews 11:1)

My soul finds rest in God alone; my salvation comes from him. He alone is my rock and my salvation; he is my fortress, I will never be shaken. (Psalm 62:1-2)

Confession of Sin   (To God)

I confess my iniquity; I am troubled by my sin. (Psalm 38:18)

Then I acknowledged my sin to you and did not cover up my iniquity. I said, "I will confess my transgressions to the Lord" — and you forgave the guilt of my sin. (Psalm 32:5)

Against you, you only, have I sinned and done what is evil in your sight, so that you are proved right when you speak and justified when you judge. (Psalm 51:4, 5)

He who conceals his sins does not prosper, but who confesses and renounces them finds mercy. (Proverbs 28:13)

If we confess our sins, he is faithful and just and will forgive us our sins and purify us from all unrighteousness. (1 John 1:9)

Our offenses are many in your sight, and our sins testify against us. Our offenses are ever with us, and we acknowledge our iniquities. (Isaiah 59:12)

Father, I have sinned against heaven and against you. I am no longer worthy to be called your son. (Luke 15:21)

Confession of Sin   (To Each Other)

Then Nathan said to David, "You are the man!"... Then David said to Nathan, "I have sinned against the Lord." Nathan replied, "The Lord has taken away your sin. You are not going to die." (2 Samuel 12:7, 13)

Therefore confess your sins to each other. (James 5:16)

If your brother sins rebuke him, and if he repents, forgive him. (Luke 17:3)

Conscience, Guilty   (See: Guilt)

Contentment

Keep your lives free from the love of money and be content with what you have, because God has said, "Never will I leave you; never will I forsake you." (Hebrews 13:5)

But godliness with contentment is great gain. For we brought nothing into the world, and we can take nothing out of it. But if we have food and clothing, we will be content with that. (1 Timothy 6:6-7)

I have learned to be content whatever the circumstances. (Philippians 4:11)

Contrition   (See: Repentance)

Covetousness   (Ninth and Tenth Commandments)   (See also: Money; Desires of the Sinful Flesh; Rich, The; Stealing; Contentment)

You shall not covet your neighbor's house. You shall not covet your neighbor's wife nor his manservant or his maidservant, his ox or donkey, or anything that belongs to your neighbor. (Exodus 20:17)

I would not have known what it is to covet if the law had not said, "Do not covet." But sin seizing the opportunity afforded by the commandment, produced in me every kind of covetous desire. (Romans 7:7-8)

Be content with what you have, because God has said, "Never will I leave you; never will I forsake you." (Hebrews 13:5)

Put to death, therefore, whatever belongs to your earthly nature: sexual immorality, impurity, lust, evil desires and greed, which is idolatry. (Colossians 3:5)

It is God's will ... that each of you should learn to control his own body in a way that is holy and honorable, not in passionate lust like the heathen, who do not know God. (1 Thessalonians 4:3a, 4-5)

Depression, Cure for (See also: Guilt, Conscience-felt)

Why are you downcast, O my soul? Why so disturbed within me? Put your hope in God, for I will yet praise him, my Savior and my God. (Psalm 42:5)

My heart is in anguish within me; the terrors of death assail me. Fear and trembling have beset me; horror has overwhelmed me. I said, "Oh, that I had the wings of a dove! I would fly away and be at rest" ... I call to God, and the Lord saves me. Evening, morning and noon I cry out in distress, and he hears my voice ... Cast your cares on the Lord and he will sustain you; he will never let the righteous fall. (Psalm 55:4-6, 16-17, 22)

I remember my affliction and my wandering, the bitterness and the gall. I well remember them, and my soul is downcast within me. Yet this I call to mind and therefore I have hope: Because of the Lord's great love we are not consumed, for his compassions never fail. They are new every morning; great is your faithfulness. I say to myself, "The Lord is my portion; therefore I will wait for him." The Lord is good to those whose hope is in him, to the one who seeks him; it is good to wait quietly for the salvation of the Lord. (Lamentations 3:19-26)

Desertion (Of One Spouse by the Other)

To the rest I say this (I, not the Lord): if any brother has a wife who is not a believer and she is willing to live with him, he must not divorce her. And if a woman has a husband who is not a believer and he is willing to live with her, she must not divorce him ... But if the unbeliever leaves let him do so. A believing man or woman is not bound in such circumstances; God has called us to live in peace. (1 Corinthians 7:12-13, 15)

Death

The wages of sin is death, but the gift of God is eternal life in Christ Jesus our Lord. (Romans 6:23)

Precious in the sight of the Lord is the death of his saints. (Psalm 116:15)

For to me, to live is Christ and to die is gain. If I am to go on living in the body, this will mean fruitful labor for me. Yet what shall I choose? I do not know! I am torn between the two: I desire to depart and to be with Christ, which is better by far. (Philippians 1:21-23)

Since the children have flesh and blood, he too shared in their humanity so that by his death he might destroy him who holds the power of death — that is, the devil — and free those who all their lives were held in slavery by their fear of death. (Hebrews 2:14-16)

Even though I walk through the valley of the shadow of death, I will fear no evil, for you are with me . . . I will dwell in the house of the Lord forever. (Psalm 23:4, 6)

"Where, O death, is your victory? Where, O death, is your sting?" The sting of death is sin, and the power of sin is the law. But thanks be to God! He gives us the victory through our Lord Jesus Christ. (1 Corinthians 15:55-56)

Then I heard a voice from heaven say, "Write: Blessed are the dead who die in the Lord from now on." "Yes," says the Spirit, "they will rest from their labor, for their deeds will follow them." (Revelation 14:13)

    Also: *Psalm 39:4-5*   The fleeting nature of life

Desires of the Sinful Flesh   (See: Flesh, Works of)

Discipline   **(Of Christians by God; A Testing of Faith)**   (See also: Illness)

Consider it pure joy, my brothers, whenever you face trials of many kinds, because you know that the testing of your faith develops perseverance . . . Blessed is the man who perseveres under trial, because when he has stood the test, he will receive the crown of life that God has promised to those who love him. (James 1:2-3, 12)

But he said to me, "My grace is sufficient for you, for my power is made perfect in weakness." (2 Corinthians 12:9)

Blessed is the man whom God corrects; so do not despise the discipline of the Almighty. (Job 5:17)

Those whom I love I rebuke and discipline. So be earnest, and repent. Here I am! I stand at the door and knock. If anyone hears my voice and opens the door, I will go in and eat with him, and he with me. To him who overcomes, I will give the right to sit with me on my throne, just as I overcame and sat down with my Father on his throne. (Revelation 3:19-21)

    Also: *Hebrews 12:1-12*   The Lord disciplines those he loves.
                  1 Peter 1:6-7   Suffering grief in all kinds of trials.
                  Proverbs 12:1   The right attitude toward discipline, correction.

Divorce   (See also: Adultery; Desertion; Marriage)

It is because the Lord is acting as the witness between you and the wife of your youth, because you have broken faith with her, though she is your partner, the wife of your marriage covenant. Has not the Lord made them one? In flesh and spirit they are his. And why one? Because he was seeking godly offspring. So guard yourself in your spirit, and do not break faith with the wife of your youth. "I hate divorce," says the Lord God of Israel. (Malachi 2:14-16a)

Some Pharisees came to him to test him. They asked, "Is it lawful for a man to divorce his wife for any and every reason?" "Haven't you read," he replied, "that at the beginning the Creator 'made them male and female,' and said, 'for this reason a man will leave his father and his mother and be united to his wife and the two will become one flesh'? So they are no longer two but one. Therefore what God has joined together, let not man separate." "Why then," they asked, "did Moses command that a man give his wife a certificate of divorce and send her away?" Jesus replied, "Moses permitted you to divorce your wives because your hearts were hard. But it was not this way from the beginning. I tell you that anyone who divorces his wife, except for marital unfaithfulness, and marries another woman commits adultery." (Matthew 19:3-8)

It has been said, "Anyone who divorces his wife must give her a certificate of divorce." But I tell you that anyone who divorces his wife, except for marital unfaithfulness, and marries another woman commits adultery." (Matthew 19:3-8)

It has been said, "Anyone who divorces his wife must give her a certificate of divorce." But I tell you that anyone who divorces his wife, except for marital unfaithfulness causes her to commit adultery and anyone who marries a woman so divorced commits adultery. (Matthew 5:31, 32)

> Also: *1 Corinthians 7:10-13, 39*   A husband must not divorce his wife — the wife is bound to her husband for life.

Drunkenness   (See also: Flesh, Works of; Idolatry)

Nor drunkards . . . will inherit the kingdom of God. And that is what some of you were. But you were washed, you were sanctified, you were justified in the name of the Lord Jesus Christ and by the Spirit of our God. "Everything is permissable for me" — but not everything is beneficial. "Everything is permissable for me" — but I will not be mastered by anything. (1 Corinthians 6:10-12)

The acts of the sinful nature are obvious . . . drunkeness, orgies, and the like. I warn you, as I did before, that those who live like this will not inherit the kingdom of God. (Galations 5:19-21)

Wine is a mocker and beer a brawler; whoever is lead astray by them is not wise. (Proverbs 20:1)

Do not get drunk on wine, which leads to debauchery. Instead, be filled with the Spirit. (Ephesians 5:18)

I pray that out of his glorious riches he may strengthen you with power through his Spirit in your inner being, so that Christ may dwell in your hearts through faith. (Ephesians 3:16)

I can do everything through him who gives me strength. (Philippians 4:14)

>Also:	Colossians 1:11-14	Strengthened with all power.
>1 Peter 5:10	God restores and makes steadfast.
>Isaiah 41:10	God will strengthen; he will uphold.

Elderly, The   (The Fourth Commandment)

Listen to your father, who gave you life, and do not despise your mother when she is old. (Proverbs 23:22)

Rise in the presence of the aged, show respect for the elderly and revere your God. I am the Lord. (Leviticus 19:32)

But if a widow has children or grandchildren, these should learn first of all to put their religion into practice by caring for their own family and so repaying their parents and grandparents, for this is pleasing to God. (1 Timothy 5:4)

Excommunication   (Of Unrepentant Persons)

If he refuses to listen to them, tell it to the church; and if he refuses to listen even to the church, treat him as you would a pagan or a tax collector. (Matthew 18:17)

When you are assembled in the name of our Lord Jesus and I am with you in spirit, and the power of the Lord Jesus is present, hand this man over to Satan, so that the sinful nature may be destroyed and his spirit saved on the day of the Lord . . . God will judge those outside. "Expel the wicked man from among you." (1 Corinthians 5:4, 5, 13)

Faith   (Salvation by Faith)   (See also: Work-righteousness; Christian Life; Unbelief)

For God so loved the world that he gave his one and only Son, that whoever believes in him shall not perish but have eternal life . . . Whoever believes in the Son has eternal life. (John 3:16, 36)

However, to the man who does not work but trusts God who justifies the wicked, his faith is credited for righteousness. (Romans 4:5)

For in the gospel a righteousness from God is revealed, a righteousness that is by faith from first to last, just as it is written: "The righteous will live by faith." (Romans 1:17)

This righteousness from God comes through faith in Jesus Christ to all who believe.

There is no difference, for all have sinned and fall short of the glory of God, and are justified freely by his grace through the redemption that came by Christ Jesus . . . for we maintain that a man is justified by faith apart from observing the law. (Romans 3:22, 23, 24, 28)

Know that a man is not justified by observing the law, but by faith in Jesus Christ. So we, too, have put our faith in Christ Jesus that we may be justified by faith in Christ and not by observing the law, because by observing the law no one will be justified. (Galations 2:16)

You are all sons of God through faith in Christ Jesus, for all of you who were baptized into Christ have been clothed with Christ. (Galations 3:26, 27)

For it is by grace you have been saved, through faith — and this not from yourselves, it is the gift of God — not by works so that no one can boast. (Ephesians 2:8, 9)

    Also: *Philippians 3:8, 9*   Paul ceased to trust in his works and trusted in Jesus.

Family   (See: Home, Christian)

Fatherless   **(Orphans)**

The Lord watches over the alien and sustains the fatherless and the widow. (Psalm 146:9)

Religion that God our Father accepts as pure and faultless is this: to look after orphans and widows in their distress and to keep oneself from being polluted by the world. (James 1:27)

Flesh, Works Of (See also: Adultery; Drunkeness; Covetousness; Sexual Immorality, Idolatry; Homosexuality, Sin)

For out of the heart come evil thoughts, murder, adultery, sexual immorality, theft, false testimony, slander. These are what make a man "unclean". (Matthew 15:19-20a)

I know that nothing good lives in me, that is, in my sinful nature (flesh). (Romans 7:18)

So I say, live by the Spirit, and you will not gratify the desires of the sinful nature . . . The acts of the sinful nature are obvious: sexual immorality, impurity and debauchery; idolatry and witchcraft; hatred, discord, jealousy, fits of rage, selfish ambition, dissensions, factions and envy; drunkenness, orgies, and the like. I warn you, as I did before, that those who live like this will not inherit the kingdom of God. (Galations 5:16, 19-21)

All of us also lived among them at one time, gratifying the cravings of our sinful nature and following its desires and thoughts. Like the rest, we were by nature objects of wrath. (Ephesians 2:3)

For if you live according to the sinful nature, you will die; but if by the Spirit you put to death the misdeeds of the body, you will live, because those who are led by the Spirit of God are sons of God. (Romans 8:13, 14)

As obedient children, do not conform to the evil desires you had when you lived in ignorance. (1 Peter 1:4)

Create in me a pure heart, O God, and renew a steadfast spirit within me. (Psalm 51:10)

I can do everything through him who gives me strength. (Philippians 4:13)

> Also:　2 Timothy 2:22　Flee the evil desires.
> Ephesians 4:19　Continual lust for more impurity.
> 1 Corinthians 6:9-11　Washed, sanctified, justified — not included with the wicked any more.
> Titus 2:12　Self-controlled lives.
> Philippians 4:8　The excellent things to think on.

Forgiveness, Divine

Blessed is he whose transgressions are forgiven, whose sins are covered. Blessed is the man whose sin the Lord does not count against him and in whose spirit is no deceit. (Psalm 32:1, 2)

If you, O Lord, kept a record of sins, O Lord, who could stand? But with you there is forgiveness; therefore you are feared. (Psalm 130:3, 4)

If we confess our sins, he is faithful and just and will forgive us our sins and purify us from all unrighteousness. (1 John 1:9)

I write to you, dear children, because your sins have been forgiven on account of his (Jesus') name. (1 John 2:12)

In him (Christ) we have redemption through his blood, the forgiveness of sins, in accordance with the riches of God's grace. (Ephesians 1:7)

Now instead, you ought to forgive and comfort him, so that he will not be overwhelmed by excessive sorrow. I urge you, therefore, to reaffirm your love for him . . . If you forgive anyone, I also forgive him. And what I have forgiven — if there was anything to forgive — I have forgiven in the sight of Christ for your sake. (2 Corinthians 2:7-10) (Office of the Keys)

If you forgive anyone his sins, they are forgiven; if you do not forgive them, they are not forgiven. (John 20:23) (Office of the Keys)

If your brother sins, rebuke him, and if he repents, forgive him. (Luke 17:3) (Office of the Keys)

I tell you the truth, whatever you bind on earth will be bound in heaven, and whatever you loose on earth will be loosed in heaven. (Matthew 18:18) (Office of the Keys)

Forgiveness, Human

For if you forgive men when they sin against you, your heavenly Father will also forgive you. But if you do not forgive men their sins, your father will not forgive your sins. (Matthew 6:14, 15)

This is how my heavenly Father will treat each of you unless you forgive your brother from your heart. (Matthew 18:35)

Get rid of all bitterness, rage and anger, brawling and slander, along with every form of malice. Be kind and compassionate to one another, forgiving each other, just as in Christ God forgave you. (Ephesians 4:31, 32)

Also: Genesis 45 Joseph forgave his brothers their sins done against him.

Gifts, Spiritual

We have different gifts, according to the grace given us. If a man's gift is prophesying, let him use it in proportion to his faith. If it is serving, let him teach; if it is encouraging, let him encourage; if it is contributing to the needs of others, let him give generously; if it is leadership, let him govern diligently; if it is showing mercy, let him do it cheerfully. (Romans 12:6-8)

There are different kinds of gifts, but the same Spirit. There are different kinds of service, but the same Lord. There are different kinds of working, but the same God works all of them in all men. Now to each one the manifestation of the Spirit is given for the common good. To one there is given through the Spirit the message of wisdom, to another the message of knowledge by means of the same Spirit, to another faith by the same Spirit, to another gifts of healing by that one Spirit, to another miraculous powers, to another prophecy, to another the ability to distinguish between spirits, to another the ability to speak in different kinds of tongues, and to still another the interpretation of tongues. All these are the work of one and the same Spirit, and he gives them to each man just as he determines. (1 Corinthians 12:4-11)

Giving, Christian (See also: Sharing with Others; Offerings, Church)

Give, and it will be given to you. A good measure, pressed down, shaken together and running over will be poured over into your lap. For with the measure you use, it will be measured to you. (Luke 6:38)

A generous man will himself be blessed, for he shares his food with the poor. (Proverbs 22:9)

Give to the one who asks you, and do not turn away from the one who wants to borrow from you. (Matthew 5:42)

If your enemy is hungry, feed him; if he is thirsty, give him something to drink. (Romans 12:20)

If anyone has material possessions and sees his brother in need but has no pity on him how can the love of God be in him? (1 John 3:17)

On the first day of every week, each one of you should set aside a sum of money in keeping with his income, saving it up, so that when I come no collections will have to be made. (1 Corinthians 16:2)

Each man should give what he has decided in his heart to give, not reluctantly nor under compulsion, for God loves a cheerful giver. And God is able to make all grace abound to you, so that in all things at all times, having all that you need, you will abound in every good work. (2 Corinthians 9:7)

>   Also: *2 Corinthians 8:3-5*   An example of Christian giving by the Macedonian churches.
>   *Philippians 4:15-19*   An example of Christian giving by the church at Philippi.
>   *Proverbs 11:24-25*   The person who gives is blessed.

Gossip   (Slander — The Eighth Commandment)

You shall not give false testimony against your neighbor. (Exodus 20:16)

Brothers, do not slander one another. Anyone who speaks against his brother or judges him, speaks against the law and judges it. When you judge the law, you are not keeping it, but sitting in judgment on it. (James 4:11)

A perverse man stirs up dissension, and a gossip separates close friends. (Proverbs 16:28)

A gossip betrays a confidence; so avoid a man who talks too much. (Proverbs 20:19)

But now I am writing you that you must not associate with anyone who calls himself a brother but is . . . a slanderer . . . With such a man do not even eat. (1 Corinthians 5:11)

Get rid of all bitterness, rage and anger, brawling and slander, along with every form of malice. (Ephesians 4:31)

Besides they (younger widows) get into the habit of being idle and going about from house to house. Not only do they become idlers, but also gossips and busybodies, saying things they ought not to. (1 Timothy 5:13)

    Also: *1 Corinthians 13:5-7*   What love does.
                  1 Peter 3:8-10   Keeping the tongue from evil.

Greed   (See: Covetousness; also: Worldliness)

Guilt **(Conscience-felt)**

When I kept silent, my bones wasted away through my groaning all the day long. For day and night your hand was heavy upon me; my strength was sapped as in the heat of summer. (Psalm 32:3, 4)

For I know my transgressions, and my sin is always before me . . . Restore to me the joy of your salvation and grant me a willing spirit, to sustain me. (Ps. 51:3, 12)

My Guilt has overwhelmed me like a burden too heavy to bear . . . I am feeble and utterly crushed; I groan in anguish of heart. All my longings lie open before you, O Lord; my sighing is not hidden from you . . . I confess my iniquity; I am troubled by my sin. (Psalm 38:4, 8, 9, 18)

    Also: *Luke 18:9-14 (esp. v. 13)*   The tax collector deeply felt his guilt.
                  Psalm 130   Out of the depths I cry to you, O Lord.

Hate   (See: Revenge)

Home, Christian   (See also: Child/Parents; Husband/Wife; Wife/Husband)

These commandments that I give you today are to be upon your hearts. Impress them on your children. Talk about them when you sit at home and when you walk along the road, when you lie down and when you get up. (Deuteronomy 6:6, 7)

For I have chosen him (Abraham), so that he will direct his children and his household after him to keep the way of the Lord by doing what is right and just so that the Lord will bring about for Abraham what he has promised him. (Genesis 18:19)

But if serving the Lord seems undesirable to you, then choose for yourselves this day whom you will serve, whether the gods your forefathers served beyond the River or the gods of the Amorites in whose land you are living. But as for me and my household we will serve the Lord. (Joshua 24:15)

    Also: *1 Timothy 5:8*   A man must provide for his family.

Homosexuality   (See also: Adultery; Sexual Immorality)

Because of this, God gave them over to shameful lusts. Even their women exchanged natural relations for unnatural ones. In the same way the men also abandoned natural relations with women and were inflamed with lust for one another. Men committed indecent acts with other men, and received in themselves the due penalty for their perversion. (Romans 1:26-27)

Then the Lord said, "The outcry against Sodom and Gomorrah is so great and their sin is so grievous that I will go down and see if what they have done is as bad as the outcry that has reached me. (Genesis 18:20, 21)

Do not lie with a man as one lies with a woman. That is detestable. (Leviticus 18:22)

If a man lies with a man as one lies with a woman, both of them have done what is detestable. They must be put to death; their blood will be upon their heads. (Leviticus 20:13)

Do you not know that the wicked will not inherit the kingdom of God? Do not be deceived: neither the sexually immoral nor idolaters nor adulterers nor male prostitutes nor homosexual offenders will inherit the kingdom of God. And that is what some of you were. But you were washed, you were sanctified, you were justified in the name of the Lord Jesus Christ and by the Spirit of our God. (1 Corinthians 6:9, 10, 11)

"Come now, let us reason together," says the Lord, "though your sins are like scarlet, they shall be as white as snow; though they are red as crimson, they shall be like wool." (Isaiah 1:18)

> Also: *Colossians 1:10, 13, 14*   He has rescued us from the dominion of darkness.
> *1 Corinthians 6:18-20*   Sexual sins are sins against one's own body, the temple of the Holy Spirit.

Humility   (See: Pride)

Husband/Wife   (See also: Home, Christian; Wife/Husband; Adultery)

Husbands, love your wives, just as Christ loved the church and gave himself up for her to make her holy, cleansing her with the washing of water through the Word, and to present her to himself as a radiant church, without stain or wrinkle or any other blemish, but holy and blameless. In this way, husbands ought to love their wives as their own bodies. He who loves his wife loves himself. After all, no one ever hated his own body, but he feeds and cares for it, just as Christ does the church — for we are members of his body. "For this reason a man will leave his father and mother and be united to his wife and the two will become one flesh" . . . However, each one of you also must love his wife as he loves himself, and the wife must respect her husband. (Ephesians 5:25-31, 33)

Husbands, in the same way be considerate as you live with your wives, and treat them with respect as the weaker partner and as heirs with you of the gracious gift of life, so that nothing will hinder your prayers. (1 Peter 3:7)

Husbands, love your wives and do not be harsh with them. (Colossians 3:19)

For this reason a man will leave his father and mother and be united to his wife and the two will be one flesh. So they are no longer two, but one. Therefore what God has joined together, let not man separate . . . I tell you that anyone who divorces his wife, except for marital unfaithfulness and marries another woman commits adultery. (Matthew 19:5, 6, 9)

Marriage should be honored by all, and the marriage bed kept pure, for God will judge the adulterer and all the sexually immoral. (Hebrews 13:4)

Idolatry   (The First Commandment)

You shall have no other gods before me. (Exodus 20:3)

No immoral, impure or greedy person — such a man is an idolater — has any inheritance in the kingdom of Christ and of God. (Ephesians 5:5)

Many live as enemies of the cross of Christ. Their destiny is destruction, their god is their stomach, and their glory is in their shame. Their mind is on earthly things. (Philippians 3:18b, 19)

Put to death, therefore, whatever belongs to your earthly nature: — greed, which is idolatry. (Colossians 3:5)

Therefore, my dear friends, flee from idolatry. (1 Corinthians 10:14)

Love the Lord your God with all your heart and with all your soul and with all your mind. (Matthew 22:37)

Illness   (See also: Discipline of Christians by God)

He forgives all my sins and heals all my diseases. (Psalm 103:3)

Blessed is the man whom God corrects; so do not despise the discipline of the Almighty. For he wounds, but he also binds up; he injuries, but his hands also heal. (Job 5:17-18)

His disciples asked him, "Rabbi, who sinned, this man or his parents, that he was born blind?" "Neither this man nor his parents sinned," said Jesus, "but this happened so that the work of God might be displayed in his life." (John 9:2-3)

Later Jesus found him at the temple and said to him, "See, you are well again. Stop sinning or something worse may happen to you." (John 5:14)

Is any one of you sick? He should call the elders (i.e. pastors) of the church to pray over him and anoint him with oil in the name of the Lord. And the prayer offered in faith will make the sick person well; the Lord will raise him up. If he has sinned, he will be forgiven. (James 5:14, 15)

(Isolation) (of a member by other members in church discipline)

I urge you, brothers, to watch out for those who cause divisions and put obstacles in your way that are contrary to the teaching you have learned. Keep away from them. (Romans 16:17)

But now I am writing you that you must not associate with anyone who calls himself a brother but is sexually immoral or greedy, an idolater or a slanderer, a drunkard or a swindler. With such a man do not even eat. (1 Corinthians 5:11)

Warn a divisive person, and then warn him a second time. After that have nothing to do with him. (Titus 3:10)

If anyone does not obey our instruction in this letter, take special note of him. Do not associate with him, in order that he may feel ashamed. Yet do not regard him as an enemy, but warn him as a brother. (2 Thessalonians 3:14, 15)

Love, Christian   (Brotherliness)

A new commandment I give you: Love one another. As I have loved you so you must love one another. (John 13:34)

Serve one another in love. (Galations 5:13)

Be completely humble and gentle; be patient, bearing with one another in love. Make every effort to keep the unity of the Spirit through the bond of peace . . . Be kind and compassionate to one another, forgiving each other just as in Christ God forgave you. (Ephesians 4:2, 3, 32)

And live a life of love, just as Christ loved us and gave himself up for us as a fragrant offering and sacrifice to God. (Ephesians 5:2)

Dear friends, let us love one another, for love comes from God. Everyone who loves has been born of God and knows God. Whoever does not love does not know God, because God is love. This is how God showed his love among us: He sent his one and only Son into the world so that we might live through him. This is love: not that we loved God, but that he loved us and sent his son as an atoning sacrifice for our sins. Dear friends, since God so loved us, we also ought to love one another. No one has ever seen God; but if we love each other, God lives in us and his love is made complete in us . . . God is love. Whoever lives in love lives in God, and God in him . . . We love because he first loved us. If anyone says, "I love God," yet hates his brother, he is a liar. For anyone who does not love his brother, whom he has seen, cannot love God, whom he has not seen. And he has given us this command: Whoever loves God must also love his brother. (1 John 4:7-12, 16b, 19-21)

Be devoted to one another in brotherly love. Honor one another above yourselves. (Romans 12:10)

And to godliness, brotherly kindness, and to brotherly kindness, love. (2 Peter 1:7)

Lust   (See: Flesh, Works of)

Marriage   (See also: Husband/Wife; Wife/Husband)

So God created man in his own image, in the image of God he created him; male and female he created them. God blessed them and said to them, "Be fruitful and increase in number; fill the earth and subdue it. (Genesis 1:27, 28)

Marriage should be honored by all, and the marriage bed kept pure, for God will judge the adulterer and all the sexually immoral. (Hebrews 13:4)

But since there is so much immorality, each man should have his own wife, and each woman should have her own husband. The husband should fulfill his marital duties to his wife, and likewise the wife to her husband. The wife's body does not belong to her alone but also to her husband. In the same way, the husband's body does not belong to him alone but also to his wife. Do not deprive each other except by mutual consent and for a time, so that you may devote yourselves to prayer. Then come together again so that Satan will not tempt you because of your lack of self-control . . . To the married I give this command (not I, but the Lord): a wife must not separate from her husband. But if she does, she must remain unmarried or else be reconciled to her husband. And her husband must not divorce his wife. (1 Corinthians 7:2-5, 10-13)

   Also: Genesis 2:18-24   God created a helper suitable for man.

Materialism   (See: Worldliness; see also: Money; Covetousness; Idolatry; Rich, The)

Minister (Ministry)   (See: Pastoral Office)

Misuse of God's Name   (The Second Commandment)

You shall not misuse the name of the Lord your God, for the Lord will not hold him guiltless who misuses his name. (Exodus 20:7)

Out of the same mouth come praise and cursing. My brothers, this should not be. (James 3:10)

Bless those who persecute you; bless and do not curse. (Romans 12:14)

Do not swear falsely by my name and so profane the name of your God. I am the Lord. (Leviticus 19:12)

>Also: Matthew 15:7, 8   The hypocrisy of professing faith in God and not having it.
>Deuteronomy 18:10-12   Detestable, devilish practices, including the occult.
>Romans 10:13; Psalm 50:15   Correct uses of God's name.

Money   (See also: Covetousness; Giving, Christian; Idolatry; Rich, The; Stealing)

A generous man will prosper; he who refreshes others will himself be refreshed. (Proverbs 11:25)

No one can serve two masters. Either he will hate the one and love the other, or he will be devoted to the one and despise the other. You cannot serve both God and money. (Matthew 6:24)

Watch out! BE on your guard against all kinds of greed; a man's life does not consist in the abundance of his possessions. (Luke 12:15)

Keep your lives free from the love of money and be content with what you have, because God has said, "Never will I leave you; never will I forsake you." (Hebrews 13:5)

Do you not know that the wicked will not inherit the kingdom of God? Do not be deceived: . . . the greedy (will not) inherit the kingdom of God. (1 Corinthians 6:9-10)

>Also: 1 Timothy 6:6-11   Contentment is gain; love of money is a root of all kinds of evil.
>Luke 12:16-21   The parable of the rich fool.

New Man   (See also: Christian Life)

For in my inner being I delight in God's law. (Romans 7:22)

Therefore we do not lost heart. Though outwardly we are wasting away, yet inwardly we are being renewed day by day. (2 Corinthians 4:16)

Therefore, if anyone is in Christ, he is a new creation; the old has gone, the new has come! All this is from God. (2 Corinthians 5:17-18)

You were taught, with regard to your former way of life, to put off your old self, which is being corrupted by its deceitful desires; to be made new in the attitude of your minds; and to put on the new self created to be like God in true righteousness and holiness. (Ephesians 4:22-24)

    Also: *Colossians 3:1-10 (esp. v. 10)*   Put on the new self.
                    John 3:3-6   Born of the Spirit

New Life in Christ   (See: Christian Life; New Man; Love, Christian)

Offerings, Church   (See also: Giving, Christian; Sharing with Others)

Jesus sat down opposite the place where the offerings were put and watched the crowd putting their money into the temple treasury. Many rich people threw in large amounts. But a poor widow came and put in two very small copper coins, worth only a fraction of a penny. Calling his disciples to him, Jesus said, "I tell you the truth, this poor widow has put more into the treasury than all the others. They all gave out of their wealth; but she, out of her poverty, put in everything — all she had to live on." (Mark 12:41-44)

On the first day of every week, each one of you should set aside a sum of money in keeping with his income. (1 Corinthians 16:2)

Each man should give what he has decided in his heart to give, not reluctantly or under compulsion, for God loves a cheerful giver. (2 Corinthians 9:7)

Even when I was in Thessalonica, you sent me aid again and again when I was in need. Not that I am looking for a gift, but I am looking for what may be credited to your account. (Philippians 4:16-17)

Office of the Keys   (See also: Excommunication; Forgiveness, Divine; Priesthood of Believers)

I will give you the keys of the kingdom of heaven; whatever you bind on earth will be bound in heaven, and whatever you loose on earth will be loosed in heaven. (Matthew 16:19)

And with that he breathed on them and said, "Receive the Holy Spirit. If you forgive anyone his sins, they are forgiven; if you do not forgive them, they are not forgiven. (John 20:22-23)

I tell you the truth, whatever you bind on earth will be bound in heaven, and whatever you loose on earth will be loosed in heaven. Again, I tell you that if two of you on earth agree about anything you ask for, it will be done for you by my Father in heaven. For where two or three come together in my name, there am I with them. (Matthew 18:18-20)

Orderliness   (In the Church)

But everything should be done in a fitting and orderly way. (1 Corinthians 14:40)

Parent/Child   (The Fourth Commandment)   (See also: Home, Christian)

These commandments that I give you today are to be on your hearts. Impress them on your children. Talk about them when you sit at home and when you walk along the road, when you lie down and when you get up. (Deuteronomy 6:6, 7)

Fathers, do not exasperate your children; instead, bring them up in the training and instruction of the Lord. (Ephesians 6:4)

Fathers, do not embitter your children or they will become discouraged. (Colossians 3:21)

He who spares the rod hates his son, but he who loves him is careful to discipline him. (Proverbs 13:24)

    Also: *2 Timothy 3:15*   The child, Timothy, instructed in Scripture.
                 Genesis 18:19   Abraham's example of directing his children.

Pastoral Office   (See also: Word of God, Hearing the; Word of God, Preaching the)

Here is a trustworthy saying: If anyone sets his heart on being an overseer, he desires a noble task. (1 Timothy 3:1)

Guard yourselves and all the flock of which the Holy Spirit has made you overseers. Be shepherds of the church of God, which he bought with his own blood. (Acts 20:28)

It was he who gave some to be apostles, some to be prophets, some to be evangelists, and some to be pastors and teachers, to prepare God's people for works of service. (Ephesians 4:11, 12)

Guard yourselves and all the flock of which the Holy Spirit has made you overseers. Be shepherds of the church of God. (Acts 20:28)

Be shepherds of God's flock that is under your care, serving as overseers — not because you must, but because you are willing, as God wants you to be. (1 Peter 5:2-3)

The elders who direct the affairs of the church well are worthy of double honor, especially those whose work is preaching and teaching. (1 Timothy 5:17)

Now we ask you, brothers, to respect those who work hard among you, who are over you in the Lord and who admonish you. Hold them in the highest regard in love because of their work. (1 Thessalonians 5:12-13)

Remember your leaders, who spoke the Word of God to you. Consider the outcome of their way of life and imitate their faith . . . Obey your leaders and submit to their authority. They keep watch over you as men who must give an account. Obey them so that their work will be a joy, not a burden, for that would be of no advantage to you. (Hebrews 13:7, 17)

Do not entertain an accusation against an elder (i.e. pastor) unless it is brought by two or three witnesses. (1 Timothy 5:19)

Patience   (See: Self-Control)

Peace With God

Peace I leave with you; my peace I give you. I do not give to you as the world gives. Do not let your hearts be troubled and do not be afraid. (John 14:27)

Therefore, since we have been justified through faith, we have peace with God through our Lord Jesus Christ. (Romans 5:1)

And the peace of God, which transcends all understanding, will guard your hearts and your minds in Christ Jesus. (Philippians 4:7)

Peace With One Another

If it is possible, as far as it depends on you, live at peace with everyone . . . Do not be overcome by evil, but overcome evil with good. (Romans 12:18, 21)

Let us therefore make every effort to do what leads to peace and to mutual edification. (Romans 14:19)

Let the peace of Christ rule in your hearts, since as members of one body you were called to peace. (Colossians 3:15)

Make every effort to live in peace with all men and to be holy; without holiness no one will see the Lord. (Hebrews 12:14)

Blessed are the peacemakers, for they will be called sons of God. (Matthew 5:9)

Peacemakers   (See: Peace With One Another)

Prayer

I tell you the truth, my Father will give you whatever you ask in my name. (John 16:23)

Ask and it will be given to you; seek and you will find; knock and the door will be opened to you. (Matthew 7:7)

Pray continually. (1 Thessalonians 5:17)

I urge, then, first of all, that requests, prayers, intercession, and thanksgiving be made for everyone. (1 Timothy 2:1)

Do not be anxious about anything, but in everything, by prayer and petition, with thanksgiving, present your requests to God. (Philippians 4:6)

For the eyes of the Lord are on the righteous and his ears are attentive to their prayer, but the face of the Lord is against those who do evil. (1 Peter 3:12)

This is the assurance we have in approaching God: that if we ask anything according to his will, he hears us. (1 John 5:14)

Call upon me in the day of trouble; I will deliver you, and you will honor me. (Psalm 50:15)

    Also: *James 1:6, 7* Prayer must be an act of faith. Doubt destroys its effectiveness.

Preaching   (See: Word of God, Preaching the)

Pride

Pride goes before destruction, a haughty spirit before a fall. (Proverbs 16:18)

Clothe yourselves with humility toward one another, because, "God opposes the proud but gives grace to the humble." Humble yourselves, therefore, under God's mighty hand. (1 Peter 5:5-6)

To fear the Lord is to hate evil; I hate pride and arrogance, evil behavior and perverse speech. (Proverbs 8:13)

When pride comes, then comes disgrace, but with humility comes wisdom. (Proverbs 11:2)

Pride only breeds quarrels, but wisdom is found in those who take advice. (Proverbs 13:10)

Before his downfall a man's heart is proud, but humility comes before honor. (Proverbs 18:12)

... he may become conceited and fall under the same judgment as the devil. (1 Timothy 3:6b)

Priesthood of Believers   (See also: Office of the Keys)

But you are a chosen people, a royal priesthood, a holy nation, a people belonging to

God, that you may declare the praises of him who called you out of darkness into his wonderful light. (1 Peter 2:9)

And has made us to be a kingdom and priests to serve his God and Father — to him be glory and power forever and ever! Amen. (Revelation 1:6)

But in your hearts set apart Christ as Lord. Always be prepared to give a reason for the hope that you have. (1 Peter 3:15)

    Also: Acts 1:8, 2:1-33   The Holy Spirit is given to the believers as Christ's witnesses.

Quarreling (Factions)   (See also: Divisiveness; Peace With One Another)

Starting a quarrel is like breeching a dam; so drop the matter before a dispute breaks out. (Proverbs 17:14)

It is to a man's honor to avoid strife, but every fool is quick to quarrel. (Proverbs 20:3)

Keep reminding them of these things. Warn them before God against quarreling about words; it is of no value, and only ruins those who listen. (2 Timothy 2:14)

Bear with each other and forgive whatever grievances you may have against one another. Forgive as the Lord forgave you. (Colossians 3:13)

I appeal to you, brothers, in the name of our Lord Jesus Christ, that all of you agree with one another so that there may be no divisions among you and that you may be perfectly united in mind and thought. (1 Corinthians 1:10)

You are still worldly. For since there is jealousy and quarreling among you, are you not worldly? Are you not acting like mere men? (1 Corinthians 3:3)

Redemption (Salvation)

(Jesus Christ) entered the Most Holy Place once for all by his own blood, having obtained eternal redemption. (Hebrews 9:12)

To (Jesus Christ) who loves us and has freed us from our sins by his blood ... to him be glory and power for ever and ever! Amen. (Revelation 1:5, 6)

In whom (Christ) we have redemption through his blood, the forgiveness of sins, in accordance with the riches of God's grace. (Ephesians 1:7)

But he was pierced for our transgressions, he was crushed for our iniquities; the punishment that brought us peace was upon him, and by his wounds we are healed. (Isaiah 53:5)

The Son of Man did not come to be served, but to serve, and to give his life a ransom for many. (Matthew 20:28)

The blood of Jesus his Son, purifies us from every sin. (1 John 1:7)

He is the atoning sacrifice for our sins, and not only for ours but also for the sins of the whole world. (1 John 2:2)

Christ died for sins once for all, the righteous for the unrighteous, to bring you to God. (1 Peter 3:18)

Christ redeemed us from the curse of the law by becoming a curse for us, for it is written: "Cursed is everyone who is hung on a tree." (Galations 3:13)

Our Savior, Christ Jesus . . . has destroyed death and has brought life and immortality to light through the gospel. (2 Timothy 1:10)

O Israel, put your hope in the Lord, for with the Lord is unfailing love and with him is full redemption. He himself will redeem Israel from all their sins. (Psalm 130:7, 8)

Therefore, there is now no condemnation for those who are in Christ Jesus. (Romans 8:1)

Also: *1 Peter 1:18, 19*   Redeemed with the precious blood of Christ.

Repentance   (See also: Confession of Sin to God; Guilt)

I confess my iniquity; I am troubled by my sin. (Psalm 38:18)

Against you, you only have I sinned and done what is evil in your sight . . . Let me hear joy and gladness; let the bones you have crushed rejoice. Hide your face from my sins and blot out all my iniquity . . . The sacrifices of God are a broken spirit; a broken and contrite heart, O God, you will not despise. (Psalm 51:4, 8, 9, 17)

Godly sorrow brings repentance that leads to salvation and leaves no regret, but worldly sorrow brings death. (2 Corinthians 7:10)

The son said to him, "Father, I have sinned against heaven and against you. I am no longer worthy to be called your son." (Luke 15:21)

Repentance and forgiveness of sins will be preached in his name to all nations. (Luke 24:47)

Repent, then, and turn to God, so that your sins may be wiped out, that times of refreshing may come from the Lord. (Acts 3:19)

(God) commands all people everywhere to repent. (Acts 17:30)

Repent! Turn away from all your offenses; then sin will not be your downfall. (Ezekiel 18:30)

"As surely as I live," declares the Sovereign Lord, "I take no pleasure in the death of the wicked, but rather that they turn from their ways and live. Turn! Turn from your evil ways! Why will you die, O house of Israel?" (Ezekiel 33:11)

Rend your heart and not your garments. Return to the Lord your God, for he is gracious and compassionate, slow to anger and abounding in love." (Joel 2:13)

I have declared to both Jews and Greeks that they must turn to God in repentance and have faith in our Lord Jesus. (Acts 20:21)

    Also: Matthew 18:15   Work to bring your brother to repentance.
                  Acts 26:20   People should repent and prove it by their deeds.
                  2 Corinthians 2:7   Forgive the repentant lest he despair.

Reproof of Sin   (See also: Admonishment (One Christian of Another))

Like an earring of gold or an ornament of fine gold is a wise man's rebuke to a listening ear. (Prov. 25:12)

If your brother sins, rebuke him, and if he repents, forgive him. (Luke 17:3)

Those who sin are to be rebuked publicly, so that the others may take warning. (1 Timothy 5:20)

All Scripture is God-breathed and is useful for teaching, rebuking, correction and training in righteousness. (2 Timothy 3:16)

Do not regard him as an enemy, but warn him as a brother. (2 Thessalonians 3:15)

Preach the Word; be prepared in season and out of season; correct, rebuke and encourage — with great patience and careful instruction. (2 Timothy 4:2)

    Also: Isaiah 59:2   The terrible effect of unrepented sin.

Resurrection

Because I live, you also will live. (John 14:19)

I am the resurrection and the life. He who believes in me will live, even though he dies. (John 11:25)

For as in Adam all die, so in Christ all will be made alive. But each in his own turn: Christ, the firstfruits; then, when he comes, those who belong to him . . . For the trumpet will sound, the dead will be raised imperishable, and we will be changed. (1 Corinthians 15:22, 23, 52)

My Father's will is that everyone who looks to the Son and believes in him shall have eternal life, and I will raise him up at the last day. (John 6:40)

(The Lord Jesus Christ) will transform our lowly bodies so that they will be like his glorious body. (Philippians 3:21b)

Revenge   (Vengeance — The Fifth Commandment)

You shall not murder. (Exodus 20:13)

"If it is possible as far as it depends on you, live at peace with everyone. Do not take revenge, my friends, but leave room for God's wrath, for it is written: "It is mine to avenge; I will repay," says the Lord . . . Do not be overcome by evil, but overcome evil with good. (Romans 12:18-21)

Get rid of all bitterness, rage and anger, brawling and slander, along with every form of malice. Be kind and compassionate to one another, forgiving each other, just as in Christ God forgave you. (Ephesians 4:31, 32)

Make sure that nobody pays back wrong for wrong, but always try to be kind to each other and to everyone else. (1 Thessalonians 5:15)

When they hurled their insults at (Jesus), he did not retaliate; when he suffered, he made no threats. (1 Peter 2:23)

    Also: *1 Peter 3:9*   Repay evil with blessing.
                  1 John 3:15   To hate is to murder.

Rich, The   (See also: Covetousness; Giving, Christian; Money)

But remember the Lord your God, for it is he who gives you the ability to produce wealth. (Deuteronomy 8:18)

Watch out! Be on your guard against all kinds of greed; a man's life does not consist in the abundance of his possessions. (Luke 12:15)

    Also: *Luke 12:16-21*   The parable of the rich fool.
                  1 Timothy 6:9-10, 17-19   The peril of loving money, of wanting to be rich.
                  Psalm 49 and Psalm 52:7   Those who trust in riches.

Self-Control   (The Fifth Commandment)

A gentle answer turns away wrath, but a harsh word stirs up anger. The tongue of the wise commends knowledge, but the mouth of the fool gushes folly. (Proverbs 15:12)

Better a patient man than a warrior, a man who controls his temper than one who takes a city. (Proverbs 16:32)

A man's wisdom gives him patience; it is his glory to overlook an offense. (Proverbs 19:11)

Like a city whose walls are broken down is a man who lacks self-control. (Proverbs 25:28)

A fool gives full vent to his anger, but a wise man keeps himself under control. (Proverbs 29:11)

>Also: *2 Timothy 4:2*   Preaching the word with great patience.
>*Psalm 37:7*   Waiting patiently for God to act.

Service   (Work Done for God)

Always give yourselves fully to the work of the Lord, because you know that your labor in the Lord is not in vain. (1 Corinthians 15:58b)

For it is God who works in you to will and to act according to his good purpose. (Philippians 2:13)

I tell you the truth, anyone who gives you a cup of water in my name because you belong to Christ will certainly not lose his reward. (Mark 9:41)

Therefore, I urge you, brothers, in view of God's mercy, to offer your bodies as living sacrifices, holy and pleasing to God — which is your spiritual worship. (Romans 12:1)

So you also, when you have done everything you were told to do, should say, "We are unworthy servants; we have only done our duty." (Luke 17:10)

>Also: *Colossians 3*   Various ways in which to serve God.

Sexual Immorality (Sixth Commandment)   (See also: Adultery; Homosexuality)

The acts of the sinful nature are obvious: sexual immorality, impurity and debauchery... I warn you, as I did before, that those who live like this will not inherit the kingdom of God. (Galations 5:19, 21b)

For out of the heart come evil thoughts, murder, adultery, sexual immorality, theft, false testimony, slander. These are what make a man "unclean". (Matthew 15:19)

I have written you in my letter not to associate with sexually immoral people... But now I am writing you that you must not associate with anyone who calls himself a brother but is sexually immoral... With such a man do not even eat. (1 Corinthians 5:9)

Do you not know that the wicked will not inherit the kingdom of God? Do not be deceived: Neither the sexually immoral nor idolaters nor adulterers nor male prostitutes nor homosexual offenders . . . will inherit the kingdom of God . . . Flee from sexual immorality. All other sins a man commits are outside his body, but he who sins sexually sins against his own body. (1 Corinthians 6:9-10, 18)

We should not commit sexual immorality, as some of them did — and in one day twenty-three thousand of them died. (1 Corinthians 10:8)

I will be grieved over many who have sinned earlier and have not repented of the impurity, sexual sin and debauchery in which they have indulged. (2 Corinthians 12:21)

Let us behave decently, as in the daytime, not in orgies and drunkenness, not in sexual immorality, not in dissension and jealousy. Rather clothe yourselves with the Lord Jesus Christ, and do not think about how to gratify the desires of the sinful nature. (Romans 13:13-14)

Dear friends, I urge you, as aliens and strangers in the world, to abstain from sinful desires, which war against your soul. (1 Peter 2:11)

    Also: Ephesians 5:3-5   Not even a hint of sexual immorality.
               1 Thessalonians 4:3-5   One must avoid sexual immorality; be in control.

Sharing with Others   (See also: Giving, Christian; Offerings, Church)

Share with God's people who are in need. Practice hospitality. (Romans 12:13)

Therefore, as we have opportunity, let us do good to all people, especially to those who belong to the family of believers. (Galations 6:10)

Give to the one who asks you, and do not turn away from the one who wants to borrow from you. (Matthew 5:42)

Command them (i.e. the rich) to do good, to be rich in good deeds, and to be generous and willing to share. (1 Timothy 6:18)

And do not forget to do good and to share with others, for with such sacrifices God is pleased. (Hebrews 13:16)

If anyone has material possessions and sees his brother in need but has no pity on him, how can the love of God be in him? Dear children, let us not love with words or tongue but with actions and in truth. (1 John 3:17-18)

Sin   (See also: Confession of Sin; Flesh, Works of; Guilt)

Never again will I curse the ground because of man, even though every inclination of his heart is evil from childhood. (Genesis 8:21)

There is not a righteous man on earth who does what is right and never sins. (Ecclesiastes 7:20)

Surely I have been a sinner from birth, sinful from the time my mother conceived me. (Psalm 51:5)

Flesh gives birth to flesh, but the Spirit gives birth to spirit. (John 3:6)

Therefore, just as sin entered the world through one man, and death through sin, and in this way death came to all men, because all sinned. (Romans 5:12)

I know that nothing good lives in me, that is, in my sinful nature (flesh). (Romans 7:18)

All of us also lived among them at one time, gratifying the cravings of our sinful nature and following its desires and thoughts. Like the rest, we were objects of wrath. (Ephesians 2:3)

    Also: 1 Corinthians 10:13   God delivers out of temptation.
                1 John 1:8-10   When we confess our sins, God forgives us.

Slander   (See: Gossip)

Stealing (The Seventh Commandment)   (See also: Covetousness; Money, Rich, The)

You shall not steal. (Exodus 20:15)

Do not use dishonest standards for measuring length, weight or quanity. (Leviticus 19:35)

The wicked borrow and do not repay but the righteous give generously. (Psalm 37:21)

Look! The wages you failed to pay the workmen who mowed your fields are crying out against you. The cries of the harvesters have reached the ears of the Lord Almighty. (James 5:4)

He who has been stealing must steal no longer, but must work, doing something useful with his own hands, that he might have something to share with those in need. (Ephesians 4:28)

But godliness with contentment is great gain. For we brought nothing into the world, and we can take nothing out of it . . . For the love of money is a root of all kinds of evil. (1 Timothy 6:6-7, 10)

Stewardship   (See also: Service (Work))

Now it is required that those who have been given a trust must prove faithful. (1 Corinthians 4:2)

Each one should use whatever gift he has received to serve others, faithfully administering God's grace in its various forms. (1 Peter 4:10)

> Also: Matthew 25:14-28   The Master settles accounts. Two kinds of stewards: faithful and unfaithful.
> Luke 17:10   No cause to boast about doing one's duty before God.

Suicide   (See also: Discipline (Of Christians by God); Illness; Worry)

Do you see a man wise in his own eyes? There is more hope for a fool than for him. (Proverbs 26:12)

I know, O Lord, that a man's life is not his own; it is not for man to direct his steps. (Jeremiah 10:23)

Do you not know that your body is a temple of the Holy Spirit, who is in you, whom you have received from God? You are not your own; you were bought at a price. Therefore honor God with your body. (1 Corinthians 6:19)

But I trust in you, O Lord; I say, "You are my God." My times are in your hands. (Psalm 31:14-15)

The Lord is a refuge for the oppressed, a stronghold in times of trouble. Those who know your name will trust in you, for you, Lord have never forsaken those who seek you. (Psalm 9:9-10)

Why are you downcast, O my soul? Why so disturbed within me? Put your hope in God, for I will yet praise him, my Savior and my God. (Psalm 42:11)

For this God is our God for ever and ever; he will be our guide even to the end. (Psalm 48:14)

But I call to God, and the Lord saves me. Evening, morning and noon I cry out in distress, and he hears my voice . . . Cast your cares on the Lord and he will sustain you; he will never let the righteous fall . . . But as for me, I trust you. (Psalm 55:16, 17, 22, 23c)

My soul finds rest in God alone; my salvation comes from him. He alone is my rock and my salvation; he is my fortress, I will never be shaken. (Psalm 62:1-2)

"Because he loves me," says the Lord, "I will rescue him; I will protect him, for he acknowledges my name. He will call upon me, and I will answer him; I will be with him in trouble, I will deliver him and honor him. With long life will I satisfy him and show him my salvation." (Psalm 91:14-16)

He gives strength to the weary and increases the power of the weak. (Isaiah 40:29)

No temptation has seized you except what is common to man. And God is faithful; he will not let you be tempted beyond what you can bear. But when you are tempted, he will also provide a way out so that you can stand up under it. (1 Corinthians 10:13)

Blessed is the man who perseveres under trial, because when he has stood the test, he will receive the crown of life that God has promised to those who love him. (James 1:12)

Listen to me, O house of Jacob, all you who remain of the house of Israel, you whom I have upheld since you were conceived, and have carried since your birth. Even to your old age and gray hairs I am he, I am he who will sustain you. I have made you and I will carry you; I will sustain you and I will rescue you. (Isaiah 46:3-4)

Therefore do not worry about tomorrow, for tomorrow will worry about itself. Each day has enough trouble of its own. (Matthew 6:34)

Do not let your hearts be troubled (Jesus said). Trust in God; trust also in me. (John 14:1)

Cast all your anxiety on him because he cares for you. (1 Peter 5:7)

You shall not murder. (Exodus 20:13)

You know that no murderer has eternal life in him. (1 John 3:15b)

For out of the heart come evil thoughts, murder, etc. (Matthew 15:19)

Temper   (See: Anger, Self-control; Revenge; Flesh, Works of; Patience)

Unbelief

Whoever does not believe will be condemned. (Mark 16:16b)

But whoever disowns me before men, I will disown him before my Father in heaven. (Matthew 10:33)

Whoever does not believe stands condemned already because he has not believed in the name of God's one and only Son ... Whoever rejects the Son will not see life, for God's wrath remains on him. (John 3:18b, 36b)

There is a judge for the one who rejects me and does not accept my Words; that very Word that I spoke will condemn him at the last day. (John 12:48)

Even denying the sovereign Lord who bought them — bringing swift destruction on themselves. (2 Peter 2:1)

Weak Brother

Be careful, however, that the exercise of your freedom does not become a stumbling block to the weak. (1 Corinthians 8:9)

Encourage the timid, help the weak, be patient with everyone. (1 Thessalonians 5:14b)

Accept him whose faith is weak, without passing judgment on disputable matters. One man's faith allows him to eat everything, but another man, whose faith is weak, eats only vegetables. (Romans 14:1-2)

We who are strong ought to bear with the failings of the weak and not to please ourselves. (Romans 15:1)

Widows

Religion that God our Father accepts as pure and faultless is this: to look after orphans and widows in their distress and to keep oneself from being polluted by the world. (James 1:27)

Wife/Husband   (See also: Adultery; Husband/Wife; Marriage)

Better to live in a desert than with a quarrelsome and ill-tempered wife. (Proverbs 21:19)

Wives, submit to your husbands as to the Lord. For the husband is the head of the wife as Christ is the head of the church, his body, of which he is the Savior. Now as the church submits to Christ, so also wives should submit to their husbands in everything . . . the wife must respect her husband. (Ephesians 5:22-24, 33b)

    Also: *1 Peter 3:1-4*   What a wife's true beauty consists in.
               Proverbs 31:10-31   The wife praised by her husband and family.

He who finds a wife finds what is good and receives favor from the Lord. (Proverbs 18:22)

Houses and wealth are inherited from parents, but a prudent wife is from the Lord. (Proverbs 19:14)

Word of God, Hearing the obeying the

But what was sown on good soil is the man who hears the Word and understands it. He produces a crop, yielding a hundred, sixty or thirty times what was sown. (Matthew 13:23)

Blessed rather are those who hear the Word of God and obey it. (Luke 11:28)

They devoted themselves to the apostles' teaching and to the fellowship, to the breaking of bread and to prayer. (Acts 2:42)

He who belongs to God hears what God says. The reason you do not hear is that you do not belong to God. (John 8:47)

Let the Word of Christ dwell in you richly as you teach and admonish one another with all wisdom, and as you sing psalms, hymns and spiritual songs with gratitude in your hearts to God. (Colossians 3:16)

Watch your life and doctrine closely. Persevere in them, because if you do, you will save both yourself and your hearers. (1 Timothy 4:16)

Therefore, get rid of all moral filth and the evil that is so prevalent, and humbly accept the word planted in you, which can save you. Do not merely listen to the word, and so deceive yourselves. Do what it says. (James 1:21-22)

And we have the word of the prophets made more certain, and you will do well to pay attention to it, as to a light shining in a dark place, until the day dawns and the morning star rises in your hearts. (2 Peter 1:19)

Word of God Works in the Believer

Sanctify them by the truth; your Word is truth. (John 17:17)

But what was sown on good soil is the man who hears the Word and understands it. He produces a crop, yielding a hundred, sixty or thirty times what was sown. (Matthew 13:23)

(The two disciples of Emmaus) asked each other, "Were not our hearts burning within us while he talked with us on the road and opened the Scriptures to us? (Luke 24:32)

Now I commit you to God and to the Word of his grace, which can build you up and give you an inheritance among all those who are sanctified. (Acts 20:32)

... When you received the Word of God, which you heard from us, you accepted it not as the word of men, but as it actually is, the Word of God, which is at work in you who believe. (1 Thessalonians 2:13)

All Scripture is God-breathed and is useful for teaching, rebuking, correcting and training in righteousness, so that the man of God may be thoroughly equipped for every good work. (2 Timothy 3:16-17)

Like newborn babies, crave pure spiritual milk, so that by it you may grow up in your salvation, now that you have tasted that the Lord is good. (1 Peter 2:2-3)

Word of God, Preaching the (See also: Church and Communion Attendance;

Word of God Works in the Believer; Word of God, Hearing and Obeying the)

Teaching them to obey everything I have commanded you. (Matthew 28:20a)

At once he began to preach in the synagogues that Jesus is the Son of God. (Acts 9:20)

We preach Christ crucified. (1 Corinthians 1:23)

How, then, can they call on the one they have not believed in? And how can they believe in the one of whom they have not heard? And how can they hear without someone preaching to them? (Romans 10:14)

Preach the Word; be prepared in season and out of season; correct, rebuke and encourage — with great patience and careful instruction. (2 Timothy 4:2)

But the Word of the Lord stands forever. And this is the Word that was preached to you. (1 Peter 1:25)

Now to him who is able to establish you by my gospel and the proclamation of Jesus Christ . . . (Romans 16:25)

And repentance and forgiveness of sins will be preached in his name to all nations. (Luke 24:47)

. . . He had the eternal gospel to proclaim to those who live on the earth. (Revelation 14:6)

Work-righteousness (See also: Faith; Forgiveness, Divine; Redemption; Sin; Unbelief; Christian Life)

This righteousness from God comes through faith in Jesus Christ to all who believe. There is no difference for all have sinned and fall short of the glory of God . . . For we maintain that a man is justified by faith apart from observing the law. (Romans 3:22-23, 28)

However, to the man who does not work but trusts God who justifies the wicked, his faith is credited as righteousness. (Romans 4:5)

Since they did not know the righteousness that comes from God and sought to establish their own, they did not submit to God's righteousness. Christ is the end of the law so that there may be righteousness for everyone who believes. (Romans 10:3-4)

And if by grace, then it is no longer by works; if it were, grace would no longer be grace. (Romans 11:6)

You who are trying to be justified by law have been alienated from Christ; you have fallen away from grace. (Galations 5:4)

For it is by grace you have been saved, through faith — and this not from yourselves, it is the gift of God — not by works, so that no one can boast. (Ephesians 2:8-9)

He saved us, not because of righteous things we had done, but because of his mercy. (Titus 3:5)

> Also: Luke 18:9-14   The parable of the Pharisee (who trusted in his works), and the tax collector (who was justified by faith).

Worldliness   (See also: Christian Life, The; Contentment; Covetousness; Idolatry; Flesh, Works of; Money)

Do not store up for yourselves treasures on earth . . . But store up for yourselves treasures in heaven . . . For where your treasure is, there your heart will be also . . . So do not worry, saying, "What shall we eat?" or "What shall we drink?" or "What shall we wear?" For the pagans run after all these things, and your heavenly Father knows that you need them. But seek first his kingdom and his righteousness, and all these things will be given to you as well. Therefore do not worry about tomorrow . . . (Matthew 6:19a, 20a, 21, 31-34a)

Be careful, or your hearts will be weighed down with dissipation, drunkenness and the anxieties of life, and that day will close on you unexpectedly like a trap. (Luke 21:34)

But the worries of this life, the deceitfulness of wealth and the desires for other things come in and choke the Word, making it unfruitful. (Mark 4:19)

Their destiny is destruction, their god is their stomach, and their glory is in their shame. Their mind is on earthly things. (Philippians 3:19)

Set your minds on things above, not on earthly things. (Colossians 3:2)

Do not love the world or anything in the world. If anyone loves the world, the love of the Father is not in him. For everything in the world — the cravings of sinful man, the lust of his eyes and the boasting of what he has and does — comes not from the Father but from the world. The world and its desires pass away, but the man who does the will of God lives forever. (1 John 2:15-17)

Demas, because he loved this world, has deserted me. (2 Timothy 4:10)

What was sown among the thorns is the man who hears the Word, but the worries of this life and the deceitfulness of wealth choke it, making it unfruitful. (Matthew 13:22)

Do not conform any longer to the pattern of this world, but be transformed by the renewing of your mind. (Romans 12:2)

Worry   (Anxiety)   (See also: Worldliness; Suicide; Discipline (Of Christians by God))

A cheerful heart is good medicine, but a crushed spirit dries up the bones. (Proverbs 17:22)

Do not be anxious about anything, but in everything, by prayer and petition, with thanksgiving, present your requests to God. And the peace of God, which transcends all understanding, will guard your hearts and your minds in Christ Jesus. (Philippians 4:6-7)

Humble yourselves, therefore, under God's mighty hand, that he may lift you up in due time. Cast all your anxiety on him because he cares for you. (1 Peter 5:6-7)

    Also: *Matthew 6:25-34*   Don't worry about tomorrow.

Worship, Public   (See also: Church and Communion Attendance; Word of God, Hearing the; Word of God, Preaching the)

I will declare your name to my brothers; in the congregation I will praise you. (Psalm 22:22)

Ascribe to the Lord the glory due his name; worship the Lord in the splendor of his holiness. (Psalm 29:2)

Come, let us sing for joy to the Lord; let us shout aloud to the Rock of our salvation. Let us come before him with thanksgiving and extol him with music and song. (Psalm 95:6)

Let the Word of Christ dwell in you richly as you teach and admonish one another with all wisdom, and as you sing psalms, hymns and spiritual songs with gratitude in your hearts to God. (Colossians 3:16)

Every day they continued to meet together in the temple courts. They broke bread in their homes and ate together with glad and sincere hearts, praising God. (Acts 2:46-47a)

ADDENDUM FIVE

SAMPLE LETTERS

LETTER #1:

To the member who has not attended church for the past month:

Dear _____ ,

We have missed seeing you at the house of God these past weeks and are writing you this brief note to let you know. (Of course, there is always the possibility that we simply overlooked you in the crowd — and if that is the case, accept our apologies. Also remind us of it.)

When a brother or sister is absent from the services it could be a matter of sickness, work or vacation that has legitimately kept him away. When there is a reason for a member's absence we — the pastor and board of elders — like to know. It is our duty and privilege to care about, and care for, *all* the members of the congregation. You are precious to us, as you are to the Lord himself.

In case there is sickness or hardship in the family, we especially want to know so that we can offer our help and our prayers. And we would urge you to contact the pastor immediately to discuss the matter with him.

Of course, it is always possible for God's children to lose some of their zeal to hear God's Word preached, to worship their loving God and to fellowship with the other saints. It is so easy for the cares, the pleasures, the busyness of life itself to interfer with heart and soul activities. Where this is the case we can only recommend the remedial action of returning at once to the house of God to hear his Word and receive the Sacrament, which alone can make one's faith and love burn hot again.

We hope that nothing of a serious matter — either physical or spiritual — has developed in your life to keep you from exercising your rights and privileges as a member of _____ Lutheran congregation. We are looking forward to enjoying your fellowship in the near future.

Blessed . . . are those who hear the Word of God and obey it. (Luke 11:28)

Yours in the Service of Our Savior,

Chairman of the board of elders   Pastor

† † † † † †

LETTER #2:

To the communicant who has not availed himself of the Lord's Supper during the first quarter of the year:

Dear _____ ,

    Your individual communion record indicates that you have not availed yourself of the Lord's Supper during the first quarter of this year. Perhaps unavoidable circumstances kept you away. Perhaps you simply forgot to hand in your announcement card so that your receipt of the Sacrament did not show up on your record. (If this is the case, please hand a communion card to the pastor with a record of the months that you communed.)

    In the Sacrament we receive with bread and wine the very things with which Christ purchased forgiveness and salvation for us sinners: his body and blood. Thus the Sacrament seals forgiveness of sins, life and salvation to us.

    Until Christ returns to take us believers home to heaven, our receiving his body and blood in the Sacrament recalls the sacrificial death he died for us and, therefore, besides assuring us of forgiveness, also renews and strengthens our faith and gives us the power and zeal to live a holy life.

    Many of our people receive the Lord's Supper regularly, thus receiving on a regular basis the wonderful blessings that it bestows. But whenever our people fail to commune they deprive themselves of these faith-life blessings. We urge you, therefore, to begin making preparation now to receive the Sacrament when next it is celebrated, which is Sunday _____(date)_____.

    Should there be some reason, unknown to us, why you have not been able to celebrate the Sacrament together with the congregation, please make arrangements to discuss it with the pastor soon.

> *"This is my body which is for you; do this in remembrance of me . . . This cup is the new covenant in my blood; do this, whenever you drink it, in remembrance of me."* *For whenever you eat this bread and drink this cup, you proclaim the Lord's death until he comes. (1 Cor. 11:24-26)*

Yours in the Service of Our Savior,

_____   _____
Chairman of the board of elders   Pastor

† † † † † †

LETTER #3:

To the delinquent, announcing a forth-coming visit by the elder:

Dear _____ ,

We are concerned about your relationship with God and with his church. Recall that we had contacted you by letter a few weeks ago to tell you that we missed sharing God's Word and Christian fellowship with you, and urged you to return at once to the house of God. We stated, in closing our letter, that we were looking forward to enjoying your fellowship in the near future.

What a weekly disappointment it has been to us, to look for you in vain in the congregation. God wants to be worshiped — has commanded that we worship him — and looks for each of his believers in the assembly of worshipers. When God's saints meet on Sunday morning to worship him, you are not there. How this grieves both God and us. Bear in mind that public worship is outward evidence of a heart that praises God. Think what we receive from him that makes us want to praise him: chief of which is his love, his forgiveness, the hope of salvation — all of which come to us through Jesus Christ.

Failure to participate in public worship — unless, of course, there are extenuating circumstances that make it impossible to participate — would indicate that a faith-problem exists. It is our privilege and duty to help find the solution to the problem. Whatever is burdening you at this time is ours to share with you. God wants us to love and care for one another, and this includes offering Christian admonishment when it is needed. In this spirit, the elder assigned to your watch care, Mr. _____ , will be visiting you in the near future. Please welcome him and feel that you can communicate freely with him.

And let us consider how we may spur one another on toward love and good deeds. (Heb. 10:24)

Yours in the Service of Our Savior,

_____   _____
Chairman of the board of elders   Pastor

Phone _____   Phone _____

† † † † † †

LETTER #4:

To communicants who have moved away: To encourage them to immediately find a church and request a transfer to it: (#1 of series)

> *All except the apostles were scattered throughout Judea and Samaria . . . Those who had been scattered preached the Word wherever they went. (Acts 8:1b, 4)*

Dear Mr. and Mrs. _____,*(name of children who are communicants also)*

    We send you greetings in behalf of your fellow saints at _____ Lutheran congregation. We were sorry to see you leave our area and now that you are gone we miss your fellowship. We pray that everything is working out well for you in your new home (and in your new job). The first month or so can be hectic and generally very trying.

    It should be a source of great comfort and encouragement to remember that the Lord has promised: "Never will I leave you; never will I forsake you" (Heb. 13:5). God is truly with you, and he will fulfill your trust by guiding and protecting you and blessing you in countless ways. And you will surely want to return your thanks and praise to him by worshipping him with other Christians at a church of our fellowship in your new community. In all your busyness, do take time to find one of our churches and begin immediately to participate in public worship and to receive the Lord's Supper. Settle into a church even while you are settling into your new home. For your convenience we are listing below the churches of our fellowship that are in, or nearest to, the community in which you now live. Also the names and phone numbers of the pastors:

    You will note that we began our letter with a quote from St. Luke's Acts of the Apostles. He told about the early Christians at Jerusalem who were forced to move from their homes and their community (Jerusalem) and take up residence in far-flung regions. They, too, were Christians on the move. And what marvelous examples they left the Christian church of all times. When they moved, they took their religion, their Lord, their hope of salvation, their love of the gospel with them. They not only gathered for worship wherever they moved, they even testified to their new neighbors of the hope of eternal life that was in them. They preached Christ wherever they went. We urge you to follow the examples they left us. Yes, take your faith with you and testify your Lord and Savior where you are, with every means available to you — including your regular attendance at public worship and the Lord's Supper.

As soon as possible send us your request for a transfer to your new church. The pastor of the church you have chosen can help you with this if you want.

We have taken the liberty of contacting one of the pastors in your area, who will then call on you to offer assistance and answer your questions about the churches there. Perhaps he has already visited with you.

We look forward to hearing from you in the near future. Let us know how things are going with you and the family. Meanwhile, rest assured that we are keeping you in our prayers.

Yours in the Service of Our Savior,

_____   _____
Chairman of the board of elders   Pastor

† † † † † †

LETTER #5:

To communicants who have moved away: They have not responded to the first letter, urging them to settle into a church and request a transfer to it: (#2 of series)

Dear Mr. and Mrs. _____, *(names of children who are communicants also)*

It has been about a month since we wrote to you, urging you to settle into a church of our fellowship in your area and request a transfer. Since to date we have not heard from you concerning this urgent matter, we thought it best to contact you again. Your silence makes us wonder whether or not you have been attending a church near your new home. Sometimes Christians lose contact with the church through a move, perhaps for the reason that they miss the familiar faces and surroundings of the home church. However, they must realize that the home church, with its pastor, can no longer serve their spiritual needs because of the distance involved. Yet their need to hear the Word, to worship God and to be involved with other Christians remains just as great as it was prior to their move. Indeed because of family and personal stress due to the move, this need may become even greater.

In your move you have had to make many adjustments, such as shopping in different stores, entrusting your health care to a strange doctor, enrolling the children in a school that is totally unfamiliar, learning to cope with the demands of a new job, etc. And you have been willing to make these adjustments. Why then should moving so adversly effect your adjusting to a different church and pastor? We pray that you will not allow your move to tempt you to become disinterested in the Christian fellowship, the preaching of the Word and the worship of God that is available to the Christian only through **active** church membership.

If you have not already found a new church home and started to worship there, we hope and pray that you will take care of this highly urgent matter within a short time, and request your transfer. Would you drop us a line right away, acknowledging our two letters, and inform us of your progress? We would also be interested to know how things are going with you.

Be assured that you remain very much in our prayers and in our hearts. Greetings in behalf of your fellow saints at _____ Lutheran congregation.

We hope that you don't mind our sending a copy of this letter to a pastor in your area, with an appeal to him to contact you in the near future.

Yours in the Service of Our Savior,

_____   _____
Chairman of the board of elders   Pastor

† † † † † †

LETTER #6:

To communicants who have moved away: They have not responded to the first and second letters, urging them to settle into a church and request a transfer to it: (#3 of series) *(Wait 2 months after letter #2)*

> *I rejoiced with those who said to me, "Let us go to the house of the Lord." (Ps. 122:1)*

Dear Mr. and Mrs. _____, *(names of children who are communicants also)*

This is now the third time that we have written to you since you moved away. Our purpose in writing remains the same: to express our interest in you, and our deep care for your spiritual welfare. Since you have not responded to our previous letters, we are all the more concerned. Please accept this letter as still another evidence of the love we have for you, and the fact that you remain in our thoughts and our prayers. You are indeed precious to God and to us.

The Holy Spirit gave you faith which trusts that your sins are washed away in Jesus' blood. Through your faith in Jesus Christ, the heavenly Father made you his own spiritual children and promised you a most wonderful inheritance, eternal life in heaven. We urge you: don't permit anything to come between you and your God.

Don't allow anything to tempt you away from serving your God with an active membership in a local church where you live. If you are growing careless about spiritual matters, stop to consider what Christ and the salvation he won for you with his own suffering and death should mean to you. Stop to consider the Word, the worship, the Lord's Supper, the public confession of sins and absolution, the Christian fellowship and the opportunities for Christian service that you are missing. These things are all priceless in their value.

If you have strayed since you have left our fellowship, we urge you to return to God, who is loving and forgiving. Read again in Luke 15:11-31 the story about the lost son who came to his senses, repented and was forgiven. God's Word tells us: "If we confess our sins, he is faithful and just and will forgive us our sins and purify us from all unrighteousness (1 John 1:9).

And when one seeks forgiveness for sin, the desire must also be there to amend one's sinful life. In your case this would involve returning to regular attendance at the house of God and all that this includes. We are not giving up hope. We are keeping you in our prayers. We are also sending a copy of this letter to the pastor nearest you, once again urging him to be our advocate so that he may counsel you concerning this most important matter.

In case you have joined a church that is not affiliated with us, please inform us in order that we might take appropriate action regarding your membership in this congregation.

We are still waiting to hear from you. We hope that all is going well.

Yours in the Service of Our Savior,

_____   _____
Chairman of the board of elders   Pastor

Name and phone number of contact pastor: _____

† † † † † †

LETTER #7:

To communicants who have moved away: They have not responded to the first three letters urging them to settle into a church and request a transfer to it: (#4 of series) *(Wait 2 months after letter #3)*

Dear Mr. and Mrs. _____, *(names of children who are communicants also)*

It has been six months and more since you moved away. Inspite of our repeated admonition through the mail to settle into a church in the area where you now live, and to request a transfer of membership, we still have no word from you. Pastor _____ of _____ Lutheran Church, _____(city)_____, whom we asked to contact you, reports that he has not made any progress in directing you to a church and persuading you to become active members. His evaluation of the situation is that you just don't seem to be interested in worshiping in the house of God. Perhaps the reason for this is that you are now involved in purely worldly matters.

By your consistent failure to respond to our letters of encouragement, you have removed yourselves from our spiritual care, leaving us no other choice than to recommend that your membership in _____ Lutheran Church be terminated. Your membership will be acted on in the forthcoming meeting of the voters on _____. Prior to this meeting, you will be contacted by phone in another attempt to convince you of what you ought to do. It is still our hope and prayer that you will yet carry out the Lord's will in this matter. We appeal to you to make first things first in your lives. Bear in mind that your lack of interest indicates that you have a very serious faith-problem. You are, in fact, placing in jeopardy your hold on eternal life.

We are taking the liberty of sending a copy of this letter to Pastor _____. Please feel free to counsel with him in this matter. And won't you please contact us? We want so much to hear from you. As always, you are precious to God and to us.

Yours in the Service of Our Savior,

_____   _____
Chairman of the board of elders   Pastor

     Name and phone number of the contact pastor: _____

† † † † † †

LETTER #8:

To communicants who have moved away: They have not responded to repeated attempts to contact them, urging them to settle into a church and request a transfer to it. Therefore, their membership had to be terminated: (Notification of congregational action) (#5 of series)

Dear Mr. and Mrs. _____, *(names of children who are communicants also)*

This letter has the purpose of informing you that your membership in

_____ Lutheran Church has been terminated as of _____(date)_____.

The voters' assembly was left with no other choice than to take this regretful action. The terminating of your membership in this congregation was simply an accomodation to reality. You chose to ignore our words of admonition repeatedly offered to you, thereby removing yourself from our spiritual care and, at the same time, giving us the message that you did not want your membership transferred to one of our sister churches. Here are the resolves adopted by the congregation through its voters' assembly:

WHEREAS 1) Mr. and Mrs. _____ (and _____) have some time ago moved outside the visitation area of _____ Lutheran Church; and

WHEREAS 2) The pastor and the board of elders have repeatedly written to them, admonishing them to become active in one of our churches in their area, and request a transfer to it; and

WHEREAS 3) Mr. and Mrs. _____ (and _____) have consistently failed to respond to the word of admonition offered by the pastor and board of elders, thus, in effect, removing themselves from their spiritual care and responsibility while declining a transfer to another church, therefore, be it

Resolved, a) That _____ Lutheran Church regretfully terminate the membership of Mr. and Mrs. _____ (and _____) and be it further

Resolved, b) That Mr. and Mrs. _____ (and _____) have herewith relinquished all their rights and privileges of membership; and be it finally

Resolved, c) That a copy of these resolves, accompanied by an admonitory letter from the board of elders, be sent to Mr. and Mrs. _____ (and, _____,) signed by the president, secretary, pastor and chairman of the board of elders.

Mr. and Mrs. _____, (and _____,) we repeat our warning, given in loving concern, that your manifest lack of interest in public worship and all that it includes, reveals a very serious condition of heart.

We hope that you haven't fallen into the false delusion that you are so good that you don't need a Savior. Every one of us is full of sin and imperfection and, therefore, every one of us needs Jesus for salvation. In church we make confession of our sins with other Christians and hear again that Jesus suffered and died to redeem us.

The matter of first importance is that you humble yourselves before God, bringing your sins to him for forgiveness. And that you believe in Jesus Christ as your personal Savior and Lord, trusting that you have remission of sins in his name. When you truly believe in Jesus with a repentant heart, you will also want to worship him publicly with other Christians and serve him.

Give this matter serious thought. God is not willing that any should perish but that all should come to repentance. Make no mistake about it, you are on a very dangerous course. Make no mistake about it, the Lord Jesus loves you, and wants you back. He is calling to you through our words of admonition. We pray that you will heed this call.

If you should be in our area, please come and visit us. Don't hesitate to contact us either in person or by mail or by phone. Pastor _____ of _____ Lutheran Church in _____(city)_____ is also eager to be of help to you.

Yours in the Service of Our Savior,

_____ _____
Chairman of the board of elders   President

copy to: Pastor _____ _____
         (phone   )   Secretary

                                    _____
                                    Pastor

† † † † † †

LETTER #9:

A commendatory letter of transfer: (#1 of series)

Dear Brothers in Christ,

On _____(date)_____, _____ Lutheran Church through its voters' assembly (or church council) granted the transfer of Mr. and Mrs. _____ and family to your fellowship and spiritual care. It is our fervant prayer and hope that they will zealously pursue the spiritual blessings available to them in their new church home through the Means of Grace.

	Names:		Dates:	
Husband	_____	Bn _____ Bapt _____ Conf _____
Wife	_____	Bn _____ Bapt _____ Conf _____

Children:

_____ Bn _____ Bapt _____ Conf _____

_____ Bn _____ Bapt _____ Conf _____

_____ Bn _____ Bapt _____ Conf _____

_____ Bn _____ Bapt _____ Conf _____

Address: _____

_____ Phone: _____

_____

The _____'s were members in good standing in this congregation: faithful in their attendance at the house of God, faithful at the Lord's Table and faithful in the financial support of Christ's church. They also served their Lord and their church in the following ways: _____

_____

_____.

While we shall miss these Christians in our fellowship, you shall surely enjoy having them in yours.

May the God who gives endurance and encouragement give you a spirit of unity among yourselves as you follow Christ Jesus, so that with one heart and mouth you may glorify the God and Father of our Lord Jesus Christ. Accept one another, then, just as Christ accepted you, in order to bring praise to God. (Rom. 15:5-7)

In the Service of Our Savior,

_____   _____

Pastor   Chairman of the board of elders

† † † † † †

LETTER #10:

A letter of transfer for one who has been lax in attendance and offerings: (#2 of series)

Dear Brothers in Christ,

On _____(date)_____, _____ Lutheran Church through its voters' assembly (or church council) granted the transfer of Mr. and Mrs. _____ and family to your fellowship and spiritual care. It is our fervent prayer and hope that they will zealously pursue the spiritual blessings available to them in them in their new church home through the means of grace.

	Names:		Dates:	
Husband	_____	Bn _____	Bapt _____	Conf _____
Wife	_____	Bn _____	Bapt _____	Conf _____
	Children:			
	_____	Bn _____	Bapt _____	Conf _____
	_____	Bn _____	Bapt _____	Conf _____
	_____	Bn _____	Bapt _____	Conf _____
	_____	Bn _____	Bapt _____	Conf _____

Address: _____

_____ Phone: _____

_____

We are sorry that we cannot recommend the _____'s to you as Christians who frequently availed themselves of the rights and privileges of church membership, or who consistently carried out their membership duties. We feel that in order to give them the spiritual care and encouragement that they need from the start, you should be apprised of the fact that they were lax in their attendance at God's House, lax in eating and drinking the Lord's Supper and lax in supporting Christ's church with their offerings. They were also inconsistent in bringing their children to Sunday School and Bible Class. You would be doing yourselves and them a favor if you made them to understand at once that good attendance and cheerful, proportionate financial support are expected in their new surroundings. In the last year that they were members of _____ congregation they communed _____ times, and attended the house of the Lord on the average of _____ times a month (every two months; every three months).

Perhaps a new start will have a salutary effect upon the _____'s. We fervently pray that this will come about and that they will reap a rich spiritual harvest through active membership in _____ Lutheran Church. We entrust them to your spiritual care.

> *All the saints send their greetings. May the grace of the Lord Jesus Christ, and the love of God, and the fellowship of the Holy Spirit be with you all. (2 Cor. 13:13, 14)*

In the Service of Our Savior,

_____   _____
Pastor   Chairman of the board of elders

† † † † † †

LETTER #11:

To the member who has evaded discipline by disassociating himself: (Notification of congregational action) *(His request to have his membership terminated came at the start of Christian discipline)*

Dear _____ ,

On _____ 19 ___, the voters' assembly considered your request that your name be removed from the membership list of _____ Lutheran Church. The pastor and board of elders explained to the voters to the best of their ability the circumstances involved in your request. Following the discussion these resolutions were adopted:

WHEREAS 1) It became necessary for the pastor and board of elders of _____ Lutheran Church to offer Christian admonishment to _____ because of his neglect of the means of grace and his failure to practice responsible Christian stewardship; and

WHEREAS 2) _____ was unwilling to accept this offer of Christian love and concern, repeatedly refusing to meet with the pastor and with the elder assigned to his case; and

WHEREAS 3) _____ has sought to evade Christian admonishment with the request that his name be removed from the congregation's membership list, therefore, be it

Resolved, a) That _____ Lutheran Church recognize that _____ has by his actions and his request disassociated himself — thereby removing himself from any further spiritual care the congregation might offer him; and be it further

Resolved, b) That _____ has herewith relinquished all his rights and privileges of membership; and be it finally

Resolved, c) That a copy of these resolutions, accompanied by an admonitory letter from the board of elders, be sent to _____, signed by the president, secretary, pastor and chairman of the board of elders.

It was with deep concern for your soul that the above-named action was taken by the voters. We therefore regard it as our duty to remind you that you have placed your faith in jeopardy for you have, in effect, cut yourself off from hearing God's Word, from remembering the Lord's death in Holy Communion and from the strengthening ties of Christian fellowship. We fear that you are allowing your sinful flesh to gain the upper hand. If you continue on the path that you have chosen you will eventually place yourself outside God's kingdom — if you haven't done so already.

Your action of disassociation does not relieve you of spiritual responsibilities: i.e. to repent of your sins, to worship God, to hear his Word preached and to support the gospel work with your offerings and prayers.

If it's a matter of feeling uncomfortable in _____ Lutheran Church, we strongly urge you to seek out another church where the Word of God is preached in its truth and purity, and request membership there.

It is our sincere hope that you will experience a change of mind and heart, and that you will soon be attending worship services on a regular basis, if not in _____ Lutheran Church, then in association with another group of Christians. If you should reconsider your move to disassociate yourself from this congregation, please contact the pastor as soon as possible so that a meeting can be arranged between you and the board of elders and the pastor.

By disassociating yourself from _____ Lutheran Church you have removed yourself from the spiritual care of the pastor and this board. This does not mean that our heart-felt care for your spiritual welfare is ended. We do love you and care for you. Be assured of this. Hence this letter from our hearts to yours.

Yours in the Service of Our Savior.

--   --
Chairman of the board of elders   President

                                                 Secretary

                                                 Pastor

† † † † † †

LETTER #12:

To the member who has disassociated himself from the congregation for no apparent reason: (Notification of congregational action)

Dear _____ ,

    Your request to be released from membership in _____ Lutheran Church was brought to the attention of the voters at their meeting held on _____(date)_____ 19 _____. Your sudden request to be released came as a surprise to the voters. They were dismayed to learn that you would not counsel with the pastor or the elders in this matter, and further dismayed by your intention not to join another church at this time. They do not understand your desire to be free of all ties to the organized church. The following resolutions were adopted by the voters:

WHEREAS 1)   _____ has asked to be released from membership in _____ Lutheran Church; and

WHEREAS 2)   No reason for this request has been given, and no counseling in the matter has been accepted; and

WHEREAS 3)   The stated intention of _____ is to remain unaffiliated at this time; and

WHEREAS 4)   It is surely God's intention that every Christian carry on active membership in a Christian congregation so as to be fed the spiritual food of God's Word (1 Thess. 2:13; Luke 11:28; 2 Pet. 1:19; James 1:21-25), and, furthermore, it is God's intention that every Christian accept Christian counseling (Heb. 13:17; Col. 3:16; 2 Tim. 4:2); therefore, be it

Resolved, a)   That, under the circumstances, _____ Lutheran

Church regretfully recognize that in asking for a release from membership, _____ has, in effect, disassociated himself, and that no further action on his request need be taken; and be it further

Resolved, b) That _____ has herewith relinquished all his rights and privileges of membership; and be it further

Resolved, c) That _____ Lutheran Church express the hope and prayer that _____ will one day seek reinstatement of his membership, accepting the Christian counseling that he has so far declined; and be it further

Resolved, d) That _____ Lutheran Church express the hope and prayer that whatever sins and sinful attitudes may be involved in this matter, _____ will be led to repent of them and ask for forgiveness; and be it finally

Resolved, e) That a copy of these resolutions, accompanied by an admonitory letter from the board of elders, be sent to _____, signed by the president, secretary, pastor and the chairman of the board of elders.

_____, we are truly sorry that you have disassociated yourself, no longer desiring to be affiliated with our Christian fellowship. But we are also saddened by the fact that you have not allowed us to advise you in this very important matter. Your decision to simply drop from the church scene is, finally, incomprehensible. While God, out of concern for the believers' souls, has given pastors to teach and preach his Word and administer the sacraments to them, he wants the believers to partake — to hear and receive. God wants us to be affiliated with a church, to fellowship with other Christians, and to have pastoral care for our souls. Please look up the following passages and give serious consideration to them: Psalm 84:1, 2, 4; Heb. 10:23-25; Col. 3:16; Acts 2:42, 46, 47; Luke 11:28; Rom. 10:17; 1 Thess. 2:13.

Do you still regard yourself as a sinner who needs the forgiveness that Jesus Christ died on the cross to give us? Are there sins that are standing in the way of your being an active member in a church? Please, if there are, we stand ready to counsel with you concerning them.

Perhaps you really do feel that you are doing the right thing under the circumstances — whatever they may be. But beware of Satan's deceptions. He can make them look so "proper." He acts like an angel of light, even arguing at times — to all appearances — from the side of God's Word. But he twists and turns Scripture to his own advantage. Remember all that you have been taught by your pastor from God's Word. Return to it. Return to the church you have chosen to leave. We, the pastor and board of elders, stand ready to help you. Please believe this.

Yours in the Service of Our Savior,

_____   _____
Chairman of the board of elders   President

                                   _____
                                   Secretary

                                   _____
                                   Pastor

† † † † † †

LETTER #13:

To the member who has been released from membership to join a church with whom the congregation is not in fellowship: (Notification of congregational action)

Dear _____ ,

    Your request for release from membership in _____ Lutheran Church was brought to the attention of the voters at their meeting held on _____ 19 ____. Although the voters expressed their reluctance to release you from membership, especially since you have indicated that you intend to affiliate with a church that does not share our confession, nonetheless, they have resolved to grant the release knowing that this is a firm decision that you have made. The following resolves were adopted by the voters:

WHEREAS 1) _____ has asked to be released from membership in _____ Lutheran Church in order to consumate membership elsewhere; and

WHEREAS 2) _____ has stated his intention to take up membership in a church with which _____ Lutheran Church is not in doctrinal agreement and with which, therefore, it does not practice fellowship; and

WHEREAS 3) _____ has indicated that he will not give further consideration to continuing his membership in _____ Lutheran Church, therefore, be it

Resolved, a) That _____ Lutheran Church regretfully release _____ from membership; and be it further

Resolved, b) That _____ Lutheran Church recognize that the bond of scriptural unity no longer exists between itself and _____, a unity that Scripture indeed calls for (1 Cor. 1:10; Eph. 4:3); and be it further

Resolved, c) That _____ has herewith relinquished all his rights and privileges of membership; and be it further

Resolved, d) That _____ Lutheran Church express the hope that _____ will one day seek reinstatement of his membership on the basis of the reestablishing of scriptural unity; and be it finally

Resolved, e) That a copy of these resolutions, accompanied by an admonitory letter from the board of elders, be sent to _____, signed by the president, secretary, pastor and chairman of the board of elders.

_____, we cannot prohibit anyone from joining the church of his choice. Finally, each has to live with his conscience in the matter. Issues of correct doctrine and practice mean more to one Christian than to another. Some Lutherans will go to great lengths and make personal sacrifices to be active in a truly confessional Lutheran Church, such as the one you are leaving. Other simply don't care. With them it is a matter of convenience rather than of conscience. As a congregation committed to Scripture, we cannot, of course, go along with some of the views held by the church you are planning to join. And it troubles us that you can. But these matters have all been explained in the private discussions that were held with you. Just this parting word: Both the pastor and the board of elders stand ready to discuss Scripture with you, and any other matter that might be involved should you once again desire to affiliate with _____ Lutheran Church.

Yours in the Service of Our Savior,

Chairman of the board of elders	President
	Secretary
	Pastor

† † † † † †

LETTER #14:

To the member under discipline (Third Step), urging him to attend a meeting of the congregation to hear the church's testimony in the matter of his impenitence: (Notification of congregational action)

Dear _____ ,

This letter is to inform you that the voters' assembly of _____ Lutheran Church, meeting on _____(date)_____, heard a brief report from _____, _____ and _____ concerning a case of discipline involving you, our brother. Acting on what has been told to the church (Matt. 18:17), the voters resolved to proceed further with the matter, respectfully and lovingly asking you to attend a meeting so that the church can carry out its Christian duty to admonish you.

In requesting a meeting with you, the voters express the sincere hope that the warning and encouragement given by a number of your brothers will persuade you to do the right thing, yes, that you will repent of your sin and confess it. The church stands ready to forgive you in God's name. The following resolves were adopted:

WHEREAS 1) _____ and his witnesses: _____ and _____ have appealed to the jurisdiction of _____ Lutheran Church in a matter of Christian discipline involving _____, basing their appeal on the Lord's command, "If he refuses to listen to them, tell it to the church" (Matt. 18:17); and

WHEREAS 2) _____ and his witnesses, in telling the matter to the church, testify that _____ failed to repent of the sin of _____ though repeatedly admonished to do so; and

WHEREAS 3) The church is constrained to accept the testimony of these witnesses, which demonstrates that the initial steps of Christian discipline ordered by our Lord have been carried out: "If your brother sins . . . go and show him his fault, just between the two of you. If he listens to you, you have won your brother over. But if he will not listen, take one or two others along, so that 'every matter may be established by the testimony of two or three witnesses'" (Matt. 18:15-16); and

WHEREAS 4) It is the Lord's will that the church, through its testimony in cases of appeal to its jurisdiction, also attempt to win the brother over (Matt. 18:18); and

WHEREAS 5) Christian love for the brother under discipline allows nothing less than this, therefore, be it

Resolved, a) That _____ Lutheran Church through its voters' assembly concurr with the appeal of these brothers and, therefore, request a meeting with _____ on _____(date)_____ 19 _____; and be it further

Resolved, b) That _____ and his witnesses be present at this meeting in order that they might state what sin has been committed and also testify that _____ has been earnestly warned to repent, but to no avail; and be it further

Resolved, c) That the prayer and hope be expressed that this meeting will result in a favorable outcome through the willingness of _____ to repent of his sin and confess it, in order that the church may forgive him (Matt. 18:18b); and be it finally

Resolved, d) That a copy of these resolutions, accompanied by a letter from the board of elders encouraging attendance at the above-posted meeting be sent "certified" or hand-delivered to _____, which letter is to be signed by the president, secretary, pastor and chairman of the board of elders.

_____, there is but one purpose behind the voters' action requesting your attendance at this meeting: the loving concern of Christians for their brother.

Your brothers are deeply concerned over your failure, up to this point, to repent and ask forgiveness. You have consistently refused to heed every admonition offered to you. Jesus died for every sin, hence, also the sin you are charged with, but so far you have told God that you don't want his forgiveness. We hope that your attitude will soon change and that you will repent in order that the congregation can assure you of divine forgiveness and help you set a course through life that is pleasing to God. What joy will be found in all of our hearts if this hope becomes reality. We pray that it will.

Consider the seriousness of the matter, and come to this meeting. It is being called for the purpose of rescuing you from impenitence and to save you from eternal death. God does not want anyone to perish, but everyone to come to repentance.

If you find it impossible to meet at the appointed time, please contact the pastor or chairman of the board of elders so that the meeting can be rescheduled to a convenient time. God loves you, and so do we.

Yours in the Service of Our Savior,

Chairman of the board of elders

President

Secretary

Pastor

† † † † † †

LETTER #15:

To the member who has been excommunicated: (Notification of congregational action)

Dear _____ ,

The purpose of this letter is to inform you of the final disciplinary action taken against you by _____ Lutheran Church at its voters' meeting, held on _____ 19 _____.

It was with deep sorrow and loving concern that the members unanimously adopted the following resolutions:

WHEREAS 1) It is recognized that _____ has committed the sin of _____; and

WHEREAS 2) Our Lord Jesus Christ has commanded that we seek to restore the erring brother (sister): "If your brother sins ... go and show him his fault, just between the two of you. If he listens to you, you have won your brother over. But if he will not listen, take one or two others along, so that 'every matter may be established by the testimony of two or three witnesses.' If he refuses to listen to them, tell it to the church; and if he refuses to listen even to the church, treat him as you would a pagan [one outside the faith] or a tax collector [one who has apostatized and is no longer in the church]. I tell you the truth, whatever you bind on earth will be bound in heaven, and whatever you loose on earth will be loosed in heaven" (Matt. 18:15-18); and

WHEREAS 3) The three steps outlined by our Lord were followed, but each time _____ failed to heed the admonition to repent and confess his sin so that he could be forgiven, and the matter thus settled; and

WHEREAS 4) In failing to hear even the church's call to repent, _____ has made it impossible for the church to admonish him any longer in the realm of fellowship as an erring brother, therefore, be it

Resolved, a) That on the basis of his refusal to repent, we affirm with deep regret that _____ is to be treated as one who no longer has the Christian faith and is no longer a member of the Holy Christian Church; and be it further

Resolved, b) That _____ Lutheran Church in the name of God the Father, Son and Holy Spirit bind his unrepented sin(s) to him,

		recognizing that it (they) is (are) bound to him in heaven itself; and be it further
Resolved,	c)	That this action be construed as excommunication or exclusion from this local fellowship of saints, known as _____ Lutheran Church; and be it further
Resolved,	d)	That _____ has herewith relinquished all his rights and privileges of membership; and be it finally
Resolved,	e)	That a copy of these resolves accompanied by an admonitory letter from the board of elders, be sent "certified", or hand delivered to _____, signed by the president, secretary, pastor and chairman of the board of elders.

_____, how we love you. How it breaks our hearts that this drastic step had to be taken. The very fact that this action was not taken in haste, but only after repeated admonition went unheeded, should confirm in your mind our genuine concern for your eternal welfare. The congregation's action in excommunicating you and binding your sin is neither hateful or spiteful. It is, in fact, the final debt of love that we can pay you. It is our fervent hope that this action taken by so many will convince you that you are indeed living with a sin that you must repent of and confess. And that you must receive forgiveness for it in order to be saved. Remember that Jesus Christ died on the cross for this sin too. God is waiting with a longing heart for you to return to him. Read again the Parable of the Lost Son, Luke 15:11-24. We urge you to read also Psalms 32, 51, 103, 130.

It is our sincere hope and prayer that you will come to your senses and return to the Lord, seek his forgiveness and amend your life. Also that you will seek reinstatement in this congregation. Remember that God is a wrathful God when it comes to unrepented sin, but a wonderfully merciful God when we approach him in contrition and faith.

Be assured that we are ready at all times to discuss God's Word with you on this matter. Do not hesitate to call on the pastor, who will be glad to arrange a meeting for you with himself and the board of elders. In the meantime we invite, even urge you to come weekly to God's house to hear the divine Word which can save your soul.

Yours in the Service of Our Savior,

_____   _____
Chairman of the board of elders   President

                                                        _____
                                                        Secretary

                                                        _____
                                                        Pastor

ADDENDUM SIX

THE ELDERS ORGANIZE

Geographical Divisions, Using Area Elders, District Elders and Elder Assistants

By now you realize that the elders have their work cut out for them. There is much work that needs to be done, and every bit of it is important. The board should be organized in such a way that it can carry on as efficiently as possible and be able to promptly address every need for spiritual care in the congregation requiring the elders' help.

To expedite spiritual care we are suggesting that the membership be apportioned along geographical lines, first into larger divisions called *areas*, and subsequently into smaller divisions called *districts*. If practical each area of the congregation should comprise four or five districts. Each district should comprise 15-25 families. Each area is under the supervision of an area elder elected by the congregation. Each district is under the care of a district elder appointed by the congregation upon the advice and recommendation of the church council and pastor(s). A separate individual is elected by the congregation to serve as chairman of the board of elders. (Note: the board selects from its own midst a secretary to record minutes and carry on official correspondence.) In congregations of moderate size the districts could be divided into fewer than 15-25 families. The number of districts in an area can also be adjusted upward or downward to fit the individual congregation. In small congregations it may be unnecessary and even impractical to subdivide the membership into districts. A few elected elders with their appointed assistants may very well suffice.

An important feature of subdividing the congregation into districts is the appointment of men to help the district elders care for the members of their districts. These men are called elder assistants. Elder assistants can be appointed by the church council at the rate of one assistant for every five to ten families. Thus each district elder will have a small force of men to help him.

But let's not count the ladies out. The wives of the district elders should be made to feel that they too take part in this work. They can help out when female members of the congregation must be contacted, and they can give special aid to female members when such aid is called for. The wives of the elders and elder assistants can accompany their husbands when making visits to the elderly and the sick, as well as to celebrants, and whenever their presence would be appreciated. The woman's touch is very much needed in church work. Note that the early church employed deaconesses to help female members, and that St. Paul spoke glowingly of service rendered the church by women in his time. Here is an excellent place for at least some of the ladies of the congregation to put their Christian zeal and feminine talents to use for the Lord.

Elder assistants — their wives too — can be used to dispense information and materials to the members. We have all been in churches which have letter boxes built into the wall of the foyer. Newsletters, devotional booklets, the official church publication, school news, financial statements and the like are placed in these recepticles for the members to retrieve when they attend services. Trouble is, printed matter has a way of piling up and becoming outdated. With an efficient elder assistant system this won't happen. Informational material is delivered regularly, while it is current, to the households. Material that cannot be hand-delivered is to be mailed out on a regular basis. This is the way it ought to be.

If it becomes necessary to change the service time, to call off services or school or other events due to storms and other emergencies, or to announce important events or special services and school doings, the district elders and the elder assistants, together with their wives, can quickly spread the word by phone or even in person. The district elders and their assistants also serve as contact people who help keep a finger on the congregation's pulse, that is, to keep aware of the ill, the troubled, the spiritually distressed, the economically depressed, new parents, celebrants, and the like. They can also see to transportation for those who need it, visit the elderly of their districts who are in nursing homes and visit the shut-ins (especially in the event the church services are not broadcast over a local radio or television station) and supply sermon tapes on a regular basis. The district elders and their assistants, with help from their wives, can deliver food and other supplies to those in need, as directed by the elder in charge of the Christian aid fund. They should maintain a prayer list of those for whom intercession before God's throne is needed. In addition, the elder assistants can serve the elders as witnesses in cases of discipline when it would be wise and suitable to do so.

An important advantage in having elder assistants (with help also from their wives whenever practical and appropriate) is that it fosters a more personal-type contact with members of the congregation — a thing so important to healthy congregational life. It also, in a highly beneficial way, solves in part the need to involve more members in the work of the church.

The pastor or shepherd of the flock has his assistants, the elders (both area and district) to help him carry on the work more efficiently and effectively. The elders, too, have need of assistants. These men, carefully chosen and well-trained, can render valuable service to the board of elders and to the members of the congregation.

The Board of Elders as Administered by the Congregation's Constitution.

A SAMPLE OF CONSTITUTIONAL WORDING GOVERNING THE BOARD OF ELDERS:

THE BYLAWS

Article_____

Section_____ The Board of Elders

A. The board members and their specialized duties:

1. The board of elders shall have a *chairman* elected by the voters' assembly to a term of _____ years. He shall:

    a) represent the board of elders on the church council and make regular reports at meetings of the voters' assembly;

    b) see that regular meetings of the board of elders are held;

    c) assist the pastor(s) in conducting the meetings of the board of elders;

    d) be ready to give counsel and assistance to the members of the board of elders;

    e) seek the advice and counsel of the pastor(s) in matters relating to the board of elders;

    f) make calls with elders and/or the pastor(s) when requested to do so;

    g) help to promote and conduct ongoing training of the elders;

    h) assist the area elders in providing for the welfare of the pastor and his family;

- i) help encourage the members of the board of elders to carry out their duties with faithfulness, promptness, efficiency, and propriety;
- j) together with the area elders comprise a Christian aid committee, of which he is then the chairman, which committee shall administer the Christian aid fund.

2. The board of elders shall have a membership of *area elders* elected by the voters' assembly to a term of _____ years. The number of area elders shall be equal to the number of geographical areas into which the congregation shall have been divided. The area elders shall:
    - a) keep accurate records of all families within their area, making certain that all members are assigned to the responsibility of a district elder;
    - b) receive all addresses and membership changes from the church office and refer them to the district elders;
    - c) promote the work of their district elders: by assisting them in maintaining accurate records of their families ● by encouraging them to make regular visits to all the families and individuals under their care and to make special visits to any who are experiencing spiritual difficulties (e.g. the delinquents), as well as visits to the sick (in consultation with the pastor(s)) ● by accompanying their district elders on visits whenever this is necessary ● by assisting the pastor(s) and chairman of the board of elders in implementing ongoing training of the area and district elders ● by reporting any vacancies among the district elders to the chairman of the board of elders;
    - d) appoint from their midst supervisors to oversee such areas as Christian life, worship, public relations, care of the pastor and his family, membership, etc.

3. The board of elders shall also have a membership of *district elders* equal in number to the districts (15-25 families each) into which the geographical areas of the congregation shall have been divided. The district elders shall be appointed by the voters' assembly upon the advice and recommendation of the church

council and the pastor(s) to a term of _____ years. The district elders shall:

a) assist the pastor(s) and church council in the spiritual care of the members of their respective districts, including cases of admonition and discipline;

b) give assistance to the stewardship board (or committee) in promoting Christian stewardship in their respective districts (e.g. carry out stewardship visitations, distribute information, etc.) in a manner agreed upon by the church council and/or voters' assembly;

c) serve in a liaison capacity, disseminating appropriate information to the membership of their respective districts when requested by the church council and/or voters' assembly;

d) receive all address and membership changes from their respective area elders and keep accurate records of all members within their districts;

e) encourage the membership within their respective districts in their spiritual growth and conduct;

f) at each regular meeting of the board of elders give a report of their visits to their respective area elders;

g) be able to inform the membership of their respective districts of important happenings in the congregation;

h) be ready to offer spiritual and moral encouragement and assistance to the membership of their respective districts;

i) recommend to the church council qualifying male communicant members to be appointed as elder assistants (at the rate of one for every 5-10 families in the district). These men are to provide assistance to their respective district elders whenever practical and appropriate (e.g. in diseminating information and printed materials, in making visits, in serving as witnesses, in affording help in cases of need, etc.).

B. The board members and their general duties.

1. The elders shall be examples in Christian knowledge and conduct,

conforming in character and behavior to the high ideals of their office (1 Timothy 3:8-13).

2. The elders shall assist the pastor(s) in assuring the general spiritual welfare of the congregation and shall assist the pastor(s) in difficult problems of the ministry. In general, the elders shall provide lay assistance to the pastor(s) in the work among the families of the parish.

3. The elders shall examine whether the ministry is adequately staffed.

4. The elders shall assist the pastor(s) in admonishing the erring, seeking through the law and the gospel to reclaim straying souls from sin and unbelief. The elders shall make every effort to induce members who have been negligent in their attendance at worship services, in the use of the Sacraments, in their Christian giving, and in the Christian education of their children, to mend their sinful ways and fully enjoy the rights and privileges, as well as perform the duties of their membership.

5. The elders shall assist the pastor(s), president and vice-president in cultivating a constant spirit of harmony among the members.

6. The elders shall accompany the pastor(s) on calls to members of the congregation when required to do so.

7. The elders shall see to it that proper decorum and order prevail at all times in the church services. They shall appoint, as well as instruct, a staff of ushers and official greeters. They shall be on hand to welcome strangers and assist them. They shall see to the procurement of needed paraments, hymn books, communion and baptismal supplies, and the like. They shall help with the recruitment of organists, choir directors and other musicians as need arises. They shall make recommendations, where needed, for improving the church services, endeavoring always to foster an environment and attitudes conducive to worship among those in attendance.

8. The elders shall be concerned for the Christian and churchly character of all congregational organizations and activities.

9. The elders shall be watchful for cases of spiritual or physical needs on the part of the members of the congregation and bring them to the attention of the pastor(s) so that appropriate action can be taken to assist the troubled individuals.

10. The elders, in consultation with the pastor(s), shall safeguard the preaching and teaching of the pure Word of God in the public services of the congregation and in its educational agencies.

11. The elders shall visit and welcome new members to the congregation.

12. The elders shall visit members of the congregation under their care on a regular basis and as often as need requires it.

13. The elders shall be responsible for the Christian aid work among the sick and needy.

14. The elders shall serve as a liaison between the membership and the pastor(s), the church council, and the voters' assembly.

15. The elders shall hold all matters discussed by them demanding confidence, in the strictest secrecy.

16. The elders shall hold regular monthly meetings — meeting oftener as is necessary.

17. The elders shall prepare an annual budget for congregational approval.

ADDENDUM SEVEN

NOTES AND BIBLIOGRAPHIES

CHAPTER ONE

1. Elmer Kettner, *Elders at Work — Manual for the Training of Elders,* St. Louis, Concordia Publishing House, Audio-Visual Aids Service, p. 31.

2. Excerpt from *Luther's Works, Vol. 3,* by Harold J. Grimm. Copyright (c) 1957, Muhlenberg Press, p. 355. Reprinted by permission of Augsburg Fortress.

3. *Enlisting and Training Kingdom Workers,* issued by the Lutheran Church — Missouri Synod, Committee on Enlisting and Training the Laity, St. Louis, Chapter I, "Lay People as Kingdom Workers," by Wm. H. Hillmer, 1952, p. 5.

4. Reprinted from *Everyone a Minister,* Copyright (c) 1974 Concordia Publishing House, p. 37. Reprinted by permission.

5. Cf. William P. Barker, *Everyone in the Bible,* Westwood, Fleming H. Revell Company, 1966.

6. *Enlisting and Training Kingdom Workers,* op. cit., p. 23. (Oscar E. Feucht quoting Dr. Wm. Dallman, Titles of the Christian.)

7. Ibid., pp. 23-24.

8. John C. Jeske, "Building Lay Leadership Within a Congregation," an essay presented to the Church Officers' Seminar, Lansing, Mich., (WELS), February 1971, p. 5.

9. Paul E. Kretzmann, *Church Government and Church Offices in a Lutheran Congregation,* a doctrinal essay read before the meeting of the South Dakota District, Lutheran Church — Missouri Synod, St. Louis, 1928, p. 31.

FURTHER READING

Donald A. Abdon, *Training and Equipping the Saints,* Indianapolis, copyright by Parish Leadership Seminars, Inc., 1977.

Guido Merkins, *Organized for Action,* St. Louis, Concordia Publishing House, 1959.

R.C.H. Lenski, *The Interpretation of St. Paul's Epistles to the Galations, to the Ephesians and to the Philippians*, Columbus, Lutheran Book Concern, 1937.

R.C.H. Lenski, *The Interpretation of the Acts of the Apostles,* Columbus, Lutheran Book Concern, 1934.

Regaining the Straying, a manual for church elders produced by the Commission on Evangelism of the Wisconsin Evangelical Lutheran Synod, 1981.

Herbert Berner, *The Board of Elders,* St. Louis, Concordia Publishing House.

CHAPTER TWO

1. Peter L. Steinke, *Sharing God's Care for One Another,* St. Louis, Concordia Publishing House, 1979, p. 4.

2. Theodore Graebner, *Handbook for Congregational Officers,* St. Louis, Concordia Publishing House, 1928, p. 19.

3. Reprinted by permission from *The Interpretation of the Acts of the Apostles* by R.C.H. Lenski, Copyright (c) Augsburg Publishing House, p. 240.

4. Harold Nichols, *The Work of the Deacon and Deaconess,* Valley Forge, The Judson Press, 1964, p. 45.

5. Cf. Armin W. Schuetze and Irwin J. Habeck, *The Shepherd Under Christ,* Milwaukee, Northwestern Publishing House, 1974, p. 90.

6. Cf. Ibid., p. 79.

7. Cf. Ibid., p. 84.

8. Donald A. Abdon, *Organized Around the Great Commission,* Indianapolis, Copyright (c) by Parish Leadership Seminars, Inc., 1977, p. 54.

9. Steinke, op. cit. p. 19.

10. Cf. Schuetze and Habeck, op. cit., pp. 42-47.

11. Elmer Kettner, *Elders at Work — Manual for the Training of Elders,* St. Louis, Concordia Publishing House, Audio-Visual Aids Service, p. 20.

12. Nichols, op. cit., p. 47.

13. Abdon, op. cit., p. 51.

FURTHER READING

Donald A. Abdon, *Training and Equipping the Saints,* Indianapolis, Copyright (c) by Parish Leadership Seminars, Inc., 1977.

Charlie W. Shedd, *The Pastoral Ministry of Church Officers,* Richmond, John Knox Press. Copyright (c) by Charlie W. Shedd.

Missionary Workman — A Manual for a Course in Missionary Training, prepared for the Congregational Call of the Cross Committee, issued by The Centennial Call of the Cross Committee of the Lutheran Church — Missouri Synod, St. Louis, Topic II.

CHAPTER THREE

1. Philip Lange, *The Approach to the Unchurched,* St. Louis, Concordia Publishing House, 1943, p. 23.

2. Lawrence J. Crabb, Jr., *Effective Biblical Counseling,* Grand Rapids, Zondervan Publishing House, 1977, pp. 44-45.

3. R.C.H. Lenski. *The Interpretation of St. Paul's First and Second Epistle to the Corinthians,* Lutheran Book Concern, p. 382.

4. Taken from *Effective Biblical Counseling* by Lawrence J. Crabb, Jr., Copyright (c) 1977 by Zondervan Corporation, p. 147. Used by permission.

5. Reprinted from *The Approach To The Unchurched,* Copyright (c) 1943 Concordia Publishing House, p. 23. Reprinted by permission.

6. *Missionary Workman — A Manual for a Course in Missionary Training,* prepared for the Congregational Call of the Cross Committee, issued by The Centennial Call of the Cross Committee of the Lutheran Church — Missouri Synod, St. Louis, Chapter II, p. 20.

7. Peter L. Steinke, *Sharing God's Care for One Another*, St. Louis, Concordia Publishing House, 1979, p. 13.

8. Reprinted from *The Approach To The Unchurched*, op. cit., p. 23. Reprinted by permission.

9. Steinke, op. cit., p. 3.

10. Lange, op. cit., p. 38.

11. Harold Nichols, *The Work of the Deacon and Deaconess,* Valley Forge, The Judson Press, 1964, p. 48.

12. Charlie W. Shedd, *The Pastoral Ministry of Church Officers,* Richmond, John Knox Press, Copyright (c) by Charlie W. Shedd, p. 31.

13. Reprinted from *A Bit of Honey — After Dinner Addresses of Inspiration, Wit and Humor,* by W.E. Thorn, Grand Rapids, Zondervan Publishing House, Copyright (c) by W.E. Thorn, p. 25. Reprinted by permission.

ADDITIONAL READING

Enlisting and Training Kingdom Workers, issued by the Lutheran Church — Missouri Synod, Committee on Enlisting and Training the Laity, St. Louis, 1952, Chapter II, "Motivating the Worker," by Oscar E. Feucht, pp. 25-26.

The Great Texts of the Bible, 1 Corinthians, New York, Charles Scribner's, 1912, edited by James Hastings, pp. 242-243.

Donald A. Abdon, *Training and Equipping the Saints,* Indianapolis, Copyright (c) by Parish Leadership Seminars, Inc., 1977.

CHAPTER FOUR

1. Milton L. Rudnick, *Authority in the Church,* Chicago, Lutheran Education Association, 1977, pp. 57-58.

2. Roger Kovaciny, "Excommunication for Fun and Profit," *Christian News Encyclopedia,* Vol. II, Washington, Missourian Publishing Co., 1983, edited by Herman Otten, p. 921.

3. Armin W. Schuetze and Irwin J. Habeck, *The Shepherd Under Christ,* Milwaukee, Northwestern Publishing House, 1974, p. 170.

4. Reprinted from *Discipling the Brother* by Marlin Jeschke, Scottdale, Herald Press, Copyright (c) 1972, p. 105. Reprinted by permission.

5. R.C.H. Lenski, *The Interpretation of St. Paul's First and Second Epistle to the Corinthians,* Columbus, Lutheran Book Concern, 1935, p. 233.

6. Ibid., p. 232.

7. Ibid., p. 234.

8. Schuetze and Habeck, op. cit., p. 173.

9. Charlie W. Shedd, *The Pastoral Ministry of Church Officers,* Richmond, John Knox Press, Copyright (c) by Charlie W. Shedd, p. 36.

10. Jon M. Mahnke, "Dealing with the Neglecter of Word and Sacrament," an unpublished essay delivered to the California Pastoral Conference, the Arizona-California District of the Wisconsin Evangelical Lutheran Synod, January 1979, pp. 7-8.

ADDITIONAL READING

R.C.H. Lenski, *The Interpretation of St. Paul's First and Second Epistle to the Corinthians*, Columbus, Lutheran Book Concern, 1935.

R.C.H. Lenski, *The Interpretation of St. Paul's Epistles to the Galations, to the Ephesians and to the Philippians*, Columbus, Lutheran Book Concern, 1937.

R.C.H. Lenski, *The Interpretation of St. Paul's Epistles to the Colossians, to the Thessalonians, to Timothy, to Titus and to Philemon*, Columbus, Lutheran Book Concern, 1937.

P.E. Kretzmann, *Popular Commentary of the Bible, The New Testament*, Vol. II, St. Louis, Concordia Publishing House, 1923, p. 256.

Dietrich Bonhoeffer, *The Cost of Discipleship*, New York, Revised Edition, MacMillan Publishing Company, Inc., Copyright (c) SCM Press Ltd., 1959, p. 324.

Regaining the Straying, a manual for church elders produced by the Commission on Evangelism of the Wisconsin Evangelical Lutheran Synod, 1981.

CHAPTER FIVE

1. Reprinted from *Discipling the Brother*, by Marlin Jeschke, Scottdale, Herald Press, Copyright (c) 1972, p. 85. Reprinted by permission.

2. Kenneth O. Gangel, *Leadership for Church Education*, Chicago, The Moody Bible Institute of Chicago, 1970, p. 265.

3. Reprinted from *Training and Equipping the Saints*, by Donald A. Abdon, Indianapolis, Copyright (c) 1977 by Parish Leadership Seminars, Inc., p. 199. Reprinted by permission.

4. On terminology used, Cf. Sue Wingard, "Communication Skills," instructions for Visitation Ministry Training at Borgess Medical Center, Kalamazoo, February, 1983.

5. Reprinted from *The Pastoral Ministry of Church Officers* by Charlie W. Shedd, Richmond, John Knox Press, Copyright (c) by Charlie W. Shedd, p. 46. Reprinted by permission.

6. Gangel, op. cit., p. 251.

7. Taken from *Competent to Counsel* by Jay E. Adams. Copyright (c) 1970 by Jay E. Adams, Grand Rapids, Zondervan, p. 120. Used by permission.

8. Jay E. Adams, *The Use of the Scripture in Counseling,* Grand Rapids, Baker Book House (Reprint). Copyright (c) by Jay E. Adams, 1975, pp. 3-4.

9. Ibid., p. 59.

10. *Advance — Information for Church Workers,* St. Louis, Concordia Publishing House, Vol. 2, February 1955, quoting Shoemaker, p. 41.

ADDITIONAL READING

William Glasser, M.D., *Reality Therapy,* New York, Harper and Row, 1965.

Milton L. Rudnick, *Authority in the Church,* Chicago, Lutheran Education Association, 1977.

Lawrence J. Crabb, Jr., *Basic Principles of Biblical Counseling,* Grand Rapids, Zondervan Publishing House, 1975.

CHAPTER SIX

1. David Witte, "Delinquency and Excommunication," an unpublished essay delivered to the Southern Pastoral Conference, Southeastern Wisconsin District of the Wisconsin Evangelical Lutheran Synod, November 1981, p. 2.

2. Ibid., p. 2.

3. John H.C. Fritz, *Pastoral Theology,* St. Louis, Concordia Publishing House, 1945, p. 234.

4. Reinhart J. Pope, "Excommunication and Removing People From the List," an unpublished essay delivered to the Southeastern Pastoral Conference, Southeastern Wisconsin District of the Wisconsin Evangelical Lutheran Synod, September 1978, p. 3.

5. Reprinted from *Organized for Action,* Copyright (c) 1959 Concordia Publishing House, p. 9. Reprinted by permission.

6. John Savage, "Interview with John Savage," *Your Church,* July/August 1983, King of Prussia, The Religious Publishing Company, 1981, pp. 6ff.

7. Lyle E. Schaller, *Assimilating New Members,* Nashville, Abingdon Press, 1978, p. 19.

8. Peter L. Steinke, *Sharing God's Care for One Another,* St. Louis, Concordia Publishing House, 1979, p. 17.

9. Reprinted from *Training and Equipping the Saints* by Donald A. Abdon, Indianapolis. Copyright (c) 1977 by Parish Leadership Seminars, Inc., p. 228. Reprinted by permission.

10. Steinke, op. cit., p. 18.

11. Reprinted from *The Pastoral Ministry of Church Officers* by Charlie W. Shedd, Richmond, John Knox Press. Copyright (c) by Charlie W. Shedd, p. 43. Reprinted by permission.

12. Martin Luther, *Luther's Large Catechism,* Minneapolis, Augsburg Publishing House, 1954, pp. 102-105, 110-111, quoted by Steinke, op. cit., p. 17.

13. Elmer Kettner, *Elders at Work — Manual for the Training of Elders,* St. Louis, Concordia Publishing House, Audio-Visual Aids Service, p. 33.

14. Jon M. Mahnke, "Dealing with the Neglecter of Word and Sacrament," an unpublished essay delivered to the California Pastoral Conference, the Arizona-California District of the Wisconsin Evangelical Lutheran Synod, January 1979, p. 8.

15. Abdon, op. cit. pp. 229-230.

16. Ibid., pp. 229-230.

17. Armin W. Schuetze and Irwin J. Habeck, *The Shepherd Under Christ,* Milwaukee, Northwestern Publishing House, 1974, p. 174.

18. Pope, op. cit., p. 2.

ADDITIONAL READING

John S. Savage, *The Apathetic and Bored Church Member,* Pittsford, Lead Consultants, 1976.

Lyle E. Schaller, *Hey, That's Our Church,* Nashville, Abingdon, 1975.

Philip Lange, *The Approach to the Unchurched,* St. Louis, Concordia Publishing House, 1943, p. 42.

Missionary Workman — A Manual for a Course in Missionary Training, prepared for

The Congregational Call of the Cross Committee, issued by The Centennial Call of the Cross Committee of the Lutheran Church — Missouri Synod, St. Louis, Topic II.

Charles S. Mueller, *The Strategy of Evangelism,* St. Louis, Concordia, 1965.

Daniel D. Walker, *Enemy in the Pew?* New York, Harper and Row, Publishers, Inc., 1967, p. 157.

CHAPTER SEVEN

1. Reprinted from *Discipling the Brother* by Marlin Jeschke. Copyright (c) 1972 by Herald Press, Scottdale, p. 86. Reprinted by permission.

2. *Missionary Workman — A Manual for a Course in Missionary Training,* prepared for The Congregational Call of the Cross Committee, issued by The Centennial Call of the Cross Committee of the Lutheran Church — Missouri Synod, St. Louis, Topic II, p. 13.

3. Ibid., p. 14.

4. Ibid., p. 14.

† † † † † †